P9-APE-097

LEARN EVERYTHING
YOU NEED TO KNOW ABOUT

- **Permanent, part-time, temp, job-sharing, flextime, independent contractor, traditional and nontraditional jobs**—an in-depth survey of the changing workplace

- **The interview**—issues to explore tactfully; interview questions, legitimate and otherwise; tests, valid and otherwise; tips for winning

- **Salary**—what is and isn't legal regarding wages and overtime; job benefits and their tax consequences

- **What it takes to win an employment discrimination claim**—kinds of illegal discrimination, your rights, what it takes to prove your claim

- **Health insurance**—an essential checklist to find out if you really understand your health insurance coverage

- **Retirement**—timing your retirement and managing your finances

FIGHT BACK!
FOR YOUR RIGHTS ON THE JOB
FIGHT BACK!
At Work

"The FIGHT BACK! series is an indispensable compass to help families navigate through complex and difficult territory. It is a wonderful antidote to the paperwork jungle."

—VAL J. HALAMANDARIS, *President,*
National Association for Home Care

Other
Fight Back! Guides
by
David Horowitz and Dana Shilling
Available from Dell:

■

The FIGHT BACK! Guide to Hospital Care

■

The FIGHT BACK! Guide to Senior Citizens' Medical Care

■

The FIGHT BACK! Guide to General Medical Care

■

The FIGHT BACK! Guide to Health Insurance

QUANTITY SALES

Most Dell books are available at special quantity discounts when purchased in bulk by corporations, organizations, or groups. Special imprints, messages, and excerpts can be produced to meet your needs. For more information, write to: Dell Publishing, 1540 Broadway, New York, NY 10036. Attention: Director, Special Markets.

INDIVIDUAL SALES

Are there any Dell books you want but cannot find in your local stores? If so, you can order them directly from us. You can get any Dell book currently in print. For a complete up-to-date listing of our books and information on how to order, write to: Dell Readers Service, Box DR, 1540 Broadway, New York, NY 10036.

AT WORK

David Horowitz

AND

Dana Shilling

A DELL TRADE PAPERBACK

A DELL TRADE PAPERBACK

Published by
Dell Publishing
a division of
Bantam Doubleday Dell Publishing Group, Inc.
1540 Broadway
New York, New York 10036

If you purchased this book without a cover you should be aware that this
book is stolen property. It was reported as "unsold and destroyed" to the
publisher and neither the author nor the publisher has received any payment
for this "stripped book."

Copyright © 1995 by David Horowitz and Dana Shilling

All rights reserved. No part of this book may be reproduced or transmitted
in any form or by any means, electronic or mechanical, including
photocopying, recording, or by any information storage and retrieval system,
without the written permission of the Publisher, except where permitted by
law.

The trademark Dell® is registered in the U.S. Patent and Trademark Office.

Library of Congress Cataloging in Publication Data
Horowitz, David, 1937–
    Fight back! at work / David Horowitz and Dana Shilling.
      p.   cm.
    ISBN 0-440-50636-0
    1. Employee rights—United States. 2. Labor laws and legislation—
United States. 3. Employee fringe benefits—Law and legislation—United
States. 4. Pensions—Law and legislation—United States. I. Shilling,
Dana. II. Title.
HD6971.8.H67 1995
331′.01′10973—dc20   94-34117
                                              CIP

Printed in the United States of America

Published simultaneously in Canada

May 1995

10 9 8 7 6 5 4 3 2

BVG

To the staff and board of directors
of the FIGHT BACK! Foundation
for Consumer Education

Contents

3   What You Earn: Salary   30

4   The Rest of the Iceberg:
Pensions and Benefits   39

5 Health Insurance: Significant Benefits, Significant Problems

65

6 Work-Family Issues

76

AT WORK

Introduction

—

For more than a century America was a nation of farmers. Then, for a while, it was a nation of factory workers. Now it's a mix, with service jobs predominating. It used to be easy to explain to your kids how you earned a living (in fact, they were probably pitching hay, milking the cows, or generally helping you do it). Now it can be awfully hard to explain what a "C-based programmer" or "commodities trader" does. Once most families had a male breadwinner and a female homemaker; today single-parent families and two-earner couples are common. Many employees have important responsibilities for the care of their children (and an increasing number have responsibilities for aging parents).

Once employers held all the cards, and slogans like "If you don't come in Sunday, don't come in Monday" were common. Pensions? Benefits? Unheard of then; today they represent about one third of what an employer pays. That little fact could explain some of the griping you hear when the subject of a raise comes up. The relationship between employers and employees has always been uneasy, but today there are more tensions than ever.

If there were no business, there would be no jobs; if there were no employees, the business couldn't sell any goods or earn any profits. On that level employers and employees have to work together. But of course lower salaries often mean higher profits. A business, especially a small one, has to devote a lot of time and money to government paperwork and mandatory ben-

1

efits. In a weak economy, with lots of national and international competition, businesses can feel pushed to the wall. We're on your side, and we'll show you how to get your legal rights and any extra benefits you can negotiate—but to be fair, we have to point out that there are two sides to the story.

In many ways employees are better off than ever; Congress, the state legislatures, and the courts have enacted strong protection for their rights. But there are also ways in which times are cold, hard, tough, and mean. New jobs being created tend to be temporary, part-time, or low-paid and short on benefits; many of the old, high-paid, benefit-rich manufacturing jobs are gone forever. In order to succeed you need diligence, patience, top-flight skills . . . and a lot of information about workplace rights.

In this book we explain the rights that you have as a job applicant, worker, or former worker. But rights don't exist in a vacuum or in the abstract. It doesn't matter **what** it says in the law book if you can't prevent someone from violating your rights, or can't at least get damages or some other form of relief after the fact. ("At least" because it's far better to avoid having your rights trampled on than to go through agonies of trouble and expense before final vindication—if, indeed, it ever comes.)

The good guys don't always win. If they do win, it doesn't come easy. There are plenty of reasons why a person who has a good claim can lose in court, or get sidetracked on the way:

- Whatever happened is unjust and unfair—but not illegal. The employer managed to stay on the right side of the law (if just barely); or there really ought to be a law, but there isn't.
- The victim just couldn't persist long enough to see the thing through.
- The victim couldn't afford to litigate the case. It's usually possible to get a lawyer who will take a discrimination case on a contingent fee basis (and lawyers are often entitled to an award of attorneys' fees when they win a discrimination case—sometimes even if they win on only some issues and lose the rest), but meanwhile the client has to pay the expenses of litigation, which can be substantial.

- The victim is afraid of retaliation.
- The victim didn't follow the right procedure. As we will explain, there's an incredibly complex and laborious process for bringing charges under Title VII, the main federal antidiscrimination law. It's much more complex than the procedure for starting an ordinary lawsuit. With minor exceptions people who claim discrimination **must** follow the process; they don't have a choice. Failure to follow the rules will doom even the most objectively serious charge.

  Under a principle called "exhaustion of remedies," if there is a state or federal agency set up to deal with a problem, it is usually required that claimants go through all of the agency's procedures (which could include four or five hearings of different kinds, and stretching over a period of years) before they go to court.

- The charge was brought against the wrong person. Oddly enough, if you believe you were sexually harassed at work, in most circumstances the right "person" to sue is the company that employed you—not the sexist pig who harassed you.
- The charge was brought too late. Once the "statute of limitations" (a period of months or years) expires, it will be too late to bring the claims. For instance, for most discrimination claims, the statute of limitations is two years from the **last** discriminatory act. Statutes of limitations can sometimes be extended, especially if the employer did something particularly bad.
- The luck of the draw. Fairly often very similar or even factually identical cases will appear in more than one court, but the courts or juries will interpret the events completely differently, with the result that one plaintiff gets a tiny award of damages and one gets a huge amount—or one plaintiff wins, and one loses.
- As if those reasons weren't enough, there is also the issue of **preemption**. Under our federal Constitutional system, the central government has enormous power, but the states also play a role, and they are allowed a significant discretion for individuality and experimentation. There are many areas in which state laws vary greatly. There are other areas where it

is deemed useful to have nationwide uniformity. In those cases the federal law is said to "preempt" the state law, and aggrieved individuals have to use the federal procedures, and be satisfied with the federal remedies, even if the state courts might give a faster or more sympathetic hearing—or a bigger payoff for the successful litigant.

There are many situations, though, in which the federal law will provide a basic, uniform minimum standard, but states will still have the power to provide even broader rights to individuals.

Speaking of payoffs, there is a belief (not entirely irrational) that juries are much more generous with the funds of a rich, "deep pocket" defendant than a judge would be hearing the same case. So you may have a sensible preference for having a jury hear your case. That's not always possible—for various technical legal reasons which you will be glad we are not explaining here, not all cases are entitled to jury trials.

Furthermore, there are some cases where you can get back whatever money you lost or expenses you incurred because of the defendant's conduct, possibly doubled or tripled, and possibly with extra damages to punish really serious misconduct. There are other cases where all you can get is a tiny amount of money, and others where you can't get any money at all—just an order that the defendant do something (e.g., give you your job back) or stop doing something (e.g., using preemployment tests that are racially discriminatory). Before you litigate, find out if you are likely to get anything besides the satisfaction of fighting for truth and justice!

The New Profile
of the Workplace

It has been said that in the last thirty years we've moved from a manufacturing economy to a service/information-driven economy. However, there are a few problems with this situation. First of all, service jobs are usually low-paid and provide few benefits. The information jobs are more sophisticated, and often better paid, but the sophistication itself is a major source of problems. The best jobs require literacy, a good education, and a variety of skills . . . skills that many U.S. workers lack. Even skilled "knowledge workers" are vulnerable to losing their job if the company decides that one person with a computer program can replace several analysts or people preparing reports, or that a couple of people with voice mail can replace an entire consumer complaint department. When big companies merge, or when one buys another, there are often duplicate jobs that become the target of "downsizing."

Many companies, forced to satisfy both stockholders (who want dividends and enhanced stock prices) and banks and other lenders (who want payments on heavy corporate debt), are cutting back on payroll in an effort to improve the bottom line. Horrible as this is for the employees who lose their jobs, ironically it may not be awfully helpful to the company. Management consultants Wyatt Co. looked at "downsizing" in September 1993 by surveying about 500 big companies. Most of the companies instituted pay freezes to accompany their employee cutbacks, but only about one fifth rated the tactic as "very effective"; incentive pay was considered more useful in keeping motivation high during the transition period. One third of the companies found that restructuring didn't even cut their costs; one third found that productivity didn't increase after the downsizing. Business professor Kenneth DeMeuse found that layoffs actually cause corporate profits to decline. In fact, half the companies in the Wyatt survey found themselves rehiring people for jobs that they had eliminated less than a year before.

Employee Priorities

In the fall of 1993 the Families and Work Institute released an important document, "The National Study of the Changing Workforce." After talking to about 3,400 people in the work force nationwide, they found a lot of insecurity among them: 42 percent worked for companies that have downsized or are implementing permanent reductions in their number of employees. When employees reported on their reasons for taking their current jobs, about one third said that it was the only job offer they got. The factor that they valued most highly in selecting a job was "open communication," followed shortly by the nature of the work, the quality of management, control over work, job security, and the chance to gain new skills.

The number two factor (cited as an important reason for taking the job by 60 percent of respondents) was the effect of the job on personal and family life; family-supportive policies were named by 46 percent, and control of work schedule by 38 percent. In a sense, these are three approaches to the same problem. But, interestingly, the survey respondents said that work/family conflicts tended to be resolved in favor of the job, which often hurt workers and families.

When the question was what they considered "success," over half named the personal satisfaction of a job well done. Thirty percent identified respect or recognition from other people. Less than a quarter plumped for getting ahead or advancing in a career, or making lots of money. This low ranking could mean that things have sure changed since the greedy, career-minded eighties—or it could mean that survey respondents want to sound like nice guys and gals instead of back-stabbing corporate clones. You call it.

Who's Who in the Workplace?

There are more people employed than ever before, but there are also plenty of layoffs, plant closings, and pink slips. Some regions are much better at holding on to jobs and creating new jobs than others. Between August 1992 and August 1993, for instance, help-wanted ads declined in one region of the country (the Pacific), and were pretty stagnant in New England, but increased by about 10–12 percent in most of the country. Things were even better in the Great Lakes area (up 17.5 percent), in the South (up 21–28 percent) and the Mountain States (up 28 percent).

In the 8/92–8/93 period, nearly three quarters of the new jobs were in service industries. Many of those jobs were temporary, part-time, or permanent full-time jobs at low pay. Yet today they are often considered good jobs (many offer decent health benefits, and even profit sharing), and there is considerable competition for them, often among people with an impressive work history that was brought to a screeching halt by a layoff or plant closing.

Another important change in the workplace has been the increasing level of diversity. No, prejudice has not disappeared, and women and people of color still complain about being "last hired, first fired" or hitting a "glass ceiling" that prevents full success, but a glance at anything from the Supreme Court bench to the police force to automobile salespersons shows that white males are not the only people now in the work force or holding responsible jobs. There is still a pay gap between women and men with similar qualifications, but it has narrowed: in 1980 women earned 60 cents for every $1.00 earned by a comparable male; in 1990 women earned almost 71 cents on the masculine dollar. Alas, most of the change was caused by declining wages for men, not golden opportunities for women . . . but there are some real female success stories. Between 1980 and 1992 the percentage of women holding the top twenty jobs in 200 of the Fortune 500 corporations went from practically zero to almost 8 percent, and some companies decided to interview only women for some major executive posts.

Between 1982 and 1992 gains for black professional women were especially dramatic. Their employment increased 8.4 percent a year, compared to 6.4 percent for white women, 4.2 percent for black men, and only 2 percent for white men. There were far more black women than black men in service, finance, and retail employment in 1992. In that year the bulk of black male employees were blue-collar, service workers or operators; most black working women were service or clerical workers.

A major *Wall Street Journal* survey, published in September 1993, showed that black workers took the brunt of the 1990–91 recession. (To be fair, we have to point out that several letters were printed shortly thereafter objecting to some of the conclusions of the study.) According to the study, blacks were the only racial group who actually had fewer workers employed after the recession than before. This was also true in earlier recessions. According to the Equal Employment Opportunity Commission (EEOC), 11.5 percent of the work force in companies large enough to make reports to the EEOC consisted of black workers in 1979, a percentage that dipped to 11 percent in the 1981–82 recession. The percentage of black workers rose steadily, peaking at 12.5 percent in 1990, then fell again to about 12.25 percent in 1991.

The survey's conclusion is that black workers took more than their share of layoffs and other job losses. It could be that, as "last hired" they were "first fired" simply for reasons of seniority; it could also be a product of unconscious racism, so that managers felt relief at getting rid of African American workers they never really felt comfortable with in the first place. On paper it looks like black technicians, professionals, and managers made big gains during 1990–91, but that's because they had so little representation in the workplace before that a small change added a big percentage.

In winter 1993 it was suggested that the Bureau of Labor Statistics' methodology may underestimate the number of unemployed workers, because the methods are too quick to assume that women who don't have paid jobs are housewives; many of them are unsuccessful job seekers.

Bad News for New Graduates

Articles published around commencement time in 1993 suggested that the 1.3 million college graduates faced a difficult time in getting entry-level jobs—perhaps the worst in decades, if the *Wall Street Journal* is right. More than a third of college graduates take jobs that don't even require college training—twice as many as five years ago. L. Patrick Scheetz, director of the College Employment Research Institute (Michigan State University) says that things haven't been this bad since the end of World War II.

In 1994 the picture was, if anything, even bleaker. A midwestern college placement counselor said that she told new graduates that $17,000 was about all they could expect as an entry-level salary; in 1993, half of the full-time workers aged 20–24 earned less than $199 per week, which was less than the $215 per week median in 1989. Unpaid internships, part-time jobs, and temping are "Generation X" facts of life.

In effect, there's a backlog of college graduates—people who got initial jobs, but got laid off; "last year's models" who still haven't gotten jobs, or at least not career-track jobs. For one thing, between 1988 and 1992, the number of college seniors grew **eleven times** as fast as the number of full-time, non-farm jobs. No way could the economy absorb them all. The process of securing a job used to take about three months; now it takes nine months to a year—especially because fewer companies are bothering to send recruiters to campus, so students have to take a more aggressive route to job seeking.

What to Do? Some teenagers (and their potentially check-writing parents) are simply bypassing college, figuring that there's no point in splashing out $80,000 or more for a four-year education if it won't result in career opportunities. But the risk is that employers, now choosier than a cat in a cat-food commercial, may begin to treat a college degree as the same kind of entry-level credential that the high school diploma used to represent.

Others are trying to use their college years to gain marketable skills. For one thing, multinational employers are looking favorably on applicants who are fluent in more than one language—or outright refusing to interview those who aren't. Of course, it helps to be good at using the major computer programs used in business, although expertise in arcade video games is not considered a fair substitute. Employers are also looking for real work experience, so collegians who have to work part-time to make ends meet may have an advantage in the post-graduation job search.

According to the Bureau of Labor Statistics, job growth can be expected in a few sectors between 1990 and 2005: people working with computers, child care workers, clerks and receptionists, R.N.s, restaurant cooks, lawyers and accountants, and security guards. (Note that, although some of these are well-paid professional jobs, most are low-paid service jobs.) Significant declines were expected in jobs for farmers, telephone repairers, switchboard operators and directory assistance operators, skilled factory workers, and household help. This reflects a deindustrialized, and more computerized economy, where sophisticated communications technologies replace the simple telephone.

Part-time and Temporary Workers

Usually when anyone from a browser through the "Help Wanted" ads to a policy wonk thinks about jobs, they think about full-time, permanent positions. There have always been workers who were outside the conventional full-time job world. But part-time and temporary employment has become an ever-increasing factor in the economy; so has the use of independent contractors and agency employees.

In the eighties and early nineties employers turned to less-than-full-time schedules for one major reason. Laws mandating pension and benefit coverage typically are limited to full-time employees who are deemed to be employees of that particular company. Usually (but not always!) the employer can get away with paying salary, but not benefits, to independent contractors, part-timers, people on temporary assignment, and those who work for "temp" agencies.

Having services performed by someone who is not an "employee" for Social Security tax (Federal Insurance Contributions Act) purposes saves the employer 7.65 percent of the employee's pay in FICA taxes. It's been estimated that one quarter to one third of a regular employee's total compensation consists of pension and other benefits and employer taxes, so avoiding regular employees makes a big difference to the cost of employment.

And even if it cost only $1 a week per employee to pay the taxes and provide the benefits, the sheer burden of paperwork makes it hard to add more employees. If an employer could earn a little more by hiring new workers, but had to add a personnel department to handle the compliance burden, it just wouldn't be worth it.

Productivity: There are some jobs that really demand the full-time services of a highly skilled person who needs extensive training plus extensive on-the-job experience. Sometimes those jobs can be handled by an independent contractor "consultant," or a very experienced person on temporary assignment (maybe even a top executive laid off by another company)—but probably a conventional employee will be required.

Other jobs are easy to learn and comparatively unskilled; the working day involves repeating tasks over and over again. Those jobs can often be filled by "temps" or part-timers with no loss of productivity. In fact, short-term workers may even be more productive, because they're less burnt out.

In the transition from a manufacturing to a service economy, unfortunately there are a lot fewer good jobs, and a higher proportion of unskilled, repetitive jobs that are suitable for casual, temporary, and part-time workers.

In the fourth quarter of 1992, there were about 350,000

temporary workers who worked in factories but were technically employees of employment agencies: about one quarter of all temp agency workers worked in factories. Many economists saw this as a bad sign. In past recessions, factory hiring spurred the recovery. This won't happen if employers get used to a flexible work force of low-wage, low-benefit temps. (Temporary workers often earn $2–$3 less per hour than permanent employees doing exactly the same thing.) Employers cheer this development and say it is the key to international competitiveness. If U.S. wages, adjusted for productivity, aren't too much higher than wages in other countries, employers will have less incentive to shift their manufacturing operations to other countries.

Voluntary Part-timers: The cost of taxes and benefits makes a big difference to the employee, too. Some people prefer staying out of the regular employment loop, trading additional freedom (and, often, additional take-home pay) for the obligation to provide their own health care and retirement funding. If it can be managed legally the employer can pay more than a full-timer's take-home pay, yet less than the entire cost of employing a full-timer. Both employer and nontraditional worker are satisfied by the deal. However, some part-time workers want, but can't get, full-time jobs.

Audition Jobs: Not all temporary gigs are low-skilled. Sometimes companies will hire a temporary worker for a skilled or professional task that once might have been handled by a permanent professional or a small department or farmed out to a higher-priced consultant. For instance, a company trying to set up an employee relations department (or, more likely, an outplacement center) might hire a personnel executive who got bumped in a merger or downsized out. If he or she does a good job of handling the start-up, a permanent offer to run the department might result. Instead of having legal work done by a law firm charging several hundred dollars an hour, a company might hire a lawyer to handle the task over the course of a few months.

If the assignment is completed successfully, it might lead to a lucrative permanent job. However, the company may not have a permanent position to offer, and short-term workers have to be prepared to think of themselves as "permanent temporaries," either doomed to wander from company to company or enjoying diverse experiences in many environments. If you find yourself in this situation, personnel professionals warn that you must never depend on a permanent job becoming available—and you must make sure to keep your health insurance current, because even if you land a permanent job, it may not come equipped with health care coverage, or you may have significant copayment responsibilities.

"Disposable Workers": In 1993 there were 118 million employed Americans—20 million of them working part-time. In February 1993, 380,000 new jobs were created . . . but 90 percent of them were part-time. In January 1993 about 1.5 million people worked through temporary agencies ("temp" agencies are a $14 billion industry), not to mention an uncounted number of people with temporary jobs who worked directly for an employer without the intervention of an agency. Those figures don't indicate how many wanted the part-time schedule or the flexibility of "temping," and how many got saddled with it involuntarily.

Some employers deliberately employ a strategy of keeping a small core of permanent workers, then filling the rest of the work force needs with independent contractors, part-timers, and temporary employees. When the company's order book is full, they add more part-time workers, or even temporary full-time workers if there seems to be enough work to justify their paychecks. At the low point in the business cycle, those workers are easily let go, because they have no expectations of permanent jobs. Employers like contingent jobs for another reason: if they pacify the union by agreeing that all workers must join after thirty days on the job, the employer can keep out the union without violating the agreement simply by chucking out one bunch of workers after twenty-nine days and starting again with new workers.

In one sense, this is sensible management and great for business. In another, it's shortsighted in business terms as well as harsh in human terms. You can't very well sell luxury goods to people living from hand to mouth. Long-range business prosperity depends on the existence of lots and lots of potential customers. A city or town's schools, fire protection, garbage disposal, and other services depend on local taxes . . . and you can't get blood out of a turnip: low-wage workers simply can't keep their homes if they have to pay taxes that approach the level of their wages.

FMLA: As we discuss in our chapter on Family and Work issues, the Family and Medical Leave Act of 1992 became effective August 5, 1993. Unless employers can set up workable flextime or job-sharing plans, or unless they can get the other employees to share the job duties of employees on leave, there will be a real need for temporary workers to cover for those who are taking leave to care for new babies, for sick children or parents, or who need some leave for their own medical problems.

Job Sharing and Flextime

Employees—especially employees with significant family responsibilities—may prefer, and even initiate, nontraditional ways to work. One way that's gotten media attention (perhaps more attention than actual implementation) is job sharing. Two employees agree to split a work schedule, either splitting the work day (preferably with some overlap so they can discuss changes, emergencies, and problems hanging over from one shift to the next) or one person working certain days, the other person working the others.

In a sense, this is an adaptation of traditional shift work, where the day shift yields to the lobster shift and the night shift. But job sharing is usually done in more upscale circumstances: say, two pediatricians who are also parents of young children sharing a practice; two magazine editors sharing responsibilities.

Another possibility is flextime: employer and employee agree on what the employee will be responsible for producing, and approximately the number of hours the employee will work per week or per month. Usually, there will be certain blocks of time when the employee will agree to be present or available on the phone or by fax. The employee will then be responsible for arranging hours so that the job tasks get done. The employee might work the same schedule all the time, just not the conventional nine-to-five; or the employee might tailor his or her hours to the actual, shifting needs of performing the job tasks.

Independent Contractors

Often employers try to avoid making the required tax payments or withholdings by claiming certain members of the company to be independent contractors instead of employees. This has been going on long enough for well-established rules to evolve. The determination of whether someone is an employee or independent contractor must be made separately, on a case-by-case basis, looking at all the facts.

The factors in the decision include:

- Where the work is done. It's a positive sign if someone works away from the employer's premises, a negative but not conclusive sign if they work at the employer's premises. It's not conclusive because, after all, you call a plumber (an independent contractor) if your bathtub backs up or your toilet gets plugged up—and the plumber doesn't sit at home waiting for you to bring in the bathtub.
- The duration of the employment relationship. If someone (like that plumber) spends five hours and then it's hasta la vista, baby, it's likely that the person was an independent contractor. If someone works nine-to-five, fifty weeks a year, for three years, it's tough to argue that the person is *not* a plain-vanilla employee. In between, it's more likely that a part-time or temporary worker will be considered an independent contractor.
- Who provides the tools and materials. Again, someone who supplies everything necessary for the job is more likely to be an independent contractor than one who uses the stuff sitting around in the workplace.
- Who controls the process and results. Of course, people who retain independent contractors don't just write a blank check and walk away; but the more control a person exer-

cises both over what is done and the way it is done, the more likely he or she is to be judged an independent contractor.

In August 1993 the Fifth Circuit pondered the challenging question of whether topless dancers were club employees or (as the club contended) independent contractors. The court decided that they were employees even though they don't receive a salary, buy their own costumes (apparently more of an expense than you'd think), and pay the club $20 per shift for the privilege of dancing for putatively tip-offering customers. To the court, the more persuasive factors were that the dancers work on schedules set by the club, follow club rules or are subject to fines, and set their rates for "table dances" and "couch dances" in accordance with the club's price schedule.

If you are an independent contractor, remember that the obligation to pay FICA taxes (**both** parts—employer and employee) belongs to you. Unless you also have a regular job (and sometimes even then) you have the obligation to make quarterly estimated tax payments that include FICA tax. Remember, if you somehow "forget" to pay your Social Security tax, you're not just violating the law—you're imperiling your own eventual Social Security benefits; you can't get benefits unless you have the necessary number of quarters of paid-up taxes for coverage. (Currently, that means forty quarters, or ten years' employment.)

You'll also have to take care of your own health insurance needs. If Congress passes a health care reform plan, employers (including small businesses) might be obligated to purchase health insurance.

Legal Implications of Temporary Work

Many of the state and federal labor laws were drafted a long time ago, and reflect a different kind of workplace. There may be difficult issues to resolve when the apparent "employer" hires the workers from a temporary agency.

Some recent court decisions prevent employers from using the temp agency as a shield to protect the employer from the consequences of job discrimination. You may have a case against the "job site employer" if you lose a temp assignment because of race, sex, religion, or nationality; if the employer refuses to offer permanent employment for one of these reasons; or if you are the victim of sexual harassment at the temporary job site. If you get hurt during a temporary assignment, you, like a permanent employee, must deal with the Workers' Compensation system (as we explain in Chapter Ten, this isn't such a great deal). You can't use your temporary status as an excuse for suing your temporary boss.

Will the Office Become Obsolete?

For a decade or more, predictions about the future of work have centered around the fully computerized, "paperless office," or even the replacement of the office by a "virtual office" where employees use electronic communications to work at home ("telecommuting") or impart information to their colleagues from business trips or conventions. The advantages of telecommuting for the employee include convenience, better coordination of work and family needs, time and energy saved by skipping long drives to work. The employer benefits if productivity goes up, if employees can devote more "face time" to making sales and keeping clients happy, and if the company can avoid renting large, expensive offices. On the other hand, employees may end up operating electronic sweatshops in their homes if they are required to meet unreasonable standards or deadlines. Some work problems are solved better by people working together face-to-face, not exchanging digitized bits of data—and people often miss the social interactions of the office culture.

2

Before You're Hired

Introduction

Applying for a job, and landing an interview, can be mundane and routine, or a delicate processes of negotiation, depending on the job you want and the size and nature of the competition. The interview itself is a tension-filled experience. It would be great if the result was always a terrific job that you keep until retirement; but it's far more likely that, sooner or later, you will face the terrors of the interview process again, perhaps over and over again.

Understandably, employers want to hire the best, and they want to get complete information about applicants' qualifications and job history. Sometimes that involves checking references, but ex-employers, afraid of lawsuits for invasion of privacy or defamation, often refuse to answer any inquiries, or merely verify that an employee had a particular title during a particular period. Without information from past employers, prospective employers have to extract as much information as they can from job applicants. Fortunately, there are some legal limits on the inquisitiveness of interviewers. You can help your chances of being offered the job by learning as much as you can about the job in question and the organization behind it, and figuring out the best way you can present yourself and your qualifications without misrepresenting yourself.

Preparing for the Interview: Best Foot Forward or Resume Fraud?

There are situations in which outright lies, even if detected, will be viewed as amusing chutzpah, or even as a sign of the kind of go-getter attitude needed for success. But don't count on it.

In most areas of enterprise, a certain amount of interpretation or flattering yourself is permissible on a resume. It might be okay to say that you "created" or "developed" an advertising campaign if you had a major role in its evolution, for instance, although it would probably be better to say something like "participated in the team" if you were one of six copywriters and eight art directors, but it would be a lie to say it if your job was mopping the floor of the conference room.

You can't award yourself an MBA if you dropped out of college, or a Harvard degree if you took a two-week summer course there—although, of course, you can feature the course on your resume (with an accurate description) if it taught you technical skills or information needed for the job you're applying for.

You can include the value of benefits in your "compensation package," as long as you don't state that your salary was $3X when it was really only $X. Salary is an objective fact that can be checked. Anyway, lying about salary can cut both ways. It **could** gain you consideration for a really high-paying job. It could just as easily get your resume thrown in the circular file because a cost-conscious employer, in these recessionary times, expects to hire a well-qualified employee for much less (something like your real salary, in fact).

So go over your resume carefully, bearing in mind that it may be reviewed by people who are suspicious or outright hostile. Have you been scrupulous about every description? Tailoring the description of your skills and experience to the demands of the job (and, if necessary, preparing several resumes, each highlighting a particular skill and appropriate for a different job category) is a good idea. Exaggeration is not; outright falsehood is unacceptable.

The odds are that, out of litigation-consciousness or sheer laziness, your resume won't be checked. But then again, it could be. It's almost certain that it will be if and when the company decides to **fire** you. That's because employers often use (or try to use) "after-acquired evidence" as a defense in a wrongful termination or employment discrimination case. That is, you say that you were fired for some unlawful reason. The employer comes back by saying it was justified in firing you, because you lied on your resume—even though the alleged misrepresentations weren't discovered until the decision had been made to fire you.

It's hard to predict the outcome of such cases, because courts have taken various approaches to the question. Sometimes they conclude that a person who commits resume fraud has no right to be hired in the first place, and therefore can't come into court with a discrimination case. They may take the middle ground, saying that the employer will win, but only if it can prove that an employer that was not guilty of discrimination would have fired the employee after discovering the employee's misrepresentation (or wouldn't have hired him or her). Most likely, they will say that an employer can't justify its own discrimination by facts that weren't even discovered until litigation began . . . but they will also punish the employee by limiting the types and/or amounts of relief that the employee can receive if he or she wins the case.

Making Interviews Productive

There are really two parts to the interview courtship process: making the interviewer want to hire you (or invite you back for further interviews) . . . and deciding if you really want the job in the first place. To manage the second part, it's best to use the interview to get meaningful information, not a lot of marshmallow fluff about the big happy workplace family, so that you can get a feeling for what the job is really like—and if you would want to take it if you had any meaningful alternatives. (Of course, if you've been out of work for a year, and debts are piling up, you may take a job even if you know perfectly well that it'll be horrible.)

Some possible issues to explore (tactfully!)

- What, exactly, does the job entail?
- Are there "regularly scheduled emergencies"—i.e., does everybody have to work long hours every tax season, before the quarterly dividends are declared, before the collections (and there are five collections a year . . .), before each monthly issue closes?
- Has the company downsized recently? Is downsizing planned? If so, have any work tasks been eliminated . . . or does the smaller employee group have to do everything the full staff used to do?
- How close to state-of-the-art is the equipment? A job that's supposed to take an hour may take days if the computer hardware can't keep pace with the software and data.
- Why did the last person to hold the job leave? Maybe he or she did a horrible job (which says something about the efficiency of the hiring process), but maybe he or she got sick of being expected to do the impossible.
- How realistic are the company's and department's budgets? What happens if there's a shortfall?
- What, if anything, are you allowed to change? Many companies **say** they want fresh, new ideas or a complete overhaul . . . but they categorically refuse to actually change anything.

Interview Questions: Legitimate and Otherwise

In theory, the job interview is supposed to pave the way for a harmonious working relationship. The potential employer is supposed to select the person best qualified, in terms of technical skills and personality—and is also supposed to make it clear exactly what the job will entail, in areas such as workload, tasks to be done, compensation, and promotion potential.

But then, also in theory, the employer is supposed to carry out hiring in a lawful manner. If the employer is large enough to be subject to the various antidiscrimination laws, there may be lawsuits or administrative penalties if the employer fails to make employment decisions objectively, viewing each applicant as an individual. With limited exceptions for affirmative action programs, the employer is supposed to choose the best individual for the job, without the assessment process being clouded by stereotypes.

There's no reason for an interviewer to ask about your ethnic or religious background, or your race (although such information may be needed later, to compile statistics showing the makeup of the work force). If the job involves a lot of weekend work, it's possible that the hours will impinge on the Sabbath observed by various religions. Even then, the legitimate inquiry is whether you are available to work weekends sometimes, always, or never . . . not the religious beliefs that inform your decision.

In order to avoid sex discrimination, employers should avoid assumptions about the way gender affects employment performance. No assumption should be made that **all** unmarried women want to get married, or that **no** married woman (or woman with children) is serious about her career, or that men **never** want to spend time being actively involved in child care, or that the mothers of small children are **not** available to travel, or that fathers of small children **always** are. It's legitimate to discuss the amount of overnight travel involved in a job, and to ask **all** applicants about their ability to travel. It may even be illegal to ask about past salaries, if the employer's motive is to pay a woman less than a man would earn for the same work, thus violating the Equal Pay Act.

Interviewers, just like everybody else, like to be friendly and exchange social chitchat—but it's a Title VII violation to ask women (but not men) about their marital status and marriage plans, much less their contraceptive habits and when they plan to have children. In fact, these inquiries would probably be unlawful even if they were made universal. Once somebody is hired, it's okay to ask about their marital status and the number of children they have—but not about those that are pending. Similarly, **after** hiring, it would be okay to ask a female applicant for her full name; but a prehiring inquiry "What was your maiden name?" could be discriminatory either as an attempt to find out whether she is indeed married (marital-status discrimination) or perhaps to find out her ethnic or religious background (which is irrelevant to hiring).

There are very limited situations in which being under forty is a bona fide occupational qualification (BFOQ), and even more limited situations in which being male or female is a BFOQ (being a dressing room attendant—but not being a nurse). Of course, it doesn't require an inquiry to see if someone is male or female, but there may be a very limited scope of inquiry about age.

Under the Americans with Disabilities Act (ADA), inquiries about medical conditions that could impede job performance are not supposed to be made until the decision has been made to offer the job. If a person is not a serious candidate, there is considered to be no legal justification for discussing handicapping conditions; but if the tentative decision to hire has been made, it becomes appropriate to determine if the individual is "qualified" (i.e., able to do the job, with or without specialized adaptations). EEOC guidelines, approved on May 19, 1994 (just in time for the expansion of the ADA to cover employers of fifteen or more), list dozens of questions that are illegal in pre-offer interviews, including:

- Do you have AIDS?
- Have you ever made a Workers' Compensation claim?
- Do you take prescription drugs? Which ones?
- Have you ever had psychiatric treatment or therapy?

Asking about education is a basic inquiry, but it can have racial implications (because of differing rates of high school and college graduation for different ethnic groups). It's **okay** for employers to ask . . . **if** educational level is relevant to the job. It's relevant to expect a speech therapist to have a degree in speech pathology, for instance; but it's not relevant to hiring a cabdriver, where the more relevant inquiry is the person's driving record and knowledge of local geography.

Questions about arrest records are improper (because, after all, being arrested doesn't prove that a person did anything wrong, just that a law enforcement officer had some reason to think the person did). Even questions about convictions are dubious, because they are not distributed evenly by race—but they can be asked if, for instance, the job involves handling money or providing security, where "nonconvictedness" would be a BFOQ (bona fide occupational qualification).

Some states do let employers ask about convictions, and even arrests, and let them do a background check as long as the applicant is warned that this is taking place. Other states consider arrest records, and records of convictions that were expunged, to be confidential; there may even be criminal penalties if the employer tries to find out about arrests and acquittals.

Stress Interviews: The so-called stress interview enables companies to see just who will stand up to the challenges of the job, using quasi-combat means like browbeating applicants, asking them impossible questions, or setting impossible tasks. Fifty candidates may be asked to interview for a senior executive job . . . at the same time. One brokerage house used to have the interviewer courteously ask the interviewee to open the window. The window had been nailed shut. Candidates did various things, from tugging at the window . . . to throwing a chair through it.

Employers are beginning to ask more of potential employees in prehire situations. After the conventional job interview, candidates may be asked to lead a meeting, develop a marketing plan, undergo psychological testing, even take written exams. Sometimes this is a sincere desire to find out how applicants tick, and what kind of jobs they'd do under real conditions. At the worst, it can be a way for companies to get valuable services for free that they would have to spend a lot to get from consultants.

What Makes an Employment Test Valid?

One of the functions of interviewing is to find out if people have the basic skills to do the job. Some of these skills are practical (can you lift 40 pounds? Okay, pick this up and put it on that shelf over there). Others are verbal or mathematical. It may be necessary to be good at technical drawing, reading blueprints, or using a particular computer program.

Employers are allowed to use professionally developed tests that really measure qualifications used in the job; but no matter how good the tests are, law-abiding employers must be sure that the tests are designed, administered, and acted on with no intent to discriminate against applicants in any protected group. It may also be necessary to make accommodations in testing for a job applicant's handicap—i.e., supplying a reader for a blind applicant for a job as a telephone operator or dictaphone typist that can be done by a blind person with reasonable accommodation.

Courts and the EEOC have accepted three standards for determining the validity of a preemployment test:

- Content validity—the test is a lot like the real job. A would-be telemarketer could be given a script and a list of telephone numbers and asked to make a sales pitch to the employees at the other end.
- Construct validity—the test identifies general mental and psychological traits needed to do the job. But psychological traits can easily become the subject of discrimination. Let's say that men who score high on aggressiveness, problem solving, individualism, and creativity are enthusiastically welcomed aboard, but women with the same traits are not hired ("unfeminine," "bad mother," "not a team player").
- Criterion-related validity—the test accurately predicts behavior at work or other characteristics of successful employees as shown by actual proficiency at the job.

The Civil Rights Act of 1991, Section 106 adds a new section to the federal statute (42 USC §2000e-2(1)). Now, it's an unlawful employment practice for an employer to "curve" or otherwise adjust test scores used in hiring or promotions, or to use different cutoff scores on employment-related tests, based on race, color, religion, sex, or national origin. It doesn't matter if the employer is trying to increase diversity in the workplace or give minorities a break—it's still illegal.

The May 19, 1994, EEOC Guidelines for the Americans with Disabilities Act, already mentioned above, also forbid preemployment medical tests until a job offer has been made, contingent on ability to perform the job. The EEOC uses several factors to decide if a test is medical, including whether a health professional is needed to give or interpret the test; if the test is given to find an impairment; and whether it measures somebody's bodily or mental responses instead of performance of specific tasks. Physical fitness tests (such as running a ten-minute mile) are generally okay, but if they screen out disabled applicants, they will be illegal unless they can be proved to be job-related and necessary for business.

Truth in Hiring: The Employer's Obligation to the Applicant

Naturally, employees are not the only ones to shade or stretch the truth. Today, employers who are guilty of misrepresentation, fraud, or both are increasingly likely to be sued by disappointed (or discharged) employees who claim violations of the employer's obligation of "truth in hiring."

A person might have a reasonable case if he or she was promised something (a job title, conditions of employment, a full-time instead of part-time job, permanent work instead of a temporary fill-in, a salary level, a benefit package) that the employer never had any intention of delivering. Of course, it isn't fraud to say something that you believe to be the truth, and which later simply doesn't pan out: company policy really could call for generous Christmas bonuses, but the year of hiring turns out to be a rotten year with no money to provide the bonuses.

The employee has to do something relying on the promise (quitting a job, moving to New Hampshire), and also has to experience some kind of harm because of the reliance (as soon as the moving van leaves, the pink slip arrives).

Just as employees have the right to express their qualifications in flattering terms as long as they are not deceptive, employers have the right to paint a rosy picture of the wonderful workplace. But if they are asked a straightforward question, and tell an outright lie, the recipient of the lie may have a case. It's not quite clear if employers have an obligation to volunteer information about their own financial problems (very few rats climb **onto** a sinking ship), but it's certainly fraudulent to lie to an interview candidate who asks.

There are two major types of claim. If there is a written employment contract (for instance, if the plaintiff is a sought-after top executive), and the terms of the contract are not followed, the employee can sue for breach of contract. This can be pretty easy to prove, just by introducing the contract and evidence that the real situation didn't match the contract terms. The other main classification is the "tort" claim, charging that the employer did not meet the duties that state law imposes on an honest party operating reasonably and in good faith. Tort claims can be pretty slippery, subjective, and hard to prove.

Another problem, as we discuss later, is that some states take the "employment at will" doctrine very seriously—in other words, they believe that unless you have an explicit employment contract, your employer can fire you for any reason or no reason. But these basically tough states may be more sympathetic to "truth in hiring" cases because other remedies are not available.

In 1990 a Colorado court upheld a $450,000-damage award ($90,000 compensatory damages, the rest punitive) to a sales manager who was laid off seven months after relocating. She said, and the jury and appellate court agreed, that she would not have relocated if the company hadn't lied to her about the serious financial problems it already had at the time of the interview. A Connecticut oil executive settled for an undisclosed, multi-million-dollar figure when he was lied to about a promised divisional presidency. It helped a lot that there was a "smoking gun": a letter from a corporate executive warning the corporation that there would be plenty of steamed-up executives willing to litigate about their unmet promises.

Clear Up Job Details

Which period do you think is more loving, harmonious, and happy . . . the engagement, or the tense weeks or months before the divorce? Think of the prehiring negotiations as the equivalent of an antenuptial agreement. It's not that you don't love each other . . . it's that you want the issues to be on the table while you're still in an affectionate and generous frame of mind. Not coincidentally, in either case, it's important to straighten out what will happen in the event there comes a parting of the ways.

- What is the base salary?
- What is the company's history of paying bonuses and awards for this job? The company will probably do its strenuous best to avoid making any promises, but at least you'll get some information. It's a hopeful sign if the company has paid big bonuses in almost every past year. If they've never done it, they probably won't start now.
- Whom do you report to? How many people report to you?
- Is the job intended to be temporary (and if so, for how long?) or permanent?
- How much notice are you entitled to if your job is eliminated?
- Is the company actually planning any downsizing, and if so, how will it affect your job? You may find yourself doing a difficult and responsible job while also covering for other employees whose jobs disappeared through attrition.
- What are the possibilities for promotion? What do you have to prove to show you're entitled to a promotion or a transfer?
- What chance will you get to learn new skills?
- Will the company pay for any kind of college or graduate course? What about conferences, in-house training, instructional videos and software?
- What can you get in the way of new equipment and/or office decoration?
- If your job involves seeing clients, what kind of expense account do you have access to? Are there limitations on business entertaining—and if so, will they make it hard to do your job?
- If you have to relocate, what will the company pay toward your expenses?
- Will the company help your spouse or companion get a job in the relocation area?

Find out if there's an employee handbook. Sophisticated employers usually add a lot of disclaimers about their rights to change job conditions whenever they want, but at least the handbook will teach you the current state of play.

It's an uphill struggle, but try to get as much put into writing as possible. Employers usually resist formal employment contracts (but if you want a contract and they agree—or they want a contract and **you** agree, have a lawyer look it over first). Some employers may be willing to give you a letter of intent or other document that is identified as purely information and not a contract. That way, at least you have some evidence of what you were told; you may not have full contractual remedies, but at least the company can't pretend that you've suddenly begun to hallucinate about the content of your long-ago job interview.

3

What You Earn: Salary

The T-shirts and bumper stickers say it all: "I owe, I owe, it's off to work I go"; "I'm having an out-of-money experience." Although there are other important factors in taking a job (interesting work, opportunities for advancement, chance to develop new skills, congenial colleagues), there's no question that salary is often the deciding factor.

If you have special, much-needed skills that are the subject of a bidding war, you can write your own ticket. If you're an educated, skillful, conscientious employee . . . well, that isn't always enough to get a well-paying job, or to hang on to the job, much less price yourself at the top of the market. Employers aren't just trying to do "more with less"; they're striving to do "less with less," as job functions disappear, and jobs right along with them. But as long as you have a job, you're entitled to certain standards of fair and equal pay.

FLSA Issues

The FLSA is the Fair Labor Standards Act, the federal law that covers minimum wages, and—more important for most of our readers—overtime. The law is enforced by the Department of Labor's Wage and Hour Division, and covers pretty much all "common-law employees" (people whose work is controlled by the employer). It doesn't cover independent contractors, which is why we are earning a lot less per hour to write this book than we would get flipping burgers at Mickey D.'s. Hey, we're artists.

The minimum wage has been $4.25 an hour since April 1, 1991. Every once in a while there is a movement to increase the minimum wage. There are good arguments for this: it's awfully hard to support yourself, much less raise a family, at that level—and it's hard for the Social Security Administration to collect enough FICA tax from a low-paid worker to fund the benefits for people who are currently retired, much less the large group of baby boomers who will retire in the future. If workers earn more, they pay more taxes (good for the deficit!) and buy more stuff (good for retailers!). But there are also valid opposing arguments.

There are plenty of small businesses that cling precariously to economic survival. Make them pay higher wages (or offer more benefits)—and they lose their grip and plummet down the precipice. If the company goes, so do the jobs. Employers also argue that employees are paid based on their productivity. If the nature of the job or the nature of the employee (limited education, few skills) keep productivity down, then the employer can't afford to pay more than the work is worth.

Minimum Wage Exceptions: There are minimum wage exceptions for teenage trainees. There's also an exception for employees who get tips—if the employee is allowed to keep all of his or her tips the employer is entitled to reduce the employee's wages to take tips into account.

The employer can credit tips against wages without violating the minimum wage laws, up to either 50 percent of the minimum wage, or the tips themselves. (State law may require restaurant owners to pay higher wages to waitstaff; the state law will prevail if it offers employees more protection than the federal law.) For tips that are charged to credit cards, it's okay for the employer to deduct the percentage it has to pay to the credit card company even before figuring out the tip credit. If employees pool their tips, federal minimum wage law says that only tips above those credited to the minimum wage can be pooled.

Overtime

The Fair Labor Standards Act requires employers to pay nonexempt employees at least time-and-a-half for overtime. Time-and-a-half is pretty straightforward: if you usually earn $8 an hour, overtime compensation must be $12 or more. It's okay for the employer to pay the normal salary rate for all hours, plus half the hourly rate for each overtime hour, instead of paying 150 percent of the hourly rate for overtime. The "regular rate" includes all hours, including overtime hours, with the result that the regular rate goes down as more hours are worked—and overtime becomes less beneficial to the employee.

There can be some tricky considerations in determining what "overtime" is, and who is "exempt" and who is "nonexempt." The normal workweek is considered forty hours. (It's not illegal to pay people for thirty-five hours a week instead of forty as long as they really do work thirty-five hours instead of working through lunch.) The employer isn't required to pay overtime just because somebody works more than eight hours in a particular day, or just because he or she works on a weekend or holiday—as long as the hours in the workweek don't exceed forty.

The employer can avoid paying overtime by giving the employee make-up "comp time" in the same workweek or pay period. That is, if you have to put in an extra three hours on Tuesday, but you get to come in three hours late on Wednesday, there's no obligation to pay overtime.

The FLSA also applies to the timing of payments, so employers can be penalized for "lag" payrolls (improving cash flow by paying later than the normal schedule).

It's perfectly legal for an employer to have a "no-overtime" policy, as long as it's enforced—as long as somebody really herds you out the front door so you don't work more than forty hours a week.

What is **not** legal is for employers to make their employees agree to waive their right to overtime compensation. If federal law gives you the right to overtime, then you're entitled. End of story.

For many years, the FLSA was considered a pretty straightforward statute; in 1993 the Department of Labor began to embroil companies like General Dynamics and Malcolm Pirnie Inc. in charges of overtime violations. The DOL theory, which found some approval in court, is that if a company docks an employee's pay when he or she takes time off (or even if the company doesn't actually do it, but maintains a policy under which it could be done), the worker is automatically converted to the status of an hourly employee. Hourly employees, of course, are entitled to overtime if they work over forty hours a week. Some firms have been handed bills for hundreds of thousands of dollars in overtime compensation.

The Family and Medical Leave Act (FMLA) is creating a whole new set of FLSA issues. In 1990 the Ninth Circuit said that the fact that fire chiefs' pay could be docked when they took partial days off meant that they were nonexempts entitled to overtime—even if no deductions were actually taken. But the District Court for the State of Michigan said just the opposite. Employers are already smarting over their FMLA obligation to offer intermittent leave—they'll be really juiced if the obligation catapults whole new classes of employees into the nonexempt category, forcing employers to pay massive overtime.

Exempt Employees

Of course, there are plenty of employees who are not entitled to overtime and are not covered by the FLSA minimum wage provisions. The test is not whether your pay is expressed in terms of a weekly, monthly, or yearly salary instead of an hourly wage; it's whether you are a plain-vanilla employee or an "administrator," "executive," "professional," or "outside salesperson." It's perfectly okay for outside salespersons' compensation to be mostly or entirely based on results, so somebody who never sells anything never gets paid. That wouldn't work for somebody who is essentially a retail salesclerk inside a store—just for the descendant of the "traveling salesman." For FLSA purposes, somebody is an outside salesperson if commissions are a significant element in compensation, if they spend at least 80 percent of their time making sales instead of doing "nonexempt" work like paperwork and stocking shelves, and if they have special sales training.

"Executives" are exempt employees—they don't have to get overtime even if they spend twenty-four hours a day at the office, breaking only for a brief nap under the desk. Federal law includes a "short test" and a "long test" of executive status. It boils down to the fact that somebody who earns more than $250 per week and who spends at least 50 percent of his or her time on managerial and administrative functions counts as an executive. That means no overtime. The $250 weekly earnings test also applies in determining if someone is an administrator or professional.

Somebody who owns 20 percent or more of a business is probably going to be considered an executive even if more than 20 percent of work time is spent on nonexempt tasks. It's understood that in a start-up business the founder is probably going to lend a hand doing everything from unplugging the toilet to sweet-talking unpaid suppliers to mailing out the invoices.

"Administrators" are also exempt. It's hard to draw a firm line between executives and administrators, but basically the administrator's primary duty is to use discretion and independent judgment in office or nonmanual work. This is the category with the biggest potential for abuse. A company too cheap to pay overtime might try to get away with calling somebody who is really a secretary or file clerk an "administrator." This is definitely illegal, but a fairly low-risk form of wrongdoing. Employees would have to be out of their minds to place an FLSA complaint while they're still working . . . but it might make sense after leaving and getting another, and let's hope better, job.

"Professionals," for purposes of exemption, are not necessarily college trained, but their work must primarily involve learned, artistic, or educational tasks, calling for consistent exercise of judgment. The work must be predominantly intellectual and varied in nature, and output or accomplishments must be the kind that can't be standardized. In 1993 it was decided that newspaper reporters, photographers, and editors **are** entitled to overtime, and are not exempt as professionals. The court ruled that some of their work does involve creativity and talent, but most doesn't.

The Equal Pay Act

The federal Equal Pay Act (29 USC §206(d)) (EPA) covers sex discrimination in pay. It doesn't cover pay discrimination based, for instance, on race, nationality, or sexual orientation. Under the EPA, it's illegal for an employer to pay one sex more than the other for doing jobs that require equal skill, effort, and responsibility, and performed under working conditions that can reasonably be compared. If one worker fixes machinery in a factory, and the other one fixes machinery while dangling from a helicopter during a Force Five gale, then it isn't sex discrimination to pay the second worker more.

For EPA purposes, the significant factor is what the employees actually do, not what their job titles are. An employer can't wriggle out of equal pay for women simply by giving male employees more exalted titles, then claiming that the title disparity explains the pay disparity. If an employer commits sex discrimination by refusing to promote a qualified woman, or by making the woman's working conditions inferior to men's working conditions, that's a Title VII violation.

But it cuts both ways. Despite a few isolated court decisions here and there, the general rule is that the EPA doesn't cover "comparable worth" cases. If day-care center workers, who are usually female, are paid less than janitors, who are usually male, that says a lot about the comparative rating given to children and trash—but it doesn't give the day-care center workers the right to sue based on the janitors' higher compensation. They're not doing the same job, and they have no legal right to sue based on the real value of their work to society.

Procedure: In addition to the federal EPA, some states have their own equal pay laws that offer even more protection to workers. The advantage of an EPA suit over a Title VII case is that someone who thinks she has an EPA case can go directly to federal court. The complex Title VII procedure is not required. However, if an employee **loses** her EPA case, she still has a right to go through the Title VII process (as long as she files in time), and can still win the Title VII case based on being paid less than a man with a similar job. In late 1992 the Eleventh Circuit ruled that the absence of an EPA violation doesn't mean that the employer was not guilty of discrimination.

Employees also have plenty of time to bring an EPA charge: two years from the date of the violation—three years, if the violation was "willful." (A willful violation is one in which the wrongdoer either knows perfectly well that the conduct violated the law, or couldn't be bothered to find out if it was lawful or not.) This is a lot longer than the time given to bring Title VII charges. Who decides whether the violation was willful? It's a factual issue, which has to be decided by the jury hearing the case—and juries are often much more sympathetic to employees than judges are.

Furthermore, **each** unequal paycheck counts as a separate EPA violation, so you get to sue for all violations that occur during the three years before you get around to filing suit. If the pay discrimination lasted longer than three years, you can only sue for the three years just before filing; but the employer can't request that your whole claim should be thrown out based on the delay.

Damages: If an EPA violation is proved, the employer has to cough up the back pay that the employee should have received but didn't. In some cases, the employee can get "front pay" to compensate her for salary she didn't receive because she lost her job improperly. Sometimes "liquidated damages" will be available. That is, the employer will have to pay double the amount of back pay. But even employers losing the EPA case can get off the hook for liquidated damages by proving that they acted in good faith and had some reason to believe their conduct was legal.

New Ways to Get Paid

Traditionally, blue-collar jobs have been paid on an hourly basis (and, as described on page 32, overtime pay is required for long workweeks). White-collar jobs are usually defined in terms of salary, perhaps with a bonus. Many jobs involve some element of incentive or contingent compensation: part or all of the compensation may involve piecework, performance standards, commissions, or quotas. In management parlance, this is called "job-based pay."

An alternative, "skill-based pay," has been gaining momentum since the 1970s. The new theory is that employees' compensation should depend on their mix of skills. That way, the company can depend on a smaller work force to do the same work as the old, larger work force—because each employee has an incentive to pick up additional skills and operate in a more flexible manner. Polaroid workers, for instance, have all been paid on a skill-based basis since April 1990. They've organized themselves into work teams and explored efficient ways to divide tasks without the bounds of traditional job titles.

Other companies, such as the furniture company Steelcase, see skill-based pay as a way to soften the impact of a demotion. An employee who learns new skills can retain the prior level of compensation, or even get a raise—even though, according to the old organization chart, he or she has been demoted to a lower-level job. (That's the optimistic, promanagement view. Then again, you could look at it as a way to force workers to do the jobs of several people for the pay of only one.)

In the eighties some companies said that they were stopped from competing effectively because they had too many long-term employees who were entitled to unrealistically high salaries. The companies' answer was to adopt a two-tier pay scale. There was no real way to take away the compensation and benefits the long-run employees had already accrued, but it was at least theoretically possible to get unions to agree to a "two-tier" contract, providing much lower compensation and benefits to new hires. Pay is often largely dependent on seniority, so the new workers got a "double whammy": they were the least senior, and they also were playing by a different, and tougher, set of rules. Conspiracy theorists might see this as a sinister plot to undermine the effectiveness of the union by setting new and old employees at one another's throats.

But in this case the conspiracy theorists often have to back down. In the 1990s few companies adopted new two-tier contracts (although the 1993 Ford Motor Company/United Auto Workers contract was two-tier); many abandoned existing two-tier contracts and went back to a single pay system for all employees. They decided that the morale problems caused by inequality of pay for workers doing exactly the same thing caused harm outweighing the money that was saved.

Off the Books

There are a lot of hassles involved in compensating an employee —lots of detailed paperwork to be completed and submitted on confusing schedules. But employers could probably cope with the nuisance if it weren't for the accompanying burden of collecting taxes for submission to the government, and actually paying taxes such as FUTA—Federal Unemployment Tax Act— (for unemployment compensation) and FICA (Social Security). Workers, especially low-paid workers, sure could live without the taxes being taken from their paychecks. So wouldn't it be convenient—and a positive benefit to employees—to pay them "off the books," without all those nuisances?

This happens very frequently: estimates of the "underground economy" go up to $500 billion a year, and that's just for the legitimate activity; crime is estimated to be twice as big a business. Isn't the underground economy a wonderful, progressive thing that puts people to work (including industrious illegal immigrants, who can't legally get an "aboveground" job)? Well, sure—except for the "tax gap" of uncollected amounts that should be going into the Treasury (plus overstated and bogus deductions)—an estimated $127 billion in 1992. Those uncollected taxes can't be used to cut the deficit, repair highways, or fund education. Instead, the burden of their payment shifts to legitimate taxpayers.

4

The Rest of the Iceberg: Pensions and Benefits

In addition to the money you can see in your paycheck, compensation also includes "hidden" elements. The amount that you receive is only part of what your employer pays. Some of the deductions are obvious: the federal, state, and local taxes which are deducted from your paycheck and itemized on the stub.

Income tax is withheld, based on the government's well-founded skepticism that the money will be available at tax time if you get paid the whole amount without deductions. You also have to pay your share of the FICA (Social Security) tax. The employer "pays" an equal amount, but it makes more sense to think of the whole amount as coming from the employee, because it naturally depresses the amount that the employer is willing to pay for the job. Initially, the Medicare tax was part of the FICA tax; since 1991 it has been a separate component, and subject to different rules: all income is subject to the Medicare tax while the FICA tax eventually "maxes out" at a set level.

The cost of pension and benefits doesn't appear on the pay stub, yet it has been estimated that the true compensation cost to an employer is about one third greater than the paycheck itself. That's because the burden of providing "deferred compensation" (pensions and profit sharing) and, especially, health benefits, is so great.

Qualified, Schmalified

To ensure that companies pay their share of employment taxes, the federal government offers them an incentive called a "qualified plan," which is a pension or benefit plan that qualifies for favorable tax treatment for the employer. The corporation that maintains the qualified plan gets a tax deduction for the amounts spent on the plan.

In fact, that's the major source of enforcement of the rules for pension and benefit plans: the threat that a noncomplying company will not only have its plan disqualified, but the disqualification will be retroactive so the company will owe a gigantic tax bill for the past years.

Companies are also allowed to have "nonqualified plans," and sometimes they do: plans that are limited to executives and/or top managers owning stock in the corporation, or plans that are much more generous to these high-paid employees than to the ordinary Joes. The deal is that the company can do anything it wants in these plans, but there won't be a tax deduction. The company has to pay for the whole thing with its after-tax income. Sometimes some or all of the benefits will also constitute taxable income for the executives. Towers Perrin, a consulting firm, looked at plans for executives in 1993. At a time when many companies were slashing benefits for rank-and-file employees, benefits for top management kept getting better and better. Of the 191 companies surveyed, 94 percent offered at least one supplemental retirement plan for top executives; the majority offered two or three supplemental plans. Additional health care coverage was also common.

One provision of the 1993 tax bill (the Revenue Reconciliation Act of 1993) was to limit the amount of compensation that could be covered by a qualified plan to $150,000. Executives earning more would have to be covered by nonqualified plans, or do without plan benefits for part of their income.

The Role of ERISA

For many years employers, and especially employers in small companies where the owners influenced the decision making, treated pension plans as their own personal piggy banks. They could set up a plan that was generous for the top management but stingy to everyone else—or, indeed, a plan that covered only the top management. There are many companies where the work force turns over frequently, because most of the jobs are low paid, boring, with little stimulation or opportunity for advancement—not much to keep people tied to the job, unless there are no jobs available with any more allure. That solved a lot of pension problems right off the bat: top management stayed put forever, but the ordinary workers quit before the ten or fifteen years they would need to earn a pension.

Major changes were created in 1974, by the federal Employee Retirement Income Security Act (ERISA). The mission of ERISA was simple: to standardize pension and benefit plans; to require some measure of fairness between high-paid and ordinary employees; and to make sure that, after a lifetime of work, the promised pension would be there for the people who earned it.

Like most statutes, ERISA has achieved some, but not complete, success. Under ERISA, there is a complex series of rules that employers must follow if they want to take advantage of the tax deductions associated with "qualified plans." If they get caught breaking an ERISA rule, however, their tax deductions can be retroactively disqualified, resulting in a gigantic tax bill and hefty penalties for the employer. Just complying with all the rules costs many hours and many dollars—a big enough burden to discourage small and start-up companies from having pension plans in the first place.

ERISA was supposed to eliminate pension inequality and create one uniform set of federal rules, instead of exposing employees (and multistate employers) to a raft of state laws that might be inconsistent. ERISA is uniform, all right—but there are many circumstances under which employees are limited to what ERISA says and to ERISA remedies. Because of preemption they often are forbidden to sue in state courts, where they might get a fairly quick ruling and generous damages.

ERISA **doesn't** require employers to have any kind of pension plan or provide any benefits at all. If a company is willing to do without the tax deduction, it's perfectly legal for the company to have only nonqualified plans that provide benefits for the top executives, but not to have any plans that cover the rank-and-file employees. What the law does say is that if an employer does have a plan, and does want to take a tax deduction for the cost of setting up, running, and funding the plan, the plan must meet at least minimal requirements as to funding, nondiscrimination (in this case, discrimination means against rank-and-file workers, not against people of a particular race, nationality, or gender), vesting (when the right to benefits becomes absolute and can't be taken away—see below), record keeping, and conduct by fiduciaries (people who manage other people's money—in this case, the pension plan, whose funds are supposed to be used exclusively for the benefit of employees and their families).

Vesting: Before ERISA too many pensions were like the proverbial treadmill. Employees kept on working, but the pension never got any closer. Before ERISA employers could impose endless delays before employees qualified for a pension, and could keep changing the rules to favor top management and disfavor ordinary workers.

Now, because of ERISA, "vesting" is required. Vesting means that employees gain increasing rights in the pension amounts reserved for them, even if they leave the company. Let's say that the plan provides for 60 percent vesting after five years of service, and the plan calculations are made based on the amount the employer contributes, not on the amount of pension the employee is scheduled to receive (in other words, it's a defined-contribution instead of a defined-benefit plan; we'll have a lot more to say about that in a minute).

Let's also say that the employee's pension account contains $10,000. After the employee has worked for five years, he or she is entitled to $6,000 of the account. (If he or she leaves before normal retirement age, the employer doesn't have to pay it immediately, but can wait until the employee reaches retirement age). If the plan is based on the size of the pension to be received at retirement, for every $100 of scheduled monthly pension benefits, a person who is 60 percent vested would be entitled to $60 a month.

ERISA sets up minimum vesting schedules that determine how fast employees will gain complete rights in their pensions. Employers do have some flexibility, but the schedule they choose must be at least as favorable to employees as one of these:

- Five-year "cliff vesting": i.e., employees who stay less than five years don't get vested at all, and have no rights in the pension money put aside for them while they worked, but employees who stay five years are immediately 100 percent vested as soon as they celebrate five years of employment with the company.
- Seven-year "graded vesting": a percentage of the pension benefit or pension account becomes vested each year, reaching 100 percent at seven years. The longer you work, the more vested you become, until you reach full vesting after seven years.

Those are the basic rules. Even faster vesting is required if the plan is "top-heavy" (has only a few employees, and a few of those earn a lot more than the others—the typical setup in a small business). Top-heavy plans have to have either three-year cliff vesting (everything vested within three years) or graded vesting ending up with 100 percent vesting after six years.

ERISA gives employers the right to amend their plans so vesting speeds up, but they're not allowed to slow down vesting —even if the plan provided for faster vesting than the law would let them get away with.

If the plan either requires or allows employees to contribute, all employees must always be 100 percent vested in the money they put into the plan. That makes sense. It's one thing for the employer to expect a certain amount of continued work in exchange for what it spends on your pension, something else entirely to make you stick around to get your own money back.

When a qualified plan terminates (either partially or totally), both ERISA and tax law require the plan to provide 100 percent vesting. If a plan merges or consolidates with another plan, or if a plan's liabilities are transferred to another plan, then each participant must be entitled to benefits at least as generous if the plan terminates after the merger or other change than if it had terminated just before the change. (If the merger takes place at a time when the plan's assets are not only big enough to meet the predictable obligations to participants who will retire in the future, but there's some money left over, the participants are entitled only to the same level of benefits they would have gotten if there hadn't been a merger; they don't get to divide up the extra money.)

Section 510: ERISA Section 510 makes it unlawful for a company to fire or lay off workers for the specific purpose of preventing them from getting benefits. There's an easy way around this for employers, though: it violates ERISA to fire an employee to avoid paying benefits (even benefits that haven't vested yet)—but it isn't an ERISA violation to keep the employee but terminate the plan.

Pension Protection: What about people who have a long but intermittent work history? They used to have to resign themselves to retirement without pensions. Today, they are more likely to gain access to pensions because of shorter schedules before they become vested, and "break-in-service" rules that make it easier to earn a pension despite several layoffs or periods out of the work force to raise children.

Another problem is pension portability. Someone may have worked for thirty, forty, fifty years—but for several employers, some of which may not have had pension plans, other jobs ending before vesting. There is still no universal system under which all pension credits can be added up to provide a larger pension, although some union members are participants in multiemployer plans that serve a similar function.

Pension, Welfare

ERISA covers both pension and welfare plans. A pension plan provides postretirement income. A welfare plan provides benefits such as health care, disability insurance, unemployment compensation, training programs, housing assistance, day care for children and dependent parents, scholarships, prepaid legal services, holiday and severance pay.

The crucial fact about welfare plans is that ERISA's vesting provisions apply only to pension plans, not to benefit plans. That modest-sounding statement has enormous consequences. If you work for an employer that has a qualified pension plan, you **have** to be allowed to participate after you've worked there for a certain time (generally a year). If you stay around long enough to "vest," you have guaranteed benefits. Employers are allowed to pick a vesting schedule; the general rule is that anyone who's worked for seven years (and most people who have worked for five years) will have vested and be entitled to at least a percentage of the full pension benefit when they reach retirement age.

But welfare benefits, including health benefits, don't vest. If your employer cuts back on medical benefits, or eliminates them entirely, you may have legal remedies—for instance, if your employer made a written or implied contract with you to maintain the benefits—but you can't bring an ERISA claim.

Benefits and Contributions

There are two major types of pension plans under ERISA. Usually, employers handle the management tasks by setting up a trust and contributing money to the trust, which is then managed by trustees who are (at least theoretically) skilled investment managers. If there are a lot of employees, or a few employees who earn six- and seven-figure salaries, the pension plan soon accumulates a lot of money. Usually it's invested in stocks —with the result that big pension plans are major stockholders, and often swing a lot of influence with corporate management simply because they can threaten to sell their stock and invest the proceeds somewhere else, and the sale of a big block of stock is almost bound to depress the stock price.

However, not all pension plans are set up in trust form; some employers choose, instead, to buy annuities for their employees from insurance companies. In that case, the security of the pension depends on the financial health of the insurance company—sometimes a good bet, sometimes not.

In a defined-contribution plan, the employer sets the level of contributions it will make for each employee in each year. There is a separate account in each year—that is, you can identify one account as Bernice's money, another as Andrew's. The money in the account is invested (the employee is frequently given some discretion about investments of his or her account). At retirement, the size of the employee's pension depends on the investment success of the pension account, so the level of the pension can rise and dip. This can be interpreted two ways: as a benefit (no risk of getting stuck with a fixed income that doesn't respond to inflation) or as a gigantic risk (the stock market hits a hiccup, and the retirement income takes a dive).

In a defined-benefit plan, the employer commits to providing a particular level of benefit for each employee, usually a percentage keyed to salary, either for the entire career or for selected years (the three years closest to retirement, for example, or the five years of highest pay—this is called a "high-five" plan). That means that the employer doesn't know how much it will have to contribute in each year; the figures have to be worked out each year, depending on investment conditions. If investments aren't yielding well, the employer will have to put in a lot more money. Defined-benefit plans are a lot harder (and more expensive) to run than defined-contribution plans, because of the need to set assumptions (who's going to retire? when? what will interest rates be like in the interim?).

PBGC Problems: When a pension plan is unable to make the necessary payments, the employees have a certain measure of protection if it's a defined-benefit plan, because a federal agency, the Pension Benefit Guaranty Corporation (PBGC) charges employers an annual premium for protection. The PBGC then uses this money to make payments when a defined-benefit plan goes under. Under federal statute, the amount of benefit that it can guarantee to any worker is limited to

$2,437.50 per month, so high-paid employees are likely to get less than their full pension.

Furthermore, the PBGC can't keep performing bailouts indefinitely; it is very short of money, and is likely to need a bailout itself unless some kind of economic miracle ensues. A federal government study published in February 1993 found that the PBGC has a large and growing deficit that is expected to grow even faster because of the prevalence of underfunded plans and the potentially inadequate premiums that PBGC charges employers. PBGC estimated that plan funding throughout the nation was about $51 billion short of employers' obligations. About $12 billion of that amount exposed PBGC to heavy risk because it was owed by financially troubled industries like steel, automobiles, and airlines; the other $39 billion was a remoter risk.

Other Types of Plans

A profit-sharing plan is a plan that has a definite formula, set in advance, for making plan contributions and deciding how much should be contributed for each employee. In years where there are no profits, the employer doesn't have to make contributions —unlike a pension plan, where contributions must be made each year or the plan will lose qualification. The profit-sharing plan must also set up a formula for distributing the money after a fixed number of years (the money must stay in the plan for at least two years—it can't be set aside one year, distributed in the next), when the employee reaches a specified age, or when an event such as death, retirement, or layoff occurs.

Stock Bonus: A stock-bonus plan is somewhat similar to a profit-sharing plan, but the benefits are paid in the form of stock in the employer corporation, not in money. An Employee Stock Ownership Plan (ESOP) is a stock-bonus plan that limits its investment (not just the payoff) to the employer's own stock. ESOPs were heavily touted in the 1970s as a big benefit for workers in the form of enhanced worker control. In the 1980s, ESOPs were big players in some of the takeover games; sometimes setting up an ESOP, and giving it a big glug of stock, could be enough to foil a raid.

CODA (401(k)): A CODA (Cash or Deferred Arrangement), also known as a 401(k) plan (because its formal rules are found in Section 401(k) of the Internal Revenue Code) is a plan allowing an employee to choose between receiving some compensation right away, or having it deposited in a profit-sharing or stock-bonus plan. For 1994 the maximum amount that can be applied to a plan is $9,200. Some 401(k) plans just let employees save their own money, with the appreciation accumulating tax free until they take money out of the account. Other plans are even more attractive: the employer "matches" the employee's contribution (let's say by contributing $1 for every $3 that the employee places in the CODA).

These plans first became available in 1982. Since then, nearly all large corporations have adopted a 401(k) plan, and they were common in smaller companies, too. In 1991, 44 percent of companies with fifty to ninety-nine employees offered 401(k) plans, as did half the companies with 100–249 employees and two thirds of larger companies. In 1992 there were some 185,000 corporate sponsors, and approximately 16 million employees had saved more than $410 billion through CODAs.

If you're living hand-to-mouth, you probably won't want a 401(k) plan even if it's offered because you need every penny to meet your obligations. But if you're a little more comfortably off, saving part of your salary each year can be a painless way to make sure your retirement years are comfortable. The money comes out of your paycheck, and goes into the CODA account, before you even notice it. (This works especially well with raises and bonuses; whisk them away, and you won't have to limit your present standard of living to help out in the future.)

However, 401(k)s can call for some hard thinking. Federal law permits employers to turn over investment control of the accounts to their employee-owners. If the plan offers at least three investment choices and permits employees to transfer funds between subaccounts at least four times a year, the employee is considered to call the shots—and the employer will probably not be liable if the account loses value when the employee's investment choices don't pan out. If your 401(k) is invested according to your instructions, you'll have to take the time to review your choices regularly, set goals, and switch when your goals are not satisfied.

Nonprofit Plans: A 403(b) plan is a pension plan for church workers, public school teachers, employees of tax-exempt nonprofit organizations, or state or municipal government workers.

WARNING Effective December 19, 1993, the banking rules changed. Under earlier law, a self-directed retirement account (such as a Keogh plan, 401(k) plan, or 403(b) plan) deposited in a bank account could get deposit insurance on an amount up to $400,000. But as of December 1993, the maximum insured deposit is only $100,000 per person per bank. If you have an account of this type and its balance hits six figures, you may need another account in another bank . . . or, in light of current abysmally low interest rates, you may need another way to invest your account instead of keeping it in a bank in the first place.

An SEP, or Simplified Employee Plan, is a system under which an employer sets up IRAs for workers and makes contributions to them. Small businesses may prefer this alternative to setting up a conventional pension plan.

A top hat plan is a nonqualified plan usually used to provide extra retirement income for top managers; because it's not a qualified plan, it's free from most of the ERISA requirements. Other nonqualified plans are sometimes described as rabbi trusts (a type of plan first used by a synagogue to provide additional compensation for its rabbi) or secular trusts (an adaptation of the rabbi trust concept). Rabbi and secular trusts are sometimes summed up as SERPs, or Supplemental Executive Retirement Plans. The trusts are used to save up funds to pay the special benefits—but the corporation doesn't get a tax deduction for contributions to the trust, or for the eventual payments to the retired executive.

Nondiscrimination Rules

There is a seemingly endless set of calculations to be performed to determine if a plan is "nondiscriminatory." In broad outline, at least 70 percent of the pension contributions must be made for, or benefit payouts must go to, the rank-and-file workers, not to highly paid employees or employees with an ownership interest in the company.

In a huge company, with 12,000 rank-and-file employees and 400 executives, this test isn't too tough to meet, even if the workers earn minimum wage and the managers get big salaries and generous retirement benefits. However, if the Ed Rothingham Chemical Company consists of ol' Eddie himself, his "outside man" sales-oriented partner, two workers who mix the glop and put it into cans, and a secretary, statistical calculations can produce some odd results. Ed and Everett are going to stay there forever, but turnover is likely among production workers and the secretary. If they leave before their pensions vest, then the amount already contributed for their pensions becomes a "forfeiture"—and, in effect, it goes back into the pot that pays for Eddie and Everett's eventual pensions. Very young workers can also lose out: pension contributions don't even have to begin until a worker is twenty-one.

The rules contain some loopholes that can be used by the owners of small businesses to increase the share of the plan's benefits that go to the owners instead of the ordinary employees. We can't explain all of the ramifications (if we did, this chapter would look like the Manhattan telephone book), so we'll just note that if your plan is "age weighted," "cross-tested," or both, your pension benefit is likely to be smaller than if the plan did not have these features. (You can find out if your plan uses these techniques by reading the Summary Plan Description or asking the plan administrator or human resources person who handles benefits.) You may need to increase your savings and personal investments to guarantee the postretirement lifestyle you want, and to make up for smaller-than-anticipated plan benefits.

Minimum Participation Rules

From the employer's viewpoint, if there is heavy turnover, it may be a waste to contribute to the plan for people who are only going to work for a few months or a few years. Employers tend to see pensions as rewards for people who put in a full career with the employer. Tax law gives this viewpoint some legitimacy. Employers can keep very young or very short-term workers out of the pension plan, but employers must stay within limits or lose qualification (and tax deductions) for the plan.

However, the "minimum participation" rules for qualified plans say that all employees who have reached age twenty-one and worked at the company for one year (or 1,000 hours) are entitled to become plan participants. There are a couple of exceptions. If the plan covers only employees of an educational institution, they can be denied plan participation until they reach age twenty-six—but they must be 100 percent vested after only one year. (See page 42 for a discussion of vesting.) Another possibility is for the employer to require three years of employment for plan participation, as long as the employee gets full, 100 percent vesting after two years.

There's a really complex set of rules about the percentage of employees participating in the plan, but it boils down to this: for the plan to remain qualified, the percentage of rank-and-file employees participating in the plan must be at least 70 percent of the percentage of highly compensated, key employees participating in the plan.

The Retirement Equity Act

ERISA was designed to decrease the number of workers left without any pension at all; the Retirement Equity Act of 1984 was designed to minimize the number of ex-wives and widows left without income because of divorce or a worker's death. (The law applies on a unisex basis, but it's more common for women to depend on their husband's pensions than the other way around.)

Under the REA the basic way that pensions must be paid to married retirees is the "qualified joint and survivor annuity."

That is, regular pension payments will be made to the retiree (usually monthly). The payments will continue as long as either the retiree or his or her spouse is still alive. It's up to the employer: either the pension can stay at the same level throughout both lifetimes, or it can be cut after the first payee dies—but it must stay at least 50 percent of the original level.

As you'd expect, most employers do cut the payment after one spouse dies, so it's possible to get a larger pension by choosing a "single-life annuity," which stops when one spouse dies. The REA requires that both spouses have to agree to the single-life annuity option.

Some people (generally, insurance agents) recommend a "pension max" strategy: take the larger single-life pension, and buy insurance or invest with the extra income. Theoretically, this will result in more income all around. But before you do this, have the figures checked by a financially knowledgeable, but objective, person. Sometimes the strategy "works" only if some very unrealistic assumptions are made.

Another important REA change is a technical one. Under pre-ERISA law, employers often kept employees from getting pensions by laying them off—and then saying that, not only would they not earn pension credits during the layoff, but the "break in service" would eliminate pension credits for all the time they worked **before** the break. The REA makes it much harder for employers to use this device, especially if the break in service was caused by maternity or parenting leave.

The REA also has important effects on divorce planning. ERISA has an "antialienation" provision to protect retirement security: you **can't** assign away your pension in advance, and your creditors can't get at it either. The most important exception is the QDRO, or Qualified Domestic Relations Order, granted in connection with a divorce or legal separation. The QDRO can relate to the worker's obligations to the ex-spouse, for child support, or both.

Several things can happen to pensions during a divorce. The nonemployee spouse can be awarded a lump sum at the time of the divorce, or extra alimony, to make up for not sharing in the pension; or a QDRO can be issued. The plan then honors the court order. It's important to note that the plan can pay over plan benefits to the ex-spouse even before the employee collects his or her pension: QDROs can be honored as soon as the employee reaches age fifty or could get benefits from the plan if he or she retired or quit.

The budget bill passed by Congress in August 1993 adds a new kind of QDRO to the arsenal of divorcing spouses. Employer group health plans have to recognize "qualified medical child support orders" issued by courts. States have a legal obligation to pass and enforce laws dealing with these orders. Congress's purpose is to get kids covered by their parents' health plans, instead of having the kids get their medical care from the Medicaid system, which has a hefty component of state funds with the balance coming from the federal government. By the way, if your ex-spouse is covered by a nonqualified plan, you will not be able to use a QDRO to get a share of benefits under that plan; QDROs affect only qualified plans. (You still may be able to get the nonqualified benefits counted as part of the marital assets that have to be divided; you just can't take advantage of the QDRO as an easy enforcement mechanism.)

The Amazing Disappearing Pension

The brain-cracking complexity of ERISA's pension rules is not supposed to keep accountants and actuaries in BMWs and Brioni—it's supposed to prevent funny business with the pension fund. Alas, despite these rules, there are a number of circumstances that prevent retirees from receiving the full amount of pension they expected, or from getting anything at all. The pension rules have been amended many times since ERISA was passed in 1974. The amendments strive to maintain a balance of power. Our society wants to encourage business success, and to allow business owners to work hard; letting top executives earn large pensions is an incentive to do this. We also want ordinary workers to get a fair shake, and to be able to retire with dignity. So the very complex system of tax and ERISA rules includes some rules to favor management and some to favor employees. In a system this complex, there are always some loopholes (such as integration with Social Security—see page 54) that can be exploited to shift a higher percentage of the company's total pension dollar from the average worker to the company's owners or top managers. The secret is to provide the absolute minimum for average workers and the absolute maximum for the bosses that the law allows.

"Integration" with Social Security means that an employer's contribution or an employee's benefit is reduced to take Social Security benefits into account. For a low-paid worker, this will either wipe out the employer's obligation to pay a pension, or cut down the amount.

Then, the pension plan could be underfunded. True, ERISA contains stringent "funding requirements" that plans are supposed to meet—but they often don't. Sometimes the companies go to the trouble of pleading financial hardship and getting permission from the IRS and DOL to take a "funding holiday." Sometimes they simply fail to make the required contributions, assuming that the PBGC (Pension Benefit Guaranty Corporation) will bail out the plan to prevent total economic hardship to employees. When employees and unions demand bigger pensions and better benefits, the path of least resistance is for the employer to say yes; but when the time comes to pay for the plan, the money may not be there.

Then again, employers can make all the contributions required by the plan's assumptions—but the assumptions can be completely nuts. In 1993, for example, General Motors acknowledged that it earned 6.4 percent on its pension funds—but made contributions on the theory that they would be earning 11 percent, creating a $14 billion gap. They weren't the only private-sector company in the same fix: Chrysler, Exxon, and Westinghouse Electric, to name just a few, had the same problem, and **most** government-employee pension funds have shortfalls. The problem got even worse when all 1992 pension results were analyzed: according to the PBGC, the 50 "most underfunded" plans had a shortfall of $38.05 billion in 1992, sinking $9 billion farther into the hole. Another factor that sometimes prevents employees from getting the full pension they expected is that an employer, acting in good faith and making rational assumptions, can still have bad luck with the investments that support the pension payments.

In May 1993, the U.S. Supreme Court slung a safety net for

employees. *Commissioner v. Keystone Consolidated Industries,* #91-1677, 62 LW 4481 (May 24, 1993)(the Commissioner is the Commissioner of IRS—it's a tax case) says employers have to use real money to satisfy their obligations to finance defined-benefit pension plans. They can't use real estate for this purpose anymore—even real estate held free and clear, without mortgages. The Supreme Court changed the rule because it's all too easy for employers to assign an inflated value to property contributed to a plan. Even if the employer provides an honest valuation, property values could decline, thus endangering the payment of benefits—especially if the plan has to hold a "fire sale" of many properties in order to satisfy its obligations.

These days, big employers have a new source of power: threatening to declare, or actually declaring, bankruptcy. The bankruptcy process may give them a chance to cast off unprofitable contracts and unfavorable deals with unions. Retiree benefits, and perhaps even pensions, can be imperiled as the bankruptcy court creates a rehabilitation plan.

Another problem is that the employer might be perfectly okay, but the insurance company providing the retirement annuities might be in severe trouble or already underwater. Theoretically, there is a bailout mechanism here too. Just as the PBGC insures pensions, all the states now have insurance guaranty funds that bail out insurers. Unfortunately, there are situations under which some insurance-funded pensions won't be covered at all (most state guaranty funds don't cover transactions outside the state) and others will be limited by maximum amounts covered.

GICs Can Be Sticky: In the 1970s and 1980s, many employers bought Guaranteed Investment Contracts (GICs) from insurance companies. The GICs promised a high interest rate. Then, it was no problem: by speculating in real estate and trading junk bonds, insurers could easily earn a return that would cover their promises under the GICs. Today, the promise is still there, but interest rates have nose-dived. If the company can't make good, the insurance guaranty fund may come to the rescue. Then again, it may not: several states exclude GICs from the insurer bailout provisions.

Pension Procedures

Somewhere amid the instruction booklets for your electronic appliances, your home mortgage, and other vital but unread documents, there probably lurks an SPD: the Summary Plan Description of your pension plan. All participants get an SPD, which is supposed to be written in understandable language.

In case after case, courts have said that whatever the SPD says, goes: it is the fundamental factor determining employees' rights under a qualified plan. If the employer chooses to modify the plan, all participants must be given a summary of the changes within 210 days of the end of the year in which the employer made the change.

The SPD must include at least this much information:

- The name of the plan.
- How it is administered (is there a trust? is it administered by an insurance company?).
- Who the administrators and trustees are.
- Requirements for participation in the plan.
- Summary of any provisions in a collective bargaining agreement (union contract) that affect the plan.
- Any circumstances that can lead to being disqualified from plan participation, or ineligible for plan benefits.
- The way the plan will be funded (including whether employee contributions are allowed—or required). If benefits are insurance-funded, the identity of the insurer has to be disclosed.
- Whether the plan's official year is a calendar year or a fiscal year—if it's a fiscal year, when it ends. This is important because a lot of funding and other issues revolve around things happening in a particular "plan year."
- Whether the PBGC guarantees plan benefits.
- An explanation of participants' rights under ERISA, including the claims and appeals procedures.

ERISA Section 503 requires all plans to have a claims procedure for participants and their beneficiaries. If a claim is denied (for instance, your employer says that you are not eligible to retire yet), you must be given a written notice of the claims denial, complete with reasons for the denial, within ninety days of the time the decision is made to deny benefits.

Miscellaneous Benefits

Cafeteria Plans: A cafeteria plan is a benefit plan that lets employees choose to get some compensation in cash or in the form of taxable or nontaxable benefits. Some cafeteria plans are wholly funded by the employer; others require contributions from the employee—these are usually taken out of salary instead of billing the employee for the cost. The theory is that employers can save money by having cafeteria plans. Employees get only the benefits they want and value; the employer doesn't have to pay for benefits the employees really don't care about.

Cafeteria plans can include:

- Accident and health insurance
- Group term life insurance
- Dependent care assistance
- Employer contributions to 401(k) plans
- Group legal services plans

Cafeteria plans are not allowed to include scholarships, educational assistance, meals and lodging, or employee discounts. Because they are benefit, and not deferred compensation plans, the benefits provided by a cafeteria plan exist on a "use it or lose it" basis—unused benefits can't be carried over to the next year.

Flexible Spending Accounts: You get to set aside some of your own money (usually, the maximum is $3,000 a year) to pay for medical expenses that are otherwise unreimbursed. The advantage is that you won't have to pay federal income tax, FICA tax, or Medicare tax on the money, and all the states except New Jersey and Pennsylvania also consider this money free of state income tax. That could add up to a powerful incentive to use pretax dollars to cover medical expenses (which could include deductibles and coinsurance under your health plan).

Company Car: This is considered a "working condition fringe benefit"—and therefore its value does not constitute taxable income—if the car is provided in connection with the employer's trade or business, and if the employee would be entitled to a deduction for providing his or her own wheels. If the employer provides parking, this is likely to be considered a working condition fringe benefit—even if parking would not be deductible because it would be considered an ordinary part of commuting.

Employee Discounts on Merchandise Made/Sold by Employer: Not counted in taxable income.

Home Office Expenses: Reimbursement from the employer is not taxable income—but only if the employee maintains an office at home for the convenience of the employer; if the home office is part of the home used exclusively for business, or is in a separate structure (e.g., a converted garage); or if the employer's patients, clients, or customers meet with the employee at the home office location.

Outplacement Assistance: It's a sad sign of the times that more and more employers offer "outplacement assistance," including career counseling and help with sending out resumes and arranging interviews for your next job, because you're about to lose the one you already have. If your employer does this (say, because a Reduction in Force is planned; your department is being eliminated), a 1992 IRS Revenue Ruling says that you will not have to pay taxes on the value of the outplacement assistance, as long as the outplacement assistance program provides valuable benefits to your **employer.** (The benefit to the employer means that the program qualifies as a "working condition fringe benefit" rather than as taxable income for the recipients.) For example, if your employer gets a better public image, morale of current workers improves, or former employees decide not to sue the employer, the program becomes a working condition fringe benefit, so nobody has extra taxable income as a result of the program.

Severance Pay: Sorry, this is compensation and therefore taxable income; and if the employer has a habit of paying severance, then the severance plan is covered by ERISA.

On the other hand, the Fifth Circuit has found that paying "golden parachutes" to some executives (a generous lump-sum payment if they lose their jobs within two years of a takeover of the employer company, designed to make the takeover process more expensive and therefore less desirable) is not an ERISA plan. The court's theory was that the golden parachutes were one-time payments, with no need for administration or making regular payments, and anyway the obligation to pay depended on an event that might never happen (the takeover). The upshot was that, when the takeover really did happen, an executive who was not included in the plan couldn't bring an ERISA suit based on the exclusion.

RRA '93: In most years, Congress passes a very long, very hard-fought bill that deals with various issues relating to the national budget. Usually the bill is called the Omnibus Budget Reconciliation Act of (whatever the year is), or "OBRA" for short. A major component in any OBRA is amendments to the Internal Revenue Code. Sometimes the tax provisions are published separately, as the Revenue Reconciliation Act (RRA) of (whatever year). RRA '93 had some interesting provisions relating to employee benefits:

- Educational assistance from the employer can be provided tax free until December 31, 1994. The educational assistance provision expired in 1992, and Congress forgot to re-enact it, but RRA '93 puts it back into the tax code retroactive to June 30, 1992. (If you had a big tax bill because of employer educational assistance, check with an accountant to see if it pays to file an amended tax return to get a refund.)
- Self-employed persons, and people who own 2 percent or more of the shares in a Subchapter S corporation, once

again have their 25 percent deduction for health insurance premiums.

- Before RRA '93, employees got a deduction if job needs forced them to move 35 miles or more; now only a 50-mile move counts. They can no longer deduct expenses of house-hunting trips, or temporary quarters at the new job site— just the cost of schlepping their possessions and traveling to a new home. However, if the employer reimburses the moving expenses, the reimbursement isn't considered taxable income for the employee, no matter how large the reimbursement.
- Do you belong to a golf club, country club, alumni club, or other comfortable spot for business discussions? As of January 1, 1994, you will no longer be able to deduct your club dues from your income taxes.
- Remember the fabled three-martini business lunch? At first business meals were fully deductible; then they were cut back to 80 percent deductible. Starting January 1, 1994, the deduction is only 50 percent.

Who Gets What? In June 1993, the Department of Labor's Bureau of Labor Statistics released data on benefits provided in 1991 for 36 million employees working for companies with one hundred or more employees. More than three quarters of employees (78 percent) participated in some kind of retirement plan—sometimes more than one plan. Defined-benefit plans were somewhat more popular than defined-contribution plans, even though they're tougher to administer, perhaps because they give the owners of small businesses an excellent chance to beef up their own pension coverage. More than 90 percent of full-time employees were entitled to paid holidays and vacations; 80 percent got paid leave for funerals and jury duty. It usually added up to ten holidays, three days for a funeral, and nine days' vacation after a year on the job, seventeen days after ten years, and twenty vacation days after twenty years.

As for leave (remember, the Bureau of Labor Statistics survey covered events in 1991, well before the effective date of the FMLA), 37 percent of surveyed workers got unpaid maternity leave of up to five weeks; 29 percent had access to unpaid paternity leave, but only 2 percent got paid maternity leave, and only one out of a hundred could take paid paternity leave.

Another survey, by market research firm Grant Thornton, reported that one third of midsized companies had qualified pension plans, and 26 percent had profit-sharing plans—but 61 percent had 401(k) plans. In other words, the shift to greater employee responsibility, and smaller employer participation, is very marked in these companies.

Unmarried Partners: Usually plans are written in terms of employees and their spouses. In March 1993, the Southern District of New York (a court that is influential on business issues because so many big companies have New York headquarters) ruled that it's okay for an employer to restrict spousal benefits to people who are legally married. In the particular case, it meant that it was okay for A T & T to deny a death benefit to a deceased employee's lesbian life partner—even though A T & T policy forbids discrimination on the basis of sexual orientation.

Some companies do provide spousal benefits for unmarried partners, including same-sex partners. As of the summer of 1994, these companies included Ben & Jerry's Homemade Ice Cream, Borland International, Levi Strauss, Lotus Development, MCA/Universal, Silicon Graphics, and Time Warner. Government employees who work for New York City, or for the state governments of New York and Vermont, are entitled to "spousal" coverage for same-sex domestic partners, and New York State is considering extending the coverage to heterosexual unmarried couples with a serious, committed domestic partnership. One problem, though: the health benefits for the spousal equivalent constitute taxable income for the employee, because tax rules, too, are limited to coverage of married couples.

Making Choices

To a large extent your role in your pension plan is a passive one: money is reserved for your benefit, and when you retire, you get it back—in a lump sum or in a series of annuity payments. However, for several reasons (including a lot of litigation centering on employers' choices), many employers give employees a more active role.

Is there a 401(k) plan? You'll have to decide how much of your salary you can afford to set aside—and whether, if the employer matches part of your contribution, this makes enough of a difference to scale down your current lifestyle in favor of more funds at retirement. If you have a cafeteria plan, you must choose which benefits you want.

Some decisions are a setup (you don't need dependent care benefits if you don't have any kids and aren't responsible for the care of a frail elderly parent); others are tougher: do you need disability coverage more or less than you need extra vacation? Health benefits under the cafeteria plan gain in importance if the company cuts back on the regular health plan by increasing your responsibility for paying premiums or by upping the level of deductibles and coinsurance.

If you are a participant in a defined-contribution plan, there's a good chance that you'll have some responsibility for allocating investments for your account. Typically, you will be given three to five mutual fund choices. The most prudent thing to do is to diversify, to avoid concentrating too heavily on your employer's own stock, and to keep reviewing the account. The usual arrangement is for you to get a chance once a year to change your investment—which could make sense, if stocks are doing great but bonds are anemic, or if the money market fund has fallen into the swamp, or whatever.

Of course, it seems that each paycheck vanishes magically within a day of payday, so it can seem laughably difficult to accumulate a retirement savings account by having your paycheck reduced further. But remember that, even though inflation has slowed down, it still exists—so you'll no doubt need more money than you think for comfortable retirement. Your Social Security benefits are likely to be lower than you expect; the pension from your employer may vanish, or fail to keep up with the real cost of living. You can get information about projected retirement income (which will influence your savings patterns) from your company's human resources department, from your union, or from a financial planner or broker.

Experts offer a caveat: if you are invited to a seminar about your benefits, find out who's sponsoring it. If it's provided by the employer, remember that their first priority is reducing the cost of the plan, so some expensive items may get little or no attention. More likely it will be offered by an independent outsider— but the speakers will be brokers and insurance people who want to sell you products and/or financial planning services. These seminars can be a great no-cost way to "audition" a financial adviser, but remember that his or her main interest is in adding new, profitable clients.

Money going into a pension plan is supposed to stay there until retirement, but there are ways to get it out if you need it. Make sure you understand the tax consequences of withdrawing money prematurely (generally, you will have to pay income tax on the amount withdrawn, plus a penalty excise tax, but there are certain hardship exceptions). Another possibility is a loan from your pension plan or 401(k). Find out the loan procedure —but remember, if you don't pay back the money as required, you may have tax problems, and you certainly won't have the level of retirement funding you were counting on.

Fiduciary Obligations

A fiduciary is someone who is in charge of someone else's money. The legal system imposes heavy responsibilities on fiduciaries. Of course, they're not allowed to steal, or commit fraud, or conceal information they're legally obligated to disclose. They also have an obligation to be prudent (i.e., not do something stupid with the money they've been entrusted with). If they violate their fiduciary obligations, they can be removed from office, or "surcharged" (made to pay money to the unfortunate people whose money it was in the first place).

Naturally, then, when it comes to pension plans, being a fiduciary is something of a hot potato, and no one really wants to handle it. The employer can't help being a fiduciary: even if it hires professional investment managers, its fiduciary responsibility remains. In mid-1993, the Supreme Court decided that an actuarial firm hired as a consultant can't be made to pay a share of compensatory or punitive damages assessed against a pension plan, because the firm was not a fiduciary. Even if the consultant helped the real fiduciary breach its duty, the consultant can appropriately be punished by being made to give back any money it received inappropriately.

On the other hand, a Third Circuit case from the end of 1993 lets plan participants or beneficiaries sue their plans' trustees or administrators for breach of fiduciary duty if the participants or beneficiaries want to enforce the terms of the pension plan.

5

Health Insurance:
Significant Benefits,
Significant Problems

There's more to a job than money, or even retirement income. For many workers, their employer provides them with health care coverage that they couldn't afford to buy for themselves. Full-time workers employed by medium-sized or large corporations usually do have some kind of health insurance, and the prevalence of employer-paid coverage is one reason why health care is so expensive. Health care providers tend to key their rates to the maximum that insurance plans will pay—which is tough luck for those with less generous insurance plans, or no insurance at all.

We've already written a book about health insurance (*The FIGHT BACK! Guide to Health Insurance,* published in 1993), so we won't reinvent the wheel. If you already have a copy, this chapter gives a summary and updates the information with post-publication developments.

Before the 1920s, there wasn't any health insurance to speak of in the United States. Health insurance became important as an employee benefit during World War II, when civilian workers were scarce and employers were not allowed to offer higher wages to attract workers, but could add employee benefits. After the war, workers, and especially unionized workers, came to consider health insurance a normal part of the compensation package. By the 1970s, after many years of health care cost inflation, health insurance represented a major part of the cost of employment.

To cut this cost, employers began to impose limits, such as forcing employees to pay higher deductibles and coinsurance, making them pay part of the insurance premium, or requiring or strongly suggesting that employees get their medical care from HMOs (Health Maintenance Organizations), PPOs (Preferred Provider Organizations), or other types of managed health care, believing that it would cut costs. (Ironically, a federal government report released in February 1994 shows that managed care did reduce health care costs for employers in the early 1990s—but at a time when all health care costs declined from their all-time high reached in 1989; managed-care and nonmanaged-care costs ended up about equal.)

In the 1980s and 1990s, employers often shifted from full-time, permanent employees entitled to health benefits to part-timers or temporary workers not entitled to coverage. Some employers simply canceled their health plans, or "self-insured" (set aside money to pay health claims, instead of buying insurance). Self-insurance also frees employers from certain legal obligations that cover employers who have health plans.

When we started writing this book, it seemed very likely that President Clinton's health reform program, the Health Security Act (HSA), would pass. The HSA included an "employer mandate," requiring employers to provide health insurance for their workers. But by the time we went to press, in late 1994, Congress had definitively rejected the HSA and was dithering about what kind of health care reform (if any) to pass.

Understanding Your Coverage

Here's a simple way to find out if you really understand your health insurance coverage. If, like most people, you have only a superficial understanding, use this checklist as a way to learn in advance of any problem.

If there's anything you still don't understand, ask the personnel department, employee assistance department, your union representative, or the person answering the (800) number maintained by your health insurer. That way, you'll be prepared to keep a medical problem from turning into a financial problem.

- Does your plan cover care from any doctor or hospital on equal terms, or do you have to pay extra if you get care outside an HMO (Health Maintenance Organization), network, or PPO (Preferred Provider Organization)?
- If you get to pick your own doctors, start asking around, and make a list of well-recommended family doctors, pediatricians, obstetricians, internists, cardiologists, or whatever kind of doctor you and your family might reasonably be expected to need.
- If you are expected to get care from a closed group of providers, make sure you know where to find them and what the procedures are.
- Do you have to pay in advance for care, then file a claim form for reimbursement, or will you get the care, then be billed later only for your coinsurance responsibility (e.g., the plan pays 80 percent—you have to pay the other 20 percent)?
- Exactly how big is your copayment responsibility, anyway? Does it vary for different kinds of procedures? How large is the deductible (amount you must pay before there is any plan coverage)? Is there a limit on the out-of-pocket payments you can be stuck with in a given year, or for a particular illness?
- If you have to file claim forms, get a blank form and work through the process a couple of times so it will be easy and automatic if you ever need to do it for real care.

- Are there any procedures that require approval from the plan? For instance, you may be denied benefits, or have benefits reduced, for nonemergency hospitalization unless you get approval from the plan's "utilization review" staff. How do you go about getting the approval? What can you do if you are turned down but you and your doctor still think you need the care? Generally, you have some kind of right to a hearing; make sure you know how to request it, and make sure that you make your application before the deadline.

- If you're married, and your spouse also has employment-related coverage, work through a few hypothetical situations involving your care, your spouse's care, your kids' care. There are various methods for "coordination of benefits"—find out how it works. Generally, the rules will be applied to make sure you never get more than you would get if there was just one insurance policy in the picture.

- Set up a bookkeeping system. You may be entitled to a deduction for health insurance premiums, or for medical expenses you pay that are not reimbursed by insurance. You'll lose the deduction if you can't figure out what you spent for what reason.

- Plan what to do in case of a real emergency. Which local hospitals have emergency rooms? Which is the closest hospital to home, work, your kids' schools, places where an accident might occur? Which is the best? What's the best way to get to the emergency room?

- What happens if someone in your family needs to be hospitalized, but the first hospital he or she goes to doesn't have a bed available? Usually, a transfer will be arranged as soon as the patient's condition is stable—but it's the patient's responsibility to arrange for transportation to the second hospital, probably via private ambulance.

Health Insurance and Career Planning: When you're hunting for your first job, or a new job, you'll probably compare health insurance and other benefits as part of the complex equation of deciding which job is better. (Which offers better salary?

More promotion possibilities? More interesting work? More congenial colleagues? A shorter commute?)

However, fewer and fewer employers are offering health care coverage at all (65 percent did so in 1988, and only 61 percent did in 1993), so you may not be able to find any job offering health coverage—especially if you are also limited to temporary or part-time work. Large companies are just about as likely to terminate or limit coverage as smaller companies, so choosing a big company in the expectation that it will have better or more consistent health benefits is not necessarily valid.

Practical Morality: There's always a temptation to describe health care services in the way that yields maximum coverage. Most plans exclude routine checkups; even plans that cover mental health services usually exclude marriage counseling. So what harm does it do if that checkup is described as "treatment of upper respiratory infection," or the family therapy is called "job-related depression"? Your doctor may gladly agree to your suggestion to "tweak" the description; the doctor may even suggest it.

First and not least, it's dishonest. If you get caught, it could be the kind of "after-acquired evidence" (see page 20) that would justify firing you. It could also be the kind of evidence that proves your discharge was for good cause, not based on race, gender, nationality, or other forbidden discrimination. So-called "harmless white lies" can also harm your entitlement to health coverage. If you have a record of frequent health claims, even for minor illnesses, you'll find it harder and more expensive to get insurance if you ever need an individual policy. Apply for disability insurance? You may be turned down, based on the maladies that appeared in your health record.

If you disguised your checkups (or your kid's checkups) as ear infections, you may find that you are denied coverage for later ear problems, because your coverage might be tailored to exclude past problem areas. If you have a lot of visits on record for vague complaints like "fatigue," a potential insurer or employer might suspect that you're hiding a serious disease such as cancer or AIDS. Yes, it is against the law to discriminate on this basis—but you will be in an impossible legal position if you try to sue, since you may have already compromised your case by lies in your medical records.

Health Insurance and ERISA: ERISA is the federal statute covering pensions and "welfare benefit plans" that provide fringe benefits for employees. Detailed information about ERISA and pensions can be found on pages 39–64. ERISA and the Tax Code explain what employers have to do to have a "qualified plan." One of the most important areas of regulation is "vesting"—the circumstances under which an employee becomes absolutely entitled to pension benefits once he or she reaches normal retirement age. Once an employer offers a pension plan, it's hard to cut back on the advantages of the plan to employees.

ERISA, however, says nothing about health insurance plans. Crucially, it doesn't provide vesting rules, and in fact health insurance plans never vest. As far as ERISA is concerned, employers can change health insurance plans at a whim, even cancel them.

The ironic part is that, because ERISA **mentions** health plans, it is interpreted to "preempt" most state regulation of health plans. That is, the subject is treated as one that is exclusively federal, and the states are supposed to keep their noses out of it. For employees in self-insured plans (plans where the employer just keeps a reserve of money for paying health claims, instead of involving an insurance policy), ERISA prevents them from bringing almost any lawsuit involving the health plan.

The Supreme Court struck another blow at employee lawsuits in 1989 by dividing ERISA plans into two groups. In the first—and by far the biggest—group, the plan administrators have discretion to make a lot of decisions. In the smaller group, the plan spells out every detail, leaving no discretion for the administrators. This group of plans is small because almost everyone recognizes that flexibility is needed to cope with practical, legal, and economic changes. If the administrator does have discretion, courts have a very limited role. All they can do is see if the administrator abused discretion by being "arbitrary and capricious"; courts can't look at the administrator's decision to see if he or she made the right decision instead of the wrong one.

For ERISA to be involved, there must be a "plan"—usually a formal, written document, but sometimes a repeated course of conduct by the employer may be considered a plan. For example, the Eleventh Circuit found an employer who helped employees buy health insurance by writing a business check for the premium and contributing part of the cost (the employees reimbursed the employer for the rest) to have an established "plan." There was a continuing subsidy from the employer, not just a one-time purchase.

These days, you may still get your medical care from kindly old Doc Jones, an independent solo practitioner—but you're far more likely to have some kind of HMO, PPO, or network involved in your care. When ERISA was passed in 1974, these forms of medical organization were embryonic or unheard-of, so ERISA's terms don't come to grips with managed care. Two courts hearing very similar cases about HMOs and ERISA reached opposite conclusions in 1992 and 1993.

The earlier case says that ERISA does not preempt a claim that the HMO should be held liable for malpractice committed by its primary doctors. The result was that the patient was allowed to pursue a state-court case against the HMO. But the later case does find ERISA preemption in a case where the survivors of an HMO participant tried to sue the HMO on the theory that the participant died because of the HMO's delay in approving the potentially lifesaving heart surgery. This time, the court said that the plaintiffs were challenging the HMO's role in plan administration, and that clearly falls under ERISA, not state wrongful-death law.

After an employer's self-insured plan went bankrupt, the plan participants tried to sue the insurance company that administered the plan. They were unsuccessful: the Second Circuit said that ERISA doesn't allow suits against plan administrators, even if the participants really believed that the insurance company sold insurance instead of just administrative services.

Health Insurance and the ADA: The Americans with Disabilities Act (ADA, PL 101-336, July 26, 1990) extends the earlier coverage of handicap discrimination under the Rehabilitation Act to include all businesses with fifteen or more employees (originally twenty-five or more; the lower limitation was phased in gradually). Employers are covered whether or not they are federal contractors or get federal funding. They are forbidden to discriminate against qualified handicapped people in hiring, promotion, or compensation. Furthermore, they must provide reasonable accommodations for disabled workers—wheelchair ramps, readers for blind people, visible signaling devices instead of sirens for deaf people, and the like.

The ADA also forbids health insurance discrimination based on a person's handicap. An employer can't prevent someone from participating in a health insurance plan because of his or her health status. On the other hand, employers **can** have plans that exclude preexisting conditions, or that deny coverage for some drugs or procedures—as long as these provisions were adopted and are applied in good faith, uniformly for all employees, and are not an improper tactic used to discriminate against the handicapped. An employer acting in good faith can also use classifications within the health plan that depend on disability, as long as they can be justified by cost or actuarial data. For instance, an employer can provide less coverage for the disabled by showing that the coverage costs as much as more comprehensive coverage for nondisabled employees.

Sometimes employers use financial rewards under "wellness programs" to motivate employees to adopt healthier lifestyles— lose weight, follow a consistent program of moderate exercise, stop smoking. In December 1992, the EEOC (Equal Employment Opportunity Commission) announced that it would not violate the ADA for an employer to offer incentives under a wellness program, as long as health benefits were not limited; the fact that some workers could derive more benefit from the program than others would not make it discriminatory. Advocates warned that employers should consider the needs of disabled employees in drafting wellness programs.

HIV, AIDS, and Health Insurance: The subject of AIDS coverage in health plans is a complex one. The Fifth Circuit allowed an employer to modify its health plan after finding out that an employee suffered from AIDS. Before, the plan provided coverage of up to $1 million for catastrophic illness; afterward, AIDS coverage was limited to $5,000. The court held that the employer had the power to modify the plan because the plan documents reserved the right to change. The discrimination claim was struck down because the court found that all employees with AIDS were treated similarly—the court didn't find the need for AIDS to be treated similarly to other illnesses. The plaintiff tried to take the case to the Supreme Court, but certiorari was denied—the Supreme Court refused to hear the case.

Employees charged that their employer violated ERISA Section 510 (the ban on firing employees to prevent their becoming eligible for benefits, or otherwise retaliating against attempts to collect benefits) by capping AIDS benefits at $25,000 at a time when five employees had already made health claims for AIDS treatment. But they, too, lost their case: the Eleventh Circuit said that ERISA Section 510 is not the equivalent of a vesting provision. It merely prevents employers from discriminating against individuals who try to assert rights under a health plan—but it doesn't forbid "discrimination relating to the plan in general."

ERISA preemption doomed another employee's case in an Indiana court. The employer's self-funded plan provided $1 million major medical coverage, but AIDS-related treatment was capped at $25,000 a year, $50,000 lifetime. The employee filed a charge of handicap discrimination with the state civil rights commissioner (at the time of the alleged discrimination, ADA wasn't in force yet, so he couldn't make a federal discrimination claim). The state court said that ERISA preempted the state law —but, because it was a self-insured plan, he didn't have any real remedies under ERISA. On the other hand, a California court let the case proceed when an employee with AIDS charged his employer with secretly changing its disability plan by switching insurers and terminating the long-term disability policy that used to cover AIDS. The court said that if the employee could prove this, he would have a valid claim under ERISA, because the employer would have violated its fiduciary duties by intentionally concealing the cancellation of the disability policy (although just canceling the policy would presumably have been OK, if employees were informed about it).

Once the ADA came on line, a whole new series of problems arose. For one thing, HIV-positive employees, and employees with AIDS, are entitled to "reasonable accommodation" from the employer if they are still able to do their jobs with some adjustments. So far, no consensus has emerged as to what employers have to do to comply with the ADA. Employees have been unsuccessful in several of the ADA cases that have already been decided by the court system. The District Court for the District of New Hampshire ruled in July 1993 that a multiemployer pension plan is not a "public accommodation" or otherwise covered by the ADA (remember, the plan is not the employer of the people covered by the plan), so limiting AIDS benefits to $25,000 while other benefits could be as high as $1 million could not be an ADA violation.

In January 1993 the EEOC announced a ruling that the agency took the position that excluding AIDS from a medical plan violates the ADA. At about the same time, the New York State Insurance Department issued regulations, effective April 1, 1993, to prevent insurers from excluding particular conditions when underwriting medical plans. But, as an article in the *New York Law Journal* pointed out, that did little practical good, because the majority of employees with health coverage work for companies with self-insured plans.

Many cases reached the courts. The Mason Tenders District Council Welfare Fund, a benefit plan affected by the EEOC ruling, filed suit on March 1, 1993, to get a declaratory judgment as to whether or not excluding AIDS and HIV-related illnesses from a plan violates the ADA. In November 1993, the fund tried to get summary judgment (a determination that their case was so strong that the matter could be resolved without a full trial), but the Southern District of New York dismissed the motion, requiring a trial and forcing the fund to prove that it had not discriminated against four workers complaining about limitations on AIDS-related health benefits.

At the very end of 1993, an ADA case was settled when the employer agreed to remove the "cap" on AIDS coverage under the plan, so that the same $500,000 maximum benefit would apply to AIDS as to other catastrophic coverage. The cap was removed retroactive to the effective date of the ADA, and the company agreed to report to the EEOC regularly for three years so the EEOC could make sure any differences in health coverage based on disability were really justified by cost differences or other reasons allowed by the ADA.

Confidentiality Issues: Another employee-plaintiff lost out when he claimed that he was fired to cut off health benefits when he was HIV positive; the Tenth Circuit accepted his employer's argument that he was fired for poor job performance. The court added a novel twist: it said that he had no symptoms, and was secretive about his HIV-positive condition, and therefore he could not be a disabled person entitled to accommodation from the employer, because the employer didn't know that any form of accommodation was required.

HIV-positive people do have good reasons not to broadcast news of their status too widely; the risk of discrimination is very great, and losing a job means not only the loss of salary but loss of health coverage that is a literal lifeline. The ADA imposes a requirement of confidentiality on information obtained at a job interview, or from an employment-related medical examination. Inappropriate disclosure of a person's HIV status may also violate a state privacy law or be an intentional tort that can give rise to a suit. In fact, a Pennsylvania doctor who obeyed a subpoena from a Workers' Compensation case and sent medical records to a patient's employer was held to have violated the New York law on protection of confidentiality of HIV status. A New York court said that the HIV information couldn't be subpoenaed in the first place, and anyway the subpoena was only good in Pennsylvania and called for information to be submitted to the Workers' Compensation hearing officer, not the employer.

6

Work-Family Issues

Some employees are single; some are married and childless by choice. Older workers may come home to an "empty nest" from which grown children have flown. Couples may be trying to have or adopt their first baby. But many, perhaps the majority, of employees combine job responsibilities with family responsibilities. Nine-to-five at the office is only part of the story: there are overtime hours, out-of-town trips, hours in front of the home computer taking care of work, commuting. Responsibilities to family members (spouse, children, and elderly, infirm parents) are a round-the-clock matter.

Being a "working father" is tough: job demands take up a lot of time and energy that could otherwise be spent with the family. But most of the burden of reconciling family and work issues falls on women who have paid jobs in addition to their family responsibilities. Sociologist Arlie Hochschild calls this "the second shift": unpaid work that has to be done to take care of kids, husbands, and parents after a day at the office, in the factory, or serving blue-plate specials at a coffee shop. (Couples who think of themselves as fully egalitarian often find that the wife does a lot more housework and child-rearing work than the husband, and does most of the repetitive daily tasks; his share tends to be seasonal tasks like putting up storm windows or enjoyable things like taking a baseball-loving kid to see the World Series.)

We dedicate this chapter, then, to the harried Mom or Dad who tries to get the monthly report compiled on time, drive the car pool, do the wash, go to Cindy's soccer game or cello recital, figure out what's wrong with the October sales figures and why the computer software isn't running properly, take Paul Jr. to the orthodontist, answer that troubling call from Mom's cardiologist, straighten out a personnel problem, apply for the in-service training program or weekend M.B.A. program, wrestle with insurance claim forms, and all the rest.

Although work-family issues affect most parents and a high percentage of employees, these issues still have a low profile, as if having family responsibilities were a rare occurrence. But according to interviews done by University of Wisconsin scholar Nadine Marks in 1987 and 1988, more than one adult out of every seven had experience as a caregiver. In fact, there were more people with experience as caregivers for elderly parents and in-laws than people with caregiving responsibilities for a sick person who was under sixty-five. Caregiving increased with age: about 20 percent of women, 14 percent of men aged thirty-five to forty-nine had caregiving experience; but one fifth of all people over fifty had this experience. Even in so-called family-friendly companies, most of the adjustments (such as flexible work schedules) were limited to executives and professionals; manufacturing workers and support staff got a lot less slack cut for them.

The Family and Medical Leave Act

One of President Clinton's first official acts was to sign the federal Family and Medical Leave Act (FMLA). (Many states already had family-leave laws in place; the federal law replaces them if it gives employees more protection, but if the state law is more protective, it remains in force.)

The FMLA applies to the companies where most U.S. workers are employed, but not to very small companies. The employer has to abide by the FMLA if it has fifty or more employees in each day of twenty or more workweeks in the year when a worker wants to take leave—or in the preceding year. Part-time workers, and people who are on leave of absence, are counted toward the total if they are on the payroll on each day of the workweek. In other words, the FMLA, like the ADA and Title VII, has a small-business exclusion, but the definitions aren't uniform throughout all the statutes.

How far does the FMLA reach? Well, virtually all employers are exempt: in 1987 (the last year for which the Census Bureau has complete statistics) there were some 3.7 million companies with employees doing business in the United States. Only about 140,000 companies—4 percent of the total—come under the FMLA. On the other hand, two thirds of **employees** worked for FMLA-covered companies, because only one third of workers were employed by a business with fifty or fewer employees. The Bureau of Labor Statistics' best guess is that there will be 2.5 million leaves taken each year—that is, about one out of every twenty eligible workers. The Department of Labor thought that a lot more employers were covered: their estimate was 300,000 companies. Some small companies planned to stay small, perhaps by turning down contracts that would require staffing up, or by using temporary or part-time employees to avoid going over the fifty-person limit.

The FMLA requires employers who are not exempt to give their employees access to up to twelve weeks' leave in each twelve-month period. The law refers to a "twelve-month period" instead of a year because employers can use several options, as long as the same approach is used uniformly for all employees. The employer can use a calendar year; a fiscal year (say, March to the following February); or a year based on your own leave history, so that if you take a leave in August, and want to take another leave, your entitlement starts again in the following July, not the following January. Any leave that was taken before the August 5, 1993, effective date of the FMLA can't be used to reduce the twelve-week amount; and an employee's eligibility for leave is counted as of the first day of leave, not the day the request was made.

Leave under the FMLA can be taken to cope with birth or adoption, or with the serious illness of the employee or a family member—but the leave is unpaid. There are some circumstances under which employers have to provide paid leave (state law or a union contract may require it), or don't have to but do it anyway. If the employer was going to provide paid leave anyway, it can count that leave toward the twelve weeks required by the FMLA. (By the way, you're only entitled to twelve weeks in every twelve months, no matter what happens—if you use up your leave after having a baby, and your mother gets very sick and needs you, you can't take extra FMLA leave because of her illness.)

Under federal law, it's allowable for the employer to require employees to substitute their accrued paid vacation time, personal leave, or family leave for part of the twelve-week FMLA allowance. That's good for employees, in a sense, because they have at least some income during the FMLA period, but it could also be a problem because, once they return to work, their vacation and leave time has been used up. If you're in this situation, and would prefer to keep your vacation and leave intact, check the state law dealing with temporary disability. It's possible that the state law forbids employers to do this—and, as we've noted, the FMLA doesn't preempt state laws that are more employee-friendly.

TIP The FMLA entitles workers to unpaid leave, which means they are out of the workplace entirely. The law doesn't make employers provide intermittent leave (a day or two off here and there) or a reduced schedule (two, three, or four days a week; working afternoons only) in cases of birth or adoption, unless the employer voluntarily agrees to the employee's request.

As for employees covered by union contracts, the FMLA can't be used to limit an employee's rights under a more expansive contract (nothing in the FMLA stops an employer from providing additional leave)—but a contract also can't be used to cut off an employee's rights under the federal statute.

After the Leave: The FMLA requires that, after returning from leave, the employee must be reinstated in his or her old job, or given an equivalent job that has equivalent duties, pension rights, and benefits. It isn't good enough to offer the employee a job that is just comparable or similar.

Furthermore, taking an FMLA leave is not allowed to result in the employee's loss of **any** benefit that was accrued before the leave, even if the benefit was not provided under a formal or written plan. On the other hand, the Senate Report published by Congress to explain the bill says that nobody accrues any seniority or additional benefits while on leave, and nobody gets anything that would not have been available if the leave had not been taken. In other words, the FMLA is intended to keep employees from losing ground, not to give them additional benefits if they choose to take the unpaid leave.

There is an exception to the reinstatement rule, though. The employer can deny reinstatement to the salaried employees who are in the highest-paid 10 percent of the employer's work force within 75 miles of the employee's old workplace, on three conditions:

- Reinstating the top executive would cause substantial economic harm to the employer's operations.
- The employer gave the employee plenty of notice of its intention not to reinstate him or her.
- After the leave starts, the employee decides that it's better not to return to work than to return without being reinstated.

Health Insurance and FMLA Leave: Companies that have a group health plan must keep up the coverage for any employee who is on leave—at the same level, and with the same conditions, as he or she would have gotten if he or she had kept on working without taking leave. However, if the employee decides not to come back after the leave (for instance, a new parent is having such a great time taking care of the baby), the employer is entitled to get back the health premiums expended during the leave—which can add up to a substantial financial penalty for the decision to take leave and then quit, instead of quitting as soon as the medical leave for childbirth runs out. (It might make sense for the employee to quit and take advantage of COBRA continuation coverage: that is, to maintain coverage under the former employer's plan by paying the insurance premiums; group premiums can be a lot lower than individual premiums.) But the employer is not allowed to deny a health **claim** that began during the leave period just because the employee decides not to come back to work.

The general rule is that the employer's obligation to provide health insurance ends if the employee is more than thirty days late in paying his or her share of the insurance premium. But if an employee who is on leave misses a payment, then comes back to work and is reinstated, the employee must also be reinstated in the health plan with no need to satisfy the eligibility requirements for the plan all over again. This is especially important for an employee whose health has deteriorated and who might otherwise be denied coverage.

New Family Members: The FMLA covers two kinds of family needs: the needs of a newly born or adopted family member, and the needs of a sick family member who needs care. Entitlement to birth or adoption leave ends one year after the birth or adoption—you can't take the leave two years after having a baby, for instance.

If the parents are unmarried, each one is entitled to twelve weeks' leave. So the mother could take three months off after the birth, then the father could stay home with the baby for three months while Mom goes back to work, all under the FMLA. This is also true if the parents are married and work for different employers. But there's an FMLA glitch: if the parents are married and work for the **same** employer, the employer can legally require the couple to split a single twelve-week leave period.

The employee has an obligation to give thirty days' notice (or as much notice as practicable) when birth or adoption leave is expected.

The Revenue Reconciliation Act of 1993 (the federal tax bill enacted in August 1993) requires that, starting August 1, 1993, employer group health plans must treat adopted children the same way as children born to employees. And coverage has to start when the child is placed with the employee's family, not when the adoption is finalized (which could be months or years later). The adopted child and adoptive parent can't be left without coverage during the transitional period.

Sick Family Members: An employee who has a "serious health condition," or who has a family member with a serious health condition, is also entitled to take FMLA leave. In this situation, unlike birth or adoption leave, the employer has to grant intermittent leave or changed schedules; but if the employee is the person with the health problem, he or she has an obligation to make a reasonable effort to schedule treatments in a way that is not unduly disruptive of the employer's schedule. Employers have a right to demand medical certification of "serious health condition leave"—but not birth/adoption leave.

A serious health condition means being hospitalized, going to a terminal-care hospice, being treated in a nursing home or related facility, or being under the continuing treatment of a doctor. The definition also extends to conditions that limit ordinary activities of daily life, so FMLA leave can be used by caregivers who take care of a frail elderly person.

It's not spelled out in the statute, but the Senate Report that accompanies the legislation says that the definition includes being impaired by Alzheimer's disease, stroke, clinical depression, recovery from surgery, or the last stage of a terminal illness.

The statute defines a family member as the employee's husband or wife, child, or parent. A person who is not a relative, but who acted in a parental role, such as a stepparent, also fits the definition. However, and perhaps surprisingly, a mother-in-law or father-in-law does not, even though many working women also have heavy care responsibilities for their in-laws.

TIP   State law may permit leave to care for a sick in-law.

Penalties and Litigation Factors: It's illegal for an employer to interfere with any employee's rights to FMLA leave, or to fire (or even discriminate against) anyone for filing a charge against the employer or participating in an investigation of a charge that FMLA violations occurred.

An employee who feels that an FMLA violation took place

has the right to sue the employer for damages or equitable relief (getting hired; getting reinstated; getting promoted), plus attorneys' fees and costs. The employee can just march to the courthouse and file the suit—the Title VII routine (see pages 93–95) isn't required. The Department of Labor can also bring a suit; if it wins, the damages will be paid to the employees who suffered the violation.

The employer who loses an FMLA case can be made to provide the compensation (including benefits) that the employee lost because of the violation—or, if compensation wasn't lost, the actual amount of unnecessary costs that the employee encountered (e.g., hiring someone to provide care because leave was improperly denied). The maximum that the employer can be ordered to pay is twice the twelve weeks' compensation, plus interest.

The statute of limitations in an FMLA case is two years from the last event that constituted an FMLA violation. If the employer committed a willful violation, the statute of limitations extends to three years.

Effective Date: The overall effective date of the FMLA is August 5, 1993, but for workers covered by a collective bargaining agreement on that date, the effective date is either the expiration date of the contract or February 5, 1994, whichever is earlier.

FMLA Effects: Before the FMLA was passed, many employers and organizations of employers predicted that they would be unable to compete in a tough world market, because too many employees would be off on leave. Many employees and unions, on the contrary, predicted that nobody would dare to take a family leave; they'd be afraid to lose their jobs, miss important assignments, or lose promotion opportunities. A survey done by the Bureau of National Affairs showed that women planned to take leaves 50–100 percent longer than men, but nobody planned to take very long leaves. Women planned an average of two and a third weeks' leave to cope with a child's serious (but not critical) illness, and eight and a half weeks for childbirth, adoption, or a life-threatening illness in the family.

Once the FMLA became law, predictions of doom were shown to be unrealistic. Aetna Life and Casualty Insurance found that giving employees access to family leave cut turnover from 23 percent to a far more manageable 9 percent; employees returning from leave were more productive than newly hired employees because they didn't need training. Not too many employees actually took advantage of leave. In California, one of the first states to adopt family leave, two thirds of employers reported that less than 1 percent of their work force was out on leave at the time of a survey done by the University of California, Berkeley, Institute of Industrial Relations. Only about 5 percent of companies had more than 2 percent of their workers on family leave when they responded to the survey. Over 90 percent of employers said that family leave did not increase their administrative costs significantly.

Some important legal questions remain to be resolved under the FMLA. It's not clear how the Americans with Disabilities Act and FMLA fit together; if employees who decide not to return to work after a leave are entitled to buy "continuation coverage" to continue the health plans they used to have at work; and what happens to a 401(k) plan during a leave. No doubt courts will resolve these issues in the next few years.

Child Care: The Employer's Role

World War II proved that day-care centers, paid for by employers, can work—if parents really need someplace to take care of kids, and if employers really need to attract workers by coping with their need for child care. Today, though, child care at the work site is often wished for, but seldom available. An estimated 10 percent of companies (generally the largest ones, of course) have on-site or nearby child-care centers. What about the other 90 percent? In the booming 1980s, high rents in business districts made it almost impossibly expensive. Today, rents are lower—there are plenty of vacant spaces—but the cost of providing child care has been estimated as $100–$200 per week, per child. Licensing requirements call for elaborate facilities, lots of staff, and lots of liability insurance—all expensive. So either corporations must limit this option to employees with high enough salaries to pay, or must provide subsidies so lower-paid workers can have access to on-site care.

There's also the question of hours. Should care be available only from nine to five, or anytime employees might be working late on a special project—or anytime the employees need reliable care while they do necessary tasks or get some recreation?

Since on-site care is scarce, most employees have to make their own arrangements (although it is fairly common for employers to provide information and referrals, and not unheardof for there to be a subsidy for care provided by an outside source; the employer may not mind paying as long as someone else has the liability and licensing headaches).

Child Care and Taxes: Employers have come up with various solutions to providing or helping to provide child care. There may be a center on-site; the employer may make direct payments to a care center; the employer may also tell the employee to pay for the child care, then submit proof of payment for partial reimbursement. Some employers also issue vouchers which are redeemable at local day-care centers.

If your employer subsidizes child care, the value of this benefit will be taxable income to you—unless the care is provided under a "qualified dependent care assistance program" as defined by Section 127(d) of the Internal Revenue Code, which includes eligibility and nondiscrimination rules similar to those imposed on other qualified benefit plans. The child-care assistance plan must:

- Be in writing.
- Give employees reasonable notification of the availability of the plan, and the plan's terms.
- Furnish each employee with a written statement by January 31 of each year, disclosing the amount the employer paid (or the expenses it incurred) for dependent care for that employee.
- Not discriminate in favor of highly compensated employees —in fact, not more than 25 percent of the dependent-care assistance furnished under the plan can go to the business's owners, their spouses, or their dependents; and the average

benefit made available to rank-and-file employees must be at least 55 percent of the average benefits furnished to highly compensated employees.

The maximum amount of dependent-care assistance that can be furnished tax-free in any year is $5,000—only $2,500 for married taxpayers who file separate returns.

Family-Friendly Employers: Since 1985, *Working Mother* magazine has published a list of the companies most receptive to working mothers. Its first list of thirty-five commended companies received comparatively little attention in the business community; but by 1993, more than 1,000 companies inquired, and 300 applied to be included in the list, now standardized at one hundred employers.

The changes in the composition of the list (more midwestern companies—but fewer on the coasts; more heavy industries) seem to show a corporate response to demands from female employees. For the record: the 1993 Top Ten, according to *Working Mother* (in alphabetical order): A T & T, Barnett Banks, Corning, Fel-Pro, Glaxo, IBM, Johnson & Johnson, NationsBank, St. Paul Companies, and Xerox.

Perhaps the changes in the list show that flexible scheduling can work for rank and filers, not just for top executives—and child care can improve productivity throughout a company, so it's worthwhile offering benefits to all, not just "under the table" for a limited population of managers and technical experts.

However, there may be career trade-offs. In 1994 when the *Wall Street Journal* looked at 38,000 companies, its conclusion was that companies can have a high percentage of women in top management jobs without offering family-friendly programs such as flextime or day care. Companies with a good program on paper may actually turn out to have few women in top roles, and employees may be reluctant to take advantage of noble-sounding policies because they're afraid that actually using day care or taking family leave will harm their careers. Before you make a career or family plan based on a corporation's nominal commitment to equality or family values, find out how the policy works in practice!

Elder Care and the Corporation

The Families and Work Institute, using surveys prepared by several corporations, estimates that one fifth of workers had some elder care responsibilities in 1992. By 1997, a dramatic increase —to about 40 percent of workers—was estimated, because of longer lifespans. University of California, Berkeley, professor Andrew Scharlach estimates that caregiving increases absenteeism by 50 percent, leading to a productivity loss of $2,500 per caregiver per year.

According to Hewitt Associates (a benefits consulting firm whose surveys are often reported in the press), 74 percent of the employers responding to one survey offered some kind of corporate child care (see page 84). But only 43 percent offered any elder-care benefits, however minimal; another survey showed only one third of employers taking an elder-care role.

Employees with parent-care responsibilities spend an average of eleven hours a week on these tasks—the equivalent of one fourth of the paid workweek. Many employees are reluctant to ask for help at work, or even to admit that they have the problem. Unlike child-care responsibilities, which diminish over time as the child grows up, elder-care burdens usually increase as the parent grows sicker and more dependent. Many "sandwich generation" women (caught between the needs of parents and children) find that they spend more time as caregivers of elderly parents than of young children.

Usually, corporations take the "I & R" route, providing "information and referrals" to their employees, but not offering care services or taking on a share of the cost of care. Still, useful information is not to be sneezed at. An overworked "sandwich generation" caregiver can save dozens or hundreds of hours of anxious research and telephoning by getting a reliable list of adult day-care programs, home-care agencies, specialized housing for the elderly, and nursing homes.

Another possibility is for the company to produce a newsletter about work-family issues. This can be a lot of work unless the company already has an in-house public relations department. An alternative is to subscribe to an outside newsletter, like "Work and Family Life" or "Working Families" (both published in New York) or "At Your Best" (Emmaus, Pennsylvania).

Another option, which employees should not shrug off too quickly, is group long-term care insurance arranged by the employer. Employees may look down their noses at this option because in nearly all of the several hundred companies arranging for this insurance, the employee has to pay the full premium. But, because of the bargaining power of the group, rates can be attractively low. Young employees may not bother to get the insurance for themselves or their spouses (even though, if purchased at an early age, the insurance costs only a couple of hundred dollars a year). But the plans often permit employees to purchase coverage for their **parents,** and the presence of the coverage can turn a caregiver's nightmare into a relatively pleasant job of arranging top-quality care for the parent, with a significant degree of insurance reimbursement.

Combining Dependent Care

A recent development is the recognition that child care and elder care aren't necessarily two distinct problems, with two solutions: the problem is really one and the same—how employees can care for those who depend on them. The strategies aren't always identical: illness, and therefore health care, is a much bigger factor in elder care than in child care. But sometimes the same strategies will work for both. A combined day-care center can provide lively companionship for the elderly, and a built-in supply of "grandparents" for preschoolers and kids in after-school programs.

Business is beginning to recognize that the dependent-care problem is best approached as a unit. A number of companies, including American Express, Philip Morris, and J.P. Morgan & Co., joined in 1988 to create The Partnership for Eldercare. By 1993 the partnership was able to support itself through fees for services. It's a public-private partnership, accessing resources from the New York City Department for the Aging to provide elder-care programs such as I & R, seminars, and counseling.

The American Business Collaboration started out in 1992 with eleven participating companies (Allstate, American Express, Amoco, A T & T, Eastman Kodak, Exxon, IBM, Johnson & Johnson, Motorola, Travelers Insurance, and Xerox); by 1993, there were 146 participating employers, and 285 dependent-care projects under way. Many of the projects involve conventional child care, but the group also has innovative projects, including training for new parents and a home-care/case management program for the elderly. (See Sue Shellenbarger's continuing *Wall Street Journal* coverage of work-family issues.)

7

Civil Rights at Work: Fighting Employment Discrimination

Introduction

There is a very clear and obvious policy: the federal government is adamantly opposed to discrimination in employment—so much so that its laws usually preempt state laws (to prevent states, especially the southern states, from passing their own, weaker, laws). In this context, "discrimination" has a wide range of meanings. It applies to conduct before someone is even hired: the "help wanted" ads that could be used to steer away members of the "wrong" race; the job interview that asks women, but not men, how they deal with their family responsibilities; the union that sends only members of the "in" group to job sites.

Once a person is hired, and an employment relationship begins, federal law covers discrimination in salary, benefits, job duties, and promotion. It covers unjust firing for discriminatory reasons, and "retaliation": punishing employees or ex-employees for filing charges or participating in investigations of their own or other people's charges.

Virtually every kind of discrimination is barred: discrimination based on race, nationality, religion, sex, pregnancy, marital status, age (over forty), handicap. Sexual harassment is defined as a kind of sex discrimination. An important exception is sexual orientation. Although six states (Connecticut, Hawaii, Massachusetts, New Jersey, Vermont, and Wisconsin) bar sexual-orientation discrimination, and many cities do as well, it remains legal under federal law to refuse to hire, to fire, or otherwise to practice job discrimination because of a person's sexual orientation. Homosexuality, bisexuality, transvestism, and transsexuality are not covered by the Americans with Disabilities Act, so the ADA can't be used to sue for sexual orientation discrimination.

Apart from the huge amount of energy it takes for employees to bring charges and maintain a lawsuit (and which tends to "strain out" employees with invalid claims—as well as employees with valid claims but limited energy), employers have formal defenses. Employers can impose "bona fide occupational qualifications" (BFOQs), legitimate requirements that are needed to get the job done efficiently. (However, employers are not allowed to claim a BFOQ defense if they are charged with racial discrimination; it's never considered necessary to job efficiency to belong to one particular race rather than another.)

Treatment/Impact

In broad terms, there are two kinds of employment discrimination that can be proved (and different legal standards for each). Disparate treatment discrimination explicitly targets a group: say, refusing to hire Hispanics for a particular job no matter what their qualifications or job experience may be. Disparate impact is more subtle. It consists of a job requirement that does not explicitly refer to a particular group, but harms members of one group more than another. If an employer insists that applicants for a particular job be at least five feet, nine inches tall, that doesn't seem to be discriminatory, but in fact it will make it hard for women of all groups, Hispanics, and Asians to qualify.

An ever-evolving set of rules has been developed to deal with the issue of discrimination. Occasionally the laws are interpreted broadly, and it's fairly easy to prove a case. Sometimes the number of statutes under which suits can be brought expands; sometimes it contracts. The statutes themselves can be and are changed; courts move this way and that. One of the major impulses behind the Civil Rights Act of 1991, Public Law 102-166, was to make it a little easier for employees to prove their cases, and to expand the kinds of remedies that can be obtained in a civil rights lawsuit.

Title VII

Federal civil rights laws began just after the Civil War, with a trio of statutes designed to prevent states from depriving their black citizens of their newly won rights, including those of voting and doing business. Attempts have been made to use these "Civil War statutes" to bring suits against employers on a variety of theories, especially the theory that people who are not "white citizens" are being deprived of the rights to make contracts that they would have if they were white.

But it's an uphill battle for several reasons—especially since the Civil War statutes were written in terms of bad actions by a state or people acting as state agents, not private parties. Therefore, in order to win, the plaintiff must show that the defendant somehow was cloaked in the powers of the state, not acting independently for personal benefit.

About thirty years ago the Civil Rights Act of 1964 was passed to expand civil rights, including job rights, and to make it clear that private conduct can also be illegal. The employment provisions are found in Title VII (lengthy statutes are often divided into Titles, which are similar to chapters) of the Civil Rights Act; the statutory cite is 42 USC Section 2000e. Title VII doesn't apply to very small companies, those with fewer than fifteen employees. But if you are the victim of discrimination in a very small company, don't give up—there may be a state or local law that protects you even if there are as few as four employees—perhaps even if you are the sole common-law employee.

If a plaintiff manages to work through the elaborate procedure described in the following pages, makes it all the way to court, and wins, the plaintiff can get "equitable relief" such as an injunction forbidding the employer to discriminate anymore; giving the plaintiff the job or reinstating a wrongfully terminated plaintiff; and back pay, for the time the plaintiff would have been working if there had been no discrimination.

If the plaintiff manages to prove disparate treatment, the plaintiff can also get compensatory damages (to make up for costs the plaintiff suffered because of the discrimination—say, job counseling or therapy) and punitive damages (extra money the defendant has to pay for especially egregious bad conduct). But the Civil Rights Act of 1991 imposes limitations on the total damages that a successful plaintiff can receive: only $50,000 if the employer has between fifteen and one hundred employees (i.e., is big enough to be subject to Title VII, but still a small business), $100,000 if there are 101–200 employees, $200,000 for 201–500 employees, and $300,000 for companies with a larger work force.

Title VII Procedure: The federal government has the Equal Employment Opportunity Commission, the EEOC. Each state has its own human rights or other antidiscrimination agency; and many cities have their own laws and ordinances, and their own bureaucracies. Theoretically, these agencies can undertake investigations, independently or based on complaints from workers—but in practice, this is not done very often; the agencies have a tremendous backlog of actual complaints to work through. (In fact, if you have what you believe to be a worthwhile case, but you took a long time bringing it, check with a lawyer—there may be a special relief statute enacted to help people who got caught up in, or might have gotten caught up in, an agency backlog.)

If another employee brings a complaint or lawsuit, it may be possible to join in the complaint or intervene in the lawsuit, and to share in the remedies awarded. These procedures are subject to complex technical rules, so once again expert legal advice should be obtained.

The theory behind the incredibly complex and byzantine Title VII procedure is that the first stage in any discrimination complaint should be investigation (to find out if any discrimination did in fact occur) and conciliation (to bring the employer and employee back into harmony, if it did occur). Therefore, a conciliation period—during which the complainant is **not** allowed to go to court to bring a suit—is built into the system.

However, not everybody is going to be satisfied with conciliation. If you have suffered a significant job loss because of discrimination, you will probably not be willing to shake hands and be friends if your employer (or ex-employer) says that it never discriminated against you, but it won't discriminate in the future.

If you want to bring a lawsuit, you must go through the state agency and/or EEOC procedure first; you must be sure to file your administrative claim on time (usually within six months; sometimes within 240 or 300 days), and you must wait for the sixty-day conciliation period to elapse before you sue. Another prerequisite of suing is a "right to sue" letter from the EEOC or state or local agency. In the federal system, you can ask for a right to sue letter at any time after 180 days have elapsed (this six-month period is supposed to give the agency time to investigate the charge, and, supposedly, settle it), then go to court. State and local rules vary. Once you get a right to sue letter, you must file your complaint in federal court within ninety days.

There are strategic reasons that may make it worthwhile to start with a state or city agency; in other cases, it makes more sense to go straight to the EEOC. Sometimes your best bet is to sue as soon as permissible; sometimes it makes more sense to let the agency use mediation and conciliation, because these methods of "alternative dispute resolution" are speedier and less expensive than litigation.

Our best advice is to tell you that if you think you are a victim of discrimination, go as soon as possible to a civil rights advocacy group or to a lawyer who is experienced in handling employment discrimination cases and find out if you have a case. Don't delay—otherwise, you might find out that you could have won big—but now you can't get anything, because it's too late to bring the claim and there are no legal factors that justify giving you extra time.

And don't forget your employer's internal grievance procedures. Sometimes you'll be able to resolve the problem this way, quickly, with little trouble, and without the expense of hiring a lawyer. You may also be able to alter an unfair policy, or turn a hostile atmosphere into a more civilized place to work, benefiting everybody. Even if you don't feel altruistic, you may lose all your other remedies if you fail to go through the grievance process.

Often, a complainant may be happier if he or she loses at the state-agency or EEOC level than if he or she wins. That's because a so-called "no-cause" determination (the agency determines that there is no cause to believe discrimination has occurred) allows the claimant to sue right away.

Furthermore, the employer isn't allowed to use the no-cause determination as evidence that there was no discrimination; the court system has to hear the whole thing over again from scratch. And if the claimant does win at the administrative level, he or she is still entitled to sue, as long as he or she meets the timing requirements. The administrative remedies don't serve as an upper limit on the amount the claimant can receive. But personnel of the local administrative agency might urge that you start your case there, promising a thorough investigation and perhaps a faster resolution than the federal system could provide.

Sue Who?   Usually, you can't go wrong if you sue your employer (or former employer, if you've quit or been fired). That doesn't always seem feasible. The employer could be bankrupt, but the person who did the real damage may have assets available. Or, you may feel that the person did something wrong; the company didn't.

Discuss the range of potential defendants with your lawyer before your complaint is filed. The proper defendant depends on the facts of the case—and the luck of the draw. Six recent cases involved fairly similar facts—in each case, the plaintiff tried to sue one or more individuals. Two of the plaintiffs were allowed to do so; four were relegated to suing the corporate employer only.

Proving and Winning a Title VII Case: The basic rule in discrimination cases is that the plaintiff has to prove a "prima facie" case. That is, the plaintiff has to introduce enough evidence to make it appear that discrimination has occurred. That can be tough: people are usually sophisticated enough about antidiscrimination laws to at least cloak their illegal actions.

Even if the plaintiff can establish a prima facie case, that won't be enough, taken by itself, to win. The employer gets a chance to defend itself. Usually, this is done by showing that the employee lacked a bona fide occupational qualification; that the employer had a valid, legal, and nondiscriminatory reason for its action; or that the plaintiff's allegations simply aren't true. This phase of the trial can get pretty hairy, with the employer using all the ammunition it can find to discredit the plaintiff.

The case doesn't end there, either. The plaintiff gets the last word, attempting to prove that the employer's defense is "pretextual": i.e., whatever the employer says is just a pretext for discrimination. The Supreme Court spent most of 1989 making it harder for plaintiffs to prove their cases. Congress spent 1990 and 1991 passing a civil rights bill that would overturn most of these cases.

But in 1993, the Supreme Court came roaring back, creating further hassles for plaintiffs. *St. Mary's Honor Center v. Hicks,* #92-602, 61 LW 4782 (Supreme Court, June 24, 1993), holds that a plaintiff can't win just because the judge or jury believes the employer's explanation for its conduct is not true: "Title VII does not award damages against employers who cannot prove a nondiscriminatory reason for adverse employment action, but only against employers who are proven to have taken adverse employment action" against someone in a protected group. In other words, it's up to the plaintiff to make the case—the employer isn't responsible for digging itself out of the hole.

Just to show that the game ain't over till it's over, consider the case of *Ezold v. Wolf, Block, Schorr and Solis-Cohen.* The plaintiff, a female lawyer, was turned down for partnership. Her contention was that the reasons cited for denying her the partnership, while granting it to male lawyers who were hired at the same time, were pretextual. The District Court agreed, but the Third Circuit overruled the District Court decision, finding it "clearly erroneous," and giving credence to the firm's assertion that Ms. Ezold was deficient in "analytic ability." To the Third Circuit, federal courts should not substitute their judgment for the employer's. True, analytic ability **is** important for a lawyer, but the Third Circuit seems to treat this as something that can be demonstrated objectively—but the firm's evaluation process is just as subjective (and just as potentially sexist) as an ice skating judge's assignment of points for "technique" or "artistry."

The Arbitration Hurdle: Theoretically, arbitration is supposed to be a down-to-earth, fair, speedy, and inexpensive way to settle disputes. However, many employees who believe they have meritorious discrimination cases find out that they can't bring a suit, because they have employment contracts or are covered by union contracts that require certain types of disputes (including discrimination claims) to be arbitrated. Employers may also require employees to sign an arbitration agreement as a condition of getting a promotion or raise. For instance, people who work in the securities industry are subject to arbitration agreements and can't sue their employers.

The problem is that arbitrators are usually older white males, with little sensitivity to modern concepts about discrimination or sexual harassment. Arbitrators don't have to be lawyers; they don't have to keep up with recent court decisions. They come from the same corporate culture as the alleged discriminators and harassers, so they may not see anything wrong with conduct that an employee finds humiliating or deeply offensive.

Furthermore, arbitrators usually can't award punitive damages, and they are not very likely to award a large amount of money to employees, even if the arbitrators agree that the employees have a good case and are entitled to be hired, rehired, or promoted.

Kinds of Illegal Discrimination

Racial Discrimination: In *Brown v. East Mississippi Electric Power Ass'n,* the court found that a black employee was constructively discharged by an unlawful demotion—he was not guilty of the misconduct that the employer fabricated to justify his demotion. A white supervisor's routine references to "niggers" (even—or perhaps especially—when there were no black people present) furnished direct evidence of racial animus in the decision to demote the plaintiff, and the employer failed to prove that the official carrying out the demotion was not influenced by racial factors. In addition to discrimination in hiring, compensation, and promotion, racial harassment (e.g., creation of a hostile environment through insults and epithets) is also unlawful.

Usually, racial discrimination is charged by a black, Hispanic, or Asian person against a white-run organization, but it's just as illegal to discriminate against a white person, or for a black person to be guilty of discrimination against another black. Black "testers" (people who apply for a job for which they are qualified, not because they want the job, but to see if they are treated differently from white applicants) have standing to sue an employment agency for its discriminatory treatment of job applicants—even though they were interested in eliminating discrimination rather than in actually getting a job.

Sex Discrimination: For a recent case that combines several relevant issues, see the *Honeywell* case from June 1993. The Department of Labor hearing officer found that Honeywell, a government contractor, discriminatorily assigned women to only a few seniority groups—and those groups got less pay and less opportunity for advancement than typically male seniority groups. It's true that there's a Title VII exemption for bona fide seniority systems, but the Department of Labor decided that seniority rules don't cover an initial assignment—nobody has seniority before being hired, so the excuse was bogus. The DOL also interpreted the relevant federal regulation—which orders federal contractors who discriminate to provide a remedy for the victims of discrimination—to give DOL the right to or-

der remedies including back pay for the female workers who lost pay because of discrimination.

There was a welcome Christmas present for workers in 1993: after a decade of struggle by female employees who alleged that they were deprived of training and access to better jobs, California grocery chain Lucky Stores, Inc., settled the employees' class action suit by agreeing to pay more than $75 million in damages (ranging between $100–$50,000 for the 14,000 employee plaintiffs, with an average of $5,000), and to establish an affirmative action program for women that would be worth another $20 million or so. This was one of the largest class-action settlements ever obtained in a sex discrimination case.

During the time the case has been under way, Lucky Stores' management went from 12 percent female to 58 percent female —but only after a ten-month trial and a ruling by a (female) federal District Court judge that "sex discrimination was standard operating procedure at Lucky's." In April 1994 the settlement was modified to $60 million—still pretty sizable. April 1994 also saw another settlement for sex discrimination plaintiffs in California: Safeway agreed to pay $5 million to settle claims made by 20,000 employees. There were also two major communications/media cases resolved in June 1994. Sixteen hundred women working for A T & T got a settlement of $1.8 million in damages and $1.5 million in attorneys' fees; one current and one former ABC employee got more than $300,000 to settle their claims of sex discrimination and racial bias.

National Origin/Language Discrimination: Nationality and national origin cannot be used by employers in making employment decisions about people who are otherwise qualified. (Of course, being either a U.S. citizen or a noncitizen legally permitted to work in the United States is a prerequisite to being hired —employers can be penalized if they hire aliens who are not legal workers, or if they keep them in the work force after having a reasonable chance to verify their immigration status.)

Several recent cases deal with a hostile environment premised on national origin. A bus driver of Arab heritage won a hostile environment case showing that he was called epithets like "rich Arab" and "camel jockey," but a Chicano employee lost his hostile environment case that was based on a supervisor's description of Hispanic employees as "Mexicans" and "wetbacks." The Fifth Circuit felt that this didn't add up to constructive discharge—the atmosphere was not unpleasant enough for a reasonable employee to believe he would have to quit. Furthermore, the employee didn't go through the employer's internal grievance procedure or file an administrative complaint. In November 1993 the Idaho-based grocery chain, Albertson's, agreed to pay nearly $30 million to settle discrimination claims brought by over 20,000 female and Hispanic employees and ex-employees.

Religious Discrimination: There are certainly some circumstances in which belonging to a particular religion is a bona fide occupational qualification—neither David nor Dana could get a job as a nun, for instance. So the law does include a common-sense exemption for situations in which a religious organization sets qualifications for a minister or other person whose job is concerned directly with religion. Usually, though, jobs must be open to people of all religions (or none). A Ninth Circuit case from 1993 involves a school that received a large bequest under a will saying that the teachers "shall forever be persons of the Protestant religion." The court found that it violates Title VII for the school to refuse to hire non-Protestants. It's a secular school, not affiliated with any religious denomination, and although it does offer some religious instruction, it's minimal.

Usually, religious discrimination cases come up in the context of accommodation. That is, a job applicant or someone who is already an employee wants a change in the work rules so that he or she can follow religious tenets, usually by resting on a Sabbath day. The employer does have a duty of reasonable accommodation to employee needs, but it isn't necessary to toss out the seniority system, or expect employees with different religious beliefs to shoulder an excessive burden.

For instance, it was reasonable for the Postal Service to accommodate a Seventh Day Adventist worker who objected to working on Saturdays by inviting him to bid on a "no-weekend" job after his old job was abolished. The P.O. wasn't being unreasonable just because the employee believed that the available jobs were "nonpreferable" and not good enough for someone with his seniority. After all, employees are expected to give a little, too: it's one thing to make them choose between earning a living and practicing their religion, another to expect some sacrifices in the interest of religious faith.

It's okay—within limits—for an employer to require employees to use their vacation days if they don't want to work on their religious Sabbath. However, employees can't be required to use up all their vacation days, because that would deprive them of a benefit that is available to workers who are not religious.

The EEOC has guidelines prohibiting employers from forcing employees to attend services or pray during working hours. Employers are forbidden to harass or behave in an offensive manner toward employees because of employees' religion. Employees are also forbidden to harass fellow employees because they are of a different religion.

Smoking: The question of smokers in the workplace says a lot about our well-intentioned but sometimes precarious system of balancing interests. In this corner, in blue trunks . . . employees who insist on a smoke-free workplace (and employers who want lower health insurance premiums by reducing smoking and other unhealthy habits among workers). In the opposite corner (or huddled in the supply closet), in the red trunks, are workers who want the right to smoke at work, at least in private offices or designated smoking areas. More than half the states have laws to bar discrimination against smokers. Surprisingly, these are not old laws that have stuck around despite increasing pressure to quit smoking—most of them are only a couple of years old.

The laws are promoted by an unusual coalition: the tobacco lobby (which naturally wants to make it possible for people who want to smoke to keep doing it) and the American Civil Liberties Union (ACLU) (which doesn't want to let employers tell employees what to do—especially in the employees' own time). A recent case from Virginia (a major tobacco-growing state) holds that the Americans with Disabilities Act (see page 117) does *not* require employers to keep the whole building smoke free to protect an asthmatic employee. The court held that the employee can perform the essential functions of the job if other reasonable accommodations are made, such as forbidding smokers to light up in hallways, conference rooms, or cafeterias, but allowing smoking in private cubicles. (The plaintiff complained that, in an open-plan office, smoke drifts out of private cubicles, but the court wasn't impressed.)

Civil Rights Act '91

Throughout the Reagan and Bush years, the Supreme Court decided a number of cases changing the technical requirements for bringing civil rights cases—generally speaking, by making it harder to win a case. Congress's response was to pass a Civil Rights Act overruling those cases. Congress first passed the act in 1990, but President Bush vetoed it, and there weren't enough votes to override his veto. In 1991, there were so many votes that the President gave in and signed the bill (PL 102-166) into law. In addition to some complex technical changes, CRA '91:

- Made it clear that in a "mixed motive" case (where discrimination was only one of several motives affecting the employer's decision), the employee can win by showing that discrimination was "a motivating factor"—not the only factor; not necessarily even the strongest factor. The employee can win even if the employer would have done the same thing if the discriminatory motive had been absent.
- Made it somewhat easier to use statistics to prove discrimination.

CRA '91 isn't a very elegant piece of drafting, and it's not clear just by reading the text whether or not the expanded rights of employees can be applied to cases of alleged discrimination occurring before the effective date of CRA '91. Most federal courts said that the statute was not retroactive, but some courts did let plaintiffs apply the new rules to their old cases. In spring 1994 the U.S. Supreme Court settled the question: CRA '91 is **not** retroactive. If the discrimination (or some discrimination in an ongoing series of wrongful acts) occurred after November 21,

pensions and employment benefits. (Lots more about ERISA on pages 39–64.) And, as we explain in connection with the Americans with Disabilities Act, the EEOC's June 1993 guidelines say that it is illegal conduct for an employer to fire someone because of the potential effect of that person, or that person's dependents, on the health care plan.

Health care coverage that seems to be complete may have serious gaps when it comes to covering pregnancy and birth. If you're planning on adding to your family, find out if your plan (or your spouse's plan):

- Covers pregnancies begun before the pregnant woman becomes covered under the health plan
- Requires mothers-to-be to take prenatal classes or have a case manager to get full maternity benefits
- Covers more than one day in the hospital for a normal delivery
- Covers the newborn nursery for normal babies—or the neonatal intensive care unit for babies with problems
- Covers midwives and birthing centers

If the plan covers less than you anticipate the full cost of pregnancy and delivery will be, you'll have to purchase additional coverage on your own, start saving up, or arrange a loan or cash advance to cover the shortfall.

Fetal Protection: The question of fair treatment for pregnant employees brings up the question of situations that are dangerous, potentially dangerous, or at least claimed to be dangerous to fetuses. One argument would be to require the employer to clean up the workplace so that it's safe enough not to prevent employees from living a normal life (including having healthy children)—but that's not likely to be enforced anytime soon.

Can the employer, citing a fear of lawsuits when abnormal babies are born, transfer or fire women to get them out of an unsafe environment? Some companies refused to hire women of childbearing age; others demanded that women be sterilized in order to get or keep jobs. The Supreme Court answered the question in 1991, in the *Johnson Controls* case, by saying that it violates Title VII to set up a "fetal protection" policy that keeps fertile women from taking jobs involving lead exposure. The Supreme Court ruled that it is not a BFOQ to be sterile (or to be a man), because fertility doesn't affect a woman's ability to do the job. There may be a risk to a situation outside the job (potential fetal damage because of lead exposure), but women must be given the right to decide what they want to do about the risk.

Sexual Harassment

Title VII has been deemed to cover sexual harassment as well as other kinds of gender-based job discrimination. There are two kinds of sexual harassment that can give rise to an enforceable claim. The first is quid pro quo harassment—either threatening an employee with firing, demotion, etc., if she doesn't provide sexual favors, or offering hiring, a raise, promotion, etc., if the sexual favors are forthcoming. The second is "hostile work environment" sexual harassment—the creation of a workplace where women feel unwelcome.

At the end of 1993 the Supreme Court decided *Harris v. Forklift Systems Inc.,* #92-1168 (November 8, 1993). The case was widely reported as making it easier to prove a sexual harassment case, but it's more accurate to say that the Supreme Court didn't make it any **harder** than before. *Harris* is a very short opinion that leaves a lot of questions unresolved.

Basically, all it says is that it isn't necessary to prove psychological injury in order to win a hostile-environment sexual harassment case, as long as a reasonable person would perceive the environment to be hostile. This makes sense: in an auto accident case your basic task is proving that the other driver was negligent. You'll get higher damages if you suffer terrible injury than if the other driver just ruined your temper and your brand-new Maud Frizon pumps, but the basic issues of negligence are the same in either case.

Of course, sexual harassment is a controversial topic. There is a risk, however minimal, that women will invent allegations of harassment against innocent men. (Title VII also bars discrimination by women against men, and by people against victims of their own gender, but political reality makes it far more likely that men will be in positions of power, that women will be the targets of unwanted sexual advances, and that people are likely to conceal the fact that they have homosexual relations even with willing partners, much less people who want to run the other way.) The risk really is pretty minimal, because even **winning** a case calls for several years of effort, during which time the woman bringing the complaint is likely to be assailed as a combination perjurer, prostitute, and prude.

There is also a much greater risk of honest misunderstanding in the sexual harassment context than in other discrimination claims. Someone who makes employment decisions on the basis of race, nationality, or age may unconsciously be affected by stereotypes, but is more likely to have a deliberate bias that is carried out against the victim of the discrimination.

A charge of sexual harassment may arise when a male supervisor or coemployee keeps asking a woman worker for dates. To **him,** this may be an honest attempt to start a relationship that will be pleasant for both of them; for **her,** this may be perceived as a constant source of tension in the job that she needs to support herself and her family. If she agrees to date the supervisor, what happens if she accompanies him on a social evening but doesn't want to have sexual relations? What if they do enter into a mutually agreeable sexual relationship, but the relationship later terminates hostilely—how can they keep working together?

Work Environment: The elements of the work environment —jokes, teasing, posters on the wall—may be intended with obvious hostility and a wish to drive women out of the workplace entirely; then again, when women enter a traditionally male workplace, the old norms may be maintained by men who think of it as "camaraderie," "being a pal," and "having a good time." The law deals with this split by imposing a standard of "reasonableness" on hostile environment claims—conduct is not illegal unless a reasonable recipient of the conduct would be offended by it.

But, in a sense, the whole concept of sexual harassment

links together two motives that are very different, even antithetical. In a quid pro quo case, the supervisor or other harasser wants sexual gratification—sometimes believing that the employee will derive gratification too, sometimes enjoying her unwillingness. In a "hostile environment" case, the motive is to drive women out of the workplace, or at least make them miserable while they're there.

Courts differ in the standard of reasonableness. Some of them refer to a "reasonable person" (unisex); others use a "reasonable woman" standard. (*Harris* uses the reasonable person, but doesn't actually forbid courts to use the reasonable woman standard.) The latter interpretation comes from an argument that men and women are brought up differently and have different responses to things like pinup pictures and four-letter words. Courts that use the "reasonable person" standard say that it's wrong to stereotype, and that women should not be considered as delicate blossoms unable to withstand dirty jokes or swearwords.

A new frontier in litigation is whether there are some jobs where sexual harassment is considered to "go with the territory." A Nevada court allowed a suit to proceed against a casino based on hassling by drunken gamblers. In April 1994 six waitresses brought suit against the Hooters chain of bar/restaurants, charging that the environment, including the sexually provocative work uniforms, was inherently hostile. The chain's defense is that the waitresses should have known at what kind of place they were applying for a job. The plaintiffs' position is that they were interviewed at another site and didn't observe the atmosphere until they started work—and anyway, a waitress's job involves schlepping burgers and suds, not providing sexual stimulation for customers.

Employer Obligations: With some exceptions, sexual harassment cases are brought against the employer, not the harasser, and the employer is entitled to defend itself by showing that it had meaningful policies to prevent sexual harassment, and that it responds promptly and appropriately to complaints. The employer is responsible for the harassing acts of employees in two circumstances. First of all, the company knew—or should have known—about the problem, but didn't bother to correct it. In the second situation, the company didn't know, but the harasser had enough power to act on behalf of the company.

For example, in the *Cortes* case the employer was held liable because a supervisor wouldn't believe a woman employee's complaints of harassment (in fact, he told her to shut up or she could be sued for slander). Transferring the woman to a department headed by the accused harasser was considered constructive discharge: the equivalent of firing her, because a reasonable person would have quit. This is not to say that all men are abusive beasts or that all women are stainless angels—only that a company has an obligation to make a reasonable investigation and discover the facts of the case.

That requirement **could** land the employer in a legal quagmire. Not disciplining a harasser could lead to a suit by the victim—but disciplining, and especially firing, the harasser could lead to a suit for wrongful termination and/or defamation. In order for companies to meet their obligation to protect their employees, they are required to:

- Create a meaningful policy to prevent discrimination.
- Provide an atmosphere where employees are free to bring complaints without fear of retaliation.
- Pursue a reasonable investigation into complaints.
- Make an honest attempt to resolve problems.

Many situations that escalate into giant lawsuits could have been cleared up by one person's explanation of why certain conduct was offensive, and another person's apology and promise to do better.

Preemption: Even a harassed employee who has the necessary proof available may not be able to bring sexual harassment claims, especially in state court. If deciding the case requires interpretation of a collective bargaining agreement, the case will be preempted by Labor-Management Relations Act (LMRA) Section 301 (see Chapter Nine for a discussion of labor law).

Equal Pay Act

The Equal Pay Act is a separate statute from Title VII; it even appears in a different part of the United States Code. The EPA requires employers to pay male and female employees the same rate for their jobs—as long as the jobs involve equal skill, efforts, and responsibility, and as long as any difference in pay is not the result of a seniority system, a merit system, or pay on the basis of piecework.

Employers are also entitled to a defense under the EPA if there was a factor other than sex motivating the disparity in pay. However, it takes more than just a title change to make jobs different: an employer that calls male workers "hygiene and sanitation technicians" and female workers "maids," and makes that the rationale for paying the men more although they do the same work, calling for the same skill, for the same number of hours a week, will violate the EPA.

There are a few exceptions, but by and large attempts to use the EPA to bring "comparable worth" cases have failed. Comparable worth is the argument that jobs should be paid based on the real value they provide to society, or the skills needed to do the job, not on the value perceived by the employer. Under this argument, elementary school teachers, who mold the minds of young people, should be highly paid because their work is valuable and requires advanced education. (As a matter of fact, on the average day-care center workers are paid less than dog kennel workers.)

A 1993 Tennessee case finds that there was a continuing violation each time a female worker was denied reclassification to a higher pay level, so her case was timely (it was brought within two years of the last incident). This was true even though the higher-paid male worker she replaced (and who served as the standard for determining whether her pay was equal) stopped working there before the last incident of pay discrimination.

Three Decades of Stasis: An article in the *Wall Street Journal,* on the thirtieth anniversary of the EPA, says that in 1963 women earned 60 cents for every dollar men earned. After thirty years of EPA protection women earned . . . 70 cents for every dollar men earned. Furthermore, much of the narrowing of the gap was due to men earning less, not to women getting raises or getting a crack at better-paid work that used to be a male preserve. (But see page 7 for some *slightly* more hopeful, newer statistics.)

According to the Bureau of Labor Statistics in 1992 women earned about two thirds of what men earned for jobs on the assembly line—and also for traditionally male work in financial management and advertising and marketing. Female doctors earned a little less than three quarters of what their male counterparts earned; woman lawyers earned a little more than three quarters of what their brothers at the bar earned. The gap was smallest in traditionally female jobs like secretarial work and data entry—but, ironically, even there, men earned a little more.

The ADEA

In our youth-oriented culture, there has always been a premium placed on being (and looking) young, and a corresponding tendency to think of old people as senile, incompetent wrecks who should be moved out of the way to give the young people a chance. Of course, once the beneficiaries of this kind of thinking get a few more turns around the block, they begin to realize the value of seasoned maturity!

Under the ADEA (Age Discrimination in Employment Act), people over forty are protected against job discrimination, including involuntary retirement at a time when they are still willing and able to do their jobs adequately although involuntary retirement can be compelled in safety-related cases (airline pilots, police officers, and firefighters). Top managers (defined by responsibility and compensation level) can also be forced to retire at age seventy. If the employer was guilty of a willful violation, the employee is entitled to double damages. However, the ADEA protects only employees, not independent contractors.

In 1993 about $100 million in age discrimination damages were awarded to successful plaintiffs. Jury Verdict Research, a Pennsylvania company, studied 515 jury verdicts handed down between 1988 and 1992. The average verdict for winning age discrimination plaintiffs was $302,914. This was much larger than the average verdict in other kinds of discrimination cases (about $175,000 for race bias, and about $150,000 for handicap discrimination).

One of the toughest questions is the "overqualified" employee. Can employers set a **maximum** level of experience for a job, saying that nobody with more than five years' relevant experience can be hired? Of course, the net effect is to make it harder for older people to get the job, even if they agree to accept a less prestigious, lower-paid job with fewer benefits than they are accustomed to, or that their resumes would seem to qualify them for. The employer's argument is that the overqualified employees will be unhappy at work, and will quit as soon as a better job turns up.

Pensions, Benefits, and Older Workers: Every year that a person spends working for the same employer brings another year of pension credits (and, often, a salary increase or higher benefits) and brings the employee a year closer to normal retirement age. Retirement plans are expensive for employers to maintain. The clash between these two facts creates a constant temptation to get rid either of the pension or benefit plan—or of the employee, before rights under the plan accrue or increase. On page 44 we talked about some of the ERISA issues involved in allegations of pension and benefit terminations and discrimination; here, we'll cope with the ADEA issues.

In 1989 the Supreme Court decided a case with serious implications for many older workers: *Public Employees Retirement System of Ohio v. Betts,* 492 U.S. 158. The Supreme Court ruled that the ADEA covers only hiring, firing, and salary, not bona fide employee benefit plans; it also ruled that a plan set up before the ADEA became law could not be an improper device to evade the ADEA, so the employer could not be punished for keeping the plan instead of amending it to deal with the post-ADEA attitudes about the rights of older workers.

Congress reacted in 1990 with the Older Workers' Benefit Protection Act (OWBPA), PL 101-433, which took effect on October 15, 1990, and in effect overruled the major part of the *Betts* decision. Since the effective date of this law, it's been clear that employee benefit plans are part of the "terms and conditions of employment" and therefore are covered by the ADEA in the same way as salary, hiring, promotion, demotion, and firing. The OWBPA lets employers provide incentives for **voluntary** early retirement (but not to force unwilling employees into retirement). Employers can also provide lesser benefits for older employees than for younger ones—just as long as the employer can prove that it spent equal amounts for the benefits of all employees, regardless of age. The clearest example is health benefits: employers can pay the same premium for each employee, even if the result is that older employees get less coverage because premiums to protect them are higher.

In 1993 the Supreme Court took on another case about retirement and the ADEA. In *Biggins v. Hazen Paper Co.,* decided April 20, 1993, the High Court said that it is not automatically age discrimination to fire an employee to avoid paying retirement benefits, but if the employee does manage to prove his case, he will be entitled to double damages because the employer's action was willful. To win, the employee must prove that age (not just being too chintzy to pay a pension) actually played a role in the employer's decision-making process, and in fact had a determining influence on the employer's final decision.

RIFs and the Older Employee: Reductions in force (RIFs) create difficult problems. In times of economic downturns, employers often eliminate jobs wholesale. This can be a valuable opportunity to clear out the deadwood—or a chance to discriminate against older workers or people other than youthful white males. Usually, to win an ADEA case, the older person must prove that he or she was replaced by someone under forty—tough to do if your job was eliminated and you weren't replaced by anybody—so special rules apply in the RIF situation. There, the older employees must prove that older employees bore a disproportionate share of the job loss.

If you think that's a tough problem to work out, consider the question of layoffs, RIFs, and early retirement. Companies often "sweeten" their retirement deals to induce older employees to retire and get off the active payroll for good. Retirement incentives can yield two sets of lawsuits for a company: one from older employees who claim that the retirement incentives are pushing them into unwanted, and unlawful, compulsory retirement—and the other from younger employees who say that it's unfair that they can't take advantage of the incentives!

A 1992 case explores some of the complexities. To save money, Boeing shut down its Houston division, laid off everyone who worked there, and then offered them the same jobs with a wholly owned subsidiary set up to take over the closed-down business. There were twenty-eight employees who were eligible for retirement, took retirement, and then were immediately rehired by the new company. They did not get the "equivalent pay" that was offered to younger workers to make up for the paid holidays and employer matching contributions to a voluntary retirement plan that were lost because of the change. The older employees sued, but lost: the Fifth Circuit said that Boeing's plan was bona fide and showed no evidence of intent to discriminate against the older workers.

Timing of ADEA Claims: Before the Civil Rights Act of 1991 the statute of limitations for ADEA cases was two years after the last discriminatory act; three years, if the act was willful. But CRA '91 sets up a new time scheme for age discrimination cases. Now, the rule is that the suit must be brought within ninety days of the time the EEOC either makes a ruling in the case or dismisses the case. This is often longer than two years, and can be longer than three years, given the amount of time it takes for a case to drag through the agency. (In fact, Congress passed two statutes extending the statute of limitations to benefit people who went to the EEOC with age discrimination claims, and who would otherwise have lost their day in court because of EEOC foot-dragging.)

Releasing a Claim: The OWBPA also settled another contentious issue: what employers have to do to get employees to release their claims. A release is a promise by the employee that he or she will not sue the employer or ex-employer (for instance, for wrongful termination; violating federal pension rules; sex or race discrimination; sexual harassment). In this lawsuit-happy climate, sensible employers try to get a signed waiver and release whenever employees depart. But if the waiver is invalid, employees can still bring a suit, so the waiver didn't help the employer in any way. On the other hand, bringing lawsuits is an inherent privilege of people who think that their legal rights have been violated—so, in order to be valid, a release must be made voluntarily, by someone who got something in return for giving up the right to sue, and who was advised about the full consequences of the document.

To be valid under the OWBPA, a release must meet all these criteria, plus a few others:

- The document must specifically refer to the ADEA—it can't be so general that employees don't understand that they're giving up many rights under the ADEA.
- The employee must be given at least twenty-one days to think things over; the employer can't suddenly spring a new program with a brief "window" period. In fact, if the employer is providing a "termination program" such as early retirement incentives to a group of employees, the employees must get written notice of who is eligible, and must be told the names and ages of everyone in the relevant job category who is **not** eligible for the program. And the waiting period must be at least forty-five days.
- A worker who does decide to sign a release must be allowed at least seven days as a "cooling off period" during which the release can be retracted.

What if the release is no good because it fails to meet these requirements? At least a few cases let the employee keep the money or other benefits given for signing the release, yet still sue the employer. After all, the employer controlled the wording of the release.

Bringing an ADEA Claim: The ADEA procedure is a little different from the Title VII procedure. Once again, the system calls for administrative charges, brought either directly to the EEOC or to the state antidiscrimination agency. Would-be plaintiffs have to get to the EEOC within 180 days of the last discriminatory act—unless they live in a so-called "deferral" state that has entered into a "work-sharing" agreement with the EEOC. In a deferral state, the filing period is longer: either 300 days after the last act of discrimination, or thirty days after the complainant is notified that the state agency has terminated its proceedings—whichever comes first.

There are some tricky issues as to just when the time clock starts ticking. In 1992 the Seventh Circuit decided that employees were not time-barred just because they failed to bring ADEA charges within 300 days of receiving bad evaluations from their supervisors. The evaluation itself was not an adverse employment decision, even though it did make the recipients more vulnerable to being RIFed out of a job.

In ADEA cases, a suit can be brought as soon as the administrative proceedings are completed; there is no need to wait 180 days (there would be in a Title VII case), and a "right to sue" letter from the EEOC is not a requirement.

Proving the ADEA Case: Basically, the employee has to prove several things: that he or she was over forty; that he or she was qualified for the job; and that the employee or applicant was denied the job, fired, demoted, underpaid, or whatever in favor of a younger person. That is called the plaintiff's prima facie case, which means something roughly like "first level" or "basic layer."

A plaintiff who can't prove a prima facie case is going to lose—often at an early stage of the case, perhaps even before the case gets to court. The defendant may be able to get the complaint dismissed as totally inadequate; or the case may begin, but be stopped at an early stage because the defendant succeeds in making a motion to throw out the case.

After the prima facie case is put in, the employer gets a chance to defend itself—for instance, by introducing evidence that the employee was not disciplined, demoted, or fired because of his or her age, but because of incompetence or misconduct.

The employee gets another chance after the employer asserts its defenses: the employee can demonstrate that the employer's statements are pretextual—that even if they're true, they just serve as a pretext for discrimination. The classic case would be an employer claiming that the older employee was fired for lateness, insubordination, or a recent bad evaluation by a supervisor. If the employee can show that younger employees did the same thing but were not punished, or that the bad evaluation came suddenly after a long history of good evaluations, raises, and promotions, the employee can win the case.

The ADA

In 1973 Congress passed the Rehabilitation Act, which did give some limited protection to handicapped people against discrimination in employment. But the Rehab Act applies only to federal contractors, and the remedies that people could get in private lawsuits are quite limited.

The Americans with Disabilities Act, on the other hand, extends broad Title VII–type protections to disabled people. That also means that the Title VII procedures also apply. The ADA covers public accommodations, too, but its employment provisions are found in Title I, 42 USC Sections 12111–12117. If the states have broader provisions, they remain in force, and are not preempted by the ADA.

For employers, the bottom line is that *qualified* individuals with disabilities cannot be discriminated against. Furthermore, the employer has to make reasonable accommodations to the physical or mental limitations of job applicants who are otherwise qualified. Although the Family and Medical Leave Act (FMLA), discussed on pages 77–84, imposes certain obligations to grant unpaid leave, the ADA doesn't require employers to make accommodations—even reasonable ones—so that nondisabled employees can care for disabled family members. Nor can disabled employees seek damages under the Civil Rights Act of 1991 if they claim that their employers discriminatorily refused to make reasonable accommodations; they have to seek their remedies under the ADA. A "reasonable" accommodation is one which meets the applicant's (or employee's) needs, but doesn't create an undue hardship in operating the employer's business.

According to the Senate Report prepared when the law was first passed, the ADA doesn't entitle disabled workers to more paid leave than their nondisabled coworkers. The law doesn't impose any obligation to pick the disabled individual if there are two or more equally qualified applicants for a position. If the disabled worker belongs to a union, and the union contract (collective bargaining agreement) sets up a grievance procedure for disability claims, the employee has to go through the grievance procedure and arbitration (instead of bringing an ADA suit) if he or she claims that the employer failed to make reasonable accommodations to the disabled worker's needs.

As with other antidiscrimination laws, small businesses are entitled to an exemption. The ADA first became effective on July 26, 1992, at which time employers of twenty-five or more were covered, and smaller employers excluded. On July 26, 1994, coverage of employers with fifteen or more employees was phased in: companies with fifteen to twenty-five employees, then, got an extra two years to work on accommodating disability in the workplace. Evidently the law addressed what was perceived as a very real problem: in the first six months the ADA was in effect, the EEOC got 4,299 complaints.

Defining Disability: A disabled person is one who has a disease or condition that limits life activities. It includes the things you'd think of as disabilities (blindness, using a wheelchair, having cancer). The statute makes it clear that some things are **not** considered handicaps. Pregnancy is one of them: as we discuss on pages 103–106, the PDA takes care of pregnancy discrimination. A predisposition to illness is not a handicap—say, a family history of developing a certain disease (which the person does not have, or doesn't have yet), or sickle cell trait (which makes it more likely that a person will have sickle cell disease). However, if a person does have a current disease or infection that creates a direct threat to the property or safety of others, employers are allowed to discriminate against that person without penalty.

Current drug use is excluded from the ADA, but it's illegal to discriminate against someone who **used** to be addicted to drugs but is now clean. Employers are allowed to maintain reasonable policies and procedures, including drug testing, to make sure that illegal drug use really is in someone's past, not present.

(More about drug testing on pages 125–129, when we talk about employee privacy rights.) Alcoholism is not considered a disability (entitled to reasonable accommodation) if the person's current use of alcohol prevents him or her from working effectively, or if alcohol use creates a threat to property or human safety, but alcoholism would be a disability if the person is not drinking currently, or can work effectively and without risks to others.

The ADA doesn't say anything one way or the other about obesity. The EEOC has taken the position for several years that obesity—anyway, "morbid" obesity, where persons weigh more than twice the normal weight for their height—is a protected disability. State courts have reached different conclusions on the issue. The jury in a federal District Court awarded $100,000 to a Rhode Island woman who was not hired for a job she was qualified for as a result of her weight; in November 1993 the First Circuit affirmed, becoming the first Court of Appeals to allow ADA claims based on obesity.

HIV/AIDS as Handicaps: Having the HIV virus is not the same thing as having AIDS (although most HIV-positive people will eventually develop AIDS); and even people with AIDS may be capable of being hired or remaining at their jobs. As far back as 1988 the courts have ruled that asserting the minimal or nonexistent risk of transmitting the HIV virus at work is not a reason for depriving a qualified person of a job.

In January 1993 a case under the Rehabilitation Act and New York State's Human Rights Law was settled for $330,000 in back pay, legal fees, and damages for emotional distress, plus a commitment to rehire a pharmacist fired for either being or being perceived as being HIV positive.

Disability and Health Plans: It's illegal to flat-out exclude a disabled employee from a group health plan, but it's legal to have a health plan that includes a preexisting-condition clause that, in effect, keeps the employee from collecting medical costs related to the disabling condition. The ADA is also violated if the employer doesn't use the preexisting-condition clause in good faith, but uses it as a "subterfuge" (unfair device) to harm handicapped workers financially. The law permits a plan that limits the payments that can be made for certain drugs or procedures, no matter how inconvenient this is for some employees with heavy health-care needs—just as long as the plan is applied uniformly to the whole work force.

In June·1993 the EEOC issued guidelines for employers. Under these rules, if the employer can meet the burden of proof, it's okay to make distinctions among employees based on disability in a benefit plan, as long as the distinctions are based on cost or actuarial data; the plan is operated in good faith, not to avoid ADA compliance; and there are no other reasonable alternatives.

Disability-based distinctions can be drawn to protect the employer or its work force from an "unacceptable change" in the health plan's coverage or the premiums charged for it. An unacceptable change would include a plan that becomes unavailable to nondisabled employees, or is so unattractive (because the employees have to contribute such high premiums and copayments) that the employer can no longer compete for good employees with other companies that offer better benefits. However, the employer can't make employment decisions (as distinct from differences in health coverage) based on an employee's or dependent's health condition. The guidelines also make it clear that the EEOC can go after a health insurance plan for ADA violations even if the plan was created before the effective date of the ADA.

Who Is Qualified? A qualified employee is one who meets any permissible standards (e.g., having an M.D. degree and a state license to practice medicine) and who is able to perform the "essential" functions of the job. The law refers to essential functions to keep employers from weaseling out, for instance, by claiming that a wheelchair user can't be a truck dispatcher in case he or she is ever called out of the office to change a truck tire or throw a side of beef into a truck.

There are a lot of factors used to determine whether a task is an essential function of the job:

- The employer's own judgment and discretion.
- Written job descriptions drafted before hiring (although em-

ployers don't have a legal obligation to have formal written job descriptions).

- The percentage of worktime spent on the function—two hours a day, or it happened once six years ago for fifteen minutes?
- What would happen if the employee weren't required to perform the function—would somebody else do it? Would anybody miss it if nobody did it?
- Terms of any collective bargaining agreement that is in effect.
- The work experience of people who hold the same or similar jobs.
- Productivity standards that the employer actually has, and enforces in all cases—not just in cases where the employer is trying to get rid of a handicapped worker.

Reasonable Accommodations: Some of the accommodations that employers can be expected to make, so that the workplace will be suitable for disabled employees and applicants, can include making facilities accessible (ramps, elevators, restrooms that will take wheelchairs), restructuring jobs, allowing part-time or modified work schedules, reassigning an employee, modifying training materials and examinations, providing readers or interpreters for employees (e.g., someone to interpret a meeting in sign language, someone to read the stock quotes to a blind employee).

However, reassignment is pretty much a last resort for employers, and the law requires an honest attempt to accommodate the employee in the current job before trying a reassignment. The reassignment should be to an equivalent position in terms of pay and status, not a demotion—as long as the person is qualified for the reassigned job and the job either is vacant or will be vacant in a reasonable time. In other words, the employer is not required to "bump" another employee so that there will be a job suitable for reassignment. But if there is absolutely no possible reasonable accommodation, and no equivalent position available, the employer won't be breaking the law by reassigning the employee to a lower-graded position. There's no obligation to pay the former, higher salary unless the employer would do the same for a nondisabled employee who was demoted.

ADA Cases: ADA cases began to travel through the court system in 1993. In March 1993 a jury made the first award of damages after a full-scale ADA trial, awarding $72,000 in back pay and compensatory damages, plus $500,000 in punitive damages, to the executive director of a commercial security service who was fired after he was diagnosed with terminal brain cancer. The plaintiff refused to give up driving, despite his doctor's advice that he might suffer a seizure while at the wheel; the company said that this meant he was a danger to others, thus justifying the firing. The jury didn't buy this argument, saying that driving was not an essential part of the plaintiff's job—and even if it was, the employer would have a duty to accommodate him by providing him with a driver. In June, though, the same court took another look at the case and found that $50,000 was an appropriate award for compensatory damages, but $500,000 in punitive damages was excessive; the punitive damage award was reduced to $150,000.

Is It Working?   By July 1993 disabled people had filed 11,500 charges with the EEOC. At that time, the law had been in effect for about a year, but the employment rate of disabled people hadn't risen much from its previous rate of 29 percent of the almost 23 million people with a disability affecting their work lives. Not all disabled people can work, even with accommodations. Others find that, taking into account preexisting-condition limitations on health insurance, and the loss of Social Security and other disability benefits, they lose money if they take a job.

After You Win

If you bring, and win, a discrimination suit, do you get to keep all the money—or is it taxable? The basic rule is that if you are awarded money based on breach of contract, or to replace taxable wages you should have earned, then the money constitutes taxable income. You would have paid taxes on it if you'd gotten it the normal way. On the other hand, if a court judgment, or a settlement, is essentially the equivalent of a personal injury judgment—the kind you would have gotten from a libeler or negligent driver—it's tax free. Therefore, if you're going to settle a case, be very careful about the wording; if the other side will agree that you're settling personal injury claims, tax will not be due (although if the IRS audits your return and finds out about the unreported settlement proceeds, it won't necessarily agree with your characterization).

In 1992 the Supreme Court decided that Title VII damages are taxable income, because Title VII doesn't really deal with the same kind of tortious conduct as a personal injury suit.

There are two basic kinds of lawsuit you can bring. In one, you claim that someone has violated a contract (breach of contract). In the other, you claim that someone has violated your legal rights—for instance, by discriminating against you; by violating your right to privacy; by wrongfully subjecting you to physical or mental injury (tort). Contract and tort cases are subject to separate technical legal rules (about whom you can sue, when you can sue, and what damages you can be awarded if you win). Tort and contract claims can be combined in the same case, if you can satisfy both sets of technical rules.

In December 1993 the IRS ruled that no tax is due on compensatory damages (including back pay) for racial or handicap discrimination. As for sex discrimination, you have to pay taxes on an award of back pay if the court finds that you were the victim of disparate impact sex discrimination; if you were the victim of disparate treatment, your back pay is not taxable. As for the punitive damages added by CRA '91, you'll have to pay taxes on whatever punitive damages you are awarded; the theory is that the purpose is to punish the employer, not to compensate you for suffering personal injuries, so the money is taxable income.

8

Privacy and Other Civil Rights Issues in the Workplace

Privacy Rights

The U.S. Constitution clearly prevents government agencies from interfering with free speech, and puts strict limits on searches and questioning of people suspected of crimes. But it's much less clear what the civil rights of employees are within the workplace. Can any limits be put on their expression of opinions? Can the workplace be searched? Can they be questioned about drug use, embezzlement, or other illegal activities? This is an emerging area of law, and many questions remain. According to the ACLU, the largest category among the 50,000 complaints they receive annually involves workplace privacy issues. This chapter sums up your rights to privacy at work—including drug testing, polygraphs, and free speech—and your right to safety at work.

If you think you have a legal claim based on violations of

your privacy rights, you may also have a legal problem in getting your case to court. There's a pretty good chance that your claim will be considered preempted by the Labor-Management Relations Act (LMRA), based on the theory that determining exactly what is or is not improper employer conduct requires an interpretation of the collective bargaining agreement.

Drug Testing

At one extreme, substance abuse (including abuse of legal substances such as alcohol and prescription drugs) can literally cost lives. Even in less dramatic circumstances, substance abuse cuts productivity and quality of work. It's therefore understandable that employers want to make sure that they have a sober work force. Employers have spent hundreds of millions of dollars on drug testing, and about one seventh of U.S. workers are required to submit to drug tests (especially at the prehire stage— job applicants aren't considered "employees" for whom the union can bargain, so the union can't fight prehire drug testing) —but the result is that employers have succeeded in cutting at-work drug use, and achieved valuable results in terms of cutting accident rates and maintaining a more stable, more productive work force.

Usually, a company that starts a testing program finds a shockingly high percentage of workers test positive; once the program has been in place for a while, the percentage of drug users is cut by two thirds or more. The American Management Association, whose members tend to be large manufacturing corporations, does an annual survey on drug testing. In 1987, only 21.5 percent of survey respondents did drug tests; the percentage rose steadily every year, reaching near universality (84.8 percent) in 1993.

But it's also understandable that employees resent being under constant suspicion; risking their jobs for leisure-time activities (but substances ingested off work can continue to have an impact during working hours); and suffering the most obvious kinds of loss of privacy: having to produce a urine specimen in front of a security guard, for instance.

That's why some scientists suggest that it makes a lot more

sense to test employees for intoxication and impairment—not
for drug use. The company's concern, after all, is employee performance, not workers' morality or good sense. For instance,
employees can be asked to play a computer game that tests
hand-eye coordination; repeated tests show improvement or de-
terioration in performance.

Impairment testing is quicker and cheaper than drug testing, and there are fewer privacy concerns. Drug testing has both
false positives (sober people, or people using legitimate prescription medication, are reported as drug users) and false nega-
tives (users of certain drugs, or users who have not yet begun to
metabolize the drug, or who have fully metabolized it, test
clean). Impairment testing also picks up employees who are too
tired or too sick to work effectively. That could be a problem if
they are treated as drug users—but is an undeniable benefit if
the company simply gets them out of situations in which they
could get injured or injure other people.

The legal status of drug testing is confusing. There are some
situations in which employers **have** to do drug tests, or face
penalties—and other situations in which the employer gets into
trouble for drug testing.

Drug-Free Workplace Act: The Drug-Free Workplace Act,
PL 100-690, 41 USC Section 701, puts an obligation on companies that are federal contractors to keep drugs out of the workplace.

Federal contractors are required to give each of their employees a written statement warning them that drug possession,
trading, and use in the workplace are forbidden—plus disclosure of what the employer will do if an employee violates these
rules. Federal contractors also have to have "awareness programs" to inform their employees about the dangers of workplace drug abuse.

It's a condition of employment that people who work for
federal contractors must notify their employers within five days
if they are convicted of a drug offense. The contractor then has
to notify the federal agency that a convicted drug user works (or
worked) there, and to impose some kind of sanctions on the
employee, or make him or her go through rehab.

Interstate Transportation: The Omnibus Transportation Employee Testing Act of 1991, PL 102-143, 45 USC Section 431, 49 USC Sections 1301, 2717, covers the operation of airplanes, railroads, trucks, and buses in interstate commerce. It's fairly obvious that people who operate these transportation devices create a great risk if they are drug-impaired; the statute goes on, more debatably, to say that "the most effective deterrent to abusers of alcohol and use of illegal drugs is increased testing, including random testing."

Under this statute, airlines, railroads, and commercial motor fleets are obligated to do drug tests of their employees who have safety-sensitive jobs. The employer has to have a program of preemployment, "reasonable suspicion," random, and postaccident testing; the secretary of transportation issues standards for lab operations and for rehabilitation programs.

Case Law: There are some cases that allow employees subjected to drug testing to sue in state court, charging deprivation of a protected right to privacy—but it's at least as likely that the court will refuse this argument, especially if an employee or job applicant had advance notice that drug testing was a condition of employment.

A drug test, like any medical test, is susceptible to tester errors, out-of-date testing chemicals, and mix-ups in identifying samples. Usually, the balance is struck this way: employers will probably be allowed to do drug testing if there is a good reason to suspect illicit drug use, or if the employee holds a job with implications for public safety (e.g., being a police officer, piloting an airplane). Where safety is involved, random testing (without particularized suspicion) is likely to be accepted.

For unionized employees the significant factor is what the collective bargaining agreement says. It has been held that a "management rights" contract clause giving the employer the right to set up and enforce reasonable rules of employee conduct is broad enough to allow the employer to impose an alcohol and drug policy that covers both at-work and off-premises conduct—even if the union is not consulted before the policy is imposed.

On the other hand, if the union and employer negotiated

about drug testing policy as a part of contract negotiations, but were unable to reach an agreement, and the collective bargaining agreement was silent about drug testing, and the employer goes ahead and unilaterally imposes drug testing, the union can require arbitration as to whether drug testing is a reasonable safety and health precaution. The difference between the two cases? In the first, the employer had a contract clause that, at least arguably, gave it the right to demand the tests without consulting the union.

An employee fired after a positive marijuana test sued the testing lab and the drug counselor to whom the specimens were sent, but the Fifth Circuit dismissed the case. It's true that a workplace drug test is related to somebody's character, reputation, and lifestyle, and affects eligibility for employment, so it's a "consumer report" regulated by the Fair Credit Reporting Act. But the FCRA contains an exemption for reports of "firsthand investigations" like the lab report—the lab and counselor couldn't be sued because they did their own investigations and didn't rely on statements made by other people.

EAPs and Confidentiality: More and more employers are setting up Employee Assistance Programs (EAPs), which are supposed to be confidential programs that counsel employees with personal problems that could affect their work performance: for example, problems with spouse or children, drinking or drug problems. Some health plans require employees to consult the EAP first, before they can get therapy visits covered under the health plan. Sometimes employees are leery about going to the EAP, worrying about whether discussions with an EAP counselor really are confidential.

These worries are sometimes valid. For example, EAP records can be used as evidence if you bring a discrimination or wrongful termination suit against your employer, or if you apply for Workers' Compensation after a workplace injury. (The rationale is that the employer might have had a valid reason for firing you if your performance was impaired by substance abuse; you might also have been partially responsible for the injury if you were intoxicated at the time you were hurt.) Does this mean you should stay away from the EAP?

Maybe, if you have a better, and more confidential, alternative for help with your problems (such as Alcoholics or Narcotics Anonymous); if you can afford psychotherapy paid out of your own pocket; or if litigation is a real possibility in the near future. But if you acknowledge that you have a serious family or substance abuse problem, and you need help right away, then you need to mobilize all the tools at your disposal; confidentiality isn't the biggest problem you face.

Lie Detectors

A polygraph—commonly known as a "lie detector"—really measures nervousness. People being examined are asked neutral questions to set a baseline (it's pretty nerve-racking being suspected of something awful, then hooked up to a bunch of gauges), and also asked questions about sensitive subjects such as theft, embezzlement, and drug use.

Theoretically, there will be a difference in the subject in respiration, heart rate, perspiration, and other measures between a neutral question, a sensitive question answered honestly, and a sensitive question answered with a lie.

There are a couple of problems with this. For one thing, not all polygraph equipment works properly, any more than all copiers or VCRs work properly. Some polygraphers are more skillful than others. Some people are just better liars than others, or are completely unconcerned with what other people think about them and thus aren't nervous.

A federal law, the Employee Polygraph Protection Act (29 USC Section §2001-2009) sets a general rule that private-sector employers are limited in the use they can make of polygraph testing. It can't be used as a general or preventive measure; it is permitted only in connection with certain investigations of actual thefts, drug problems, and so forth. (Public-sector employers such as government agencies are not covered by this statute.)

The polygrapher (the person who carries out the test) may be liable to the same penalties as the employer if the law is violated—but only if the polygrapher has some degree of control over the way the actual employer carries out the testing and complies (or fails to comply) with the statute.

Don't forget to check state law: it may provide you with more protection than the federal legislation. In Rhode Island, for instance, it's flat-out illegal for an employer to impose a requirement of polygraph **testing** as a condition of getting or keeping a job—even if the employee won't be disciplined for refusing to take the test. And don't forget to check any documents you signed in connection with employment. People who work in the securities industry, for instance, sign a standard contract that calls for disputes to be arbitrated instead of handled by the court system—and that goes for disputes about polygraphy, too.

Surveillance

When George Orwell wrote *1984,* the nightmare of being observed constantly by electronic monitoring devices resided firmly in the realm of unpleasant fantasy. Today, it isn't even expensive for a store owner to train a video camera on potentially light-fingered customers—or for an office or factory to keep a camera trained constantly on employees.

When *Macworld* magazine surveyed employers, it discovered that 20 percent of employers examined computer files, voice mail, or E-mail used by employees; 30 percent of companies with 1,000 or more employees did this—but less than one third of the companies told employees that they were subject to electronic snooping, and less than one company out of five had a written policy controlling the use of surveillance.

If you ask the employers, intermittent or never-ending surveillance by camera (or by a computer that monitors the performance of word processors) is a necessity to keep employees honest, competent, and hardworking. Without this ability, employers say they would become the target of pilfering; employees would waste time instead of working; and it would be impossible to determine how effective training programs are, because they wouldn't be able to monitor employee performance of the tasks they had been trained to do.

Some employees don't mind, but most prefer not to be observed—especially in locations traditionally considered private, such as locker rooms and bathrooms. No doubt some employees, somewhere, use these refuges to indulge in drugs, or to hide merchandise they have stolen—but most employees would be indignant to know that they are subjected to surveillance on a random basis, with no reason to suspect them of any wrongdoing.

There is already a law called the Electronic Communications Privacy Act of 1986, which is designed to make it illegal to intercept someone else's electronic communications. However, it doesn't offer employees much privacy protection because the law doesn't cover communications "in the ordinary course of business." To change that situation, bills were introduced in both houses of Congress in 1993, called the Privacy for Consumers and Workers Act. If the law is passed, it will:

- Limit surveillance of "privacy areas" like locker rooms and dressing rooms to situations in which the employer has a reasonable suspicion of theft or other wrongdoing.
- Make employers disclose to their employees when surveillance will take place.
- Exempt employees with five years' experience from random or periodic monitoring; any kind of monitoring would be permitted for probationary employees, those working less than sixty days. In between, only two hours' surveillance would be allowed each week—and only with advance notice.
- Let workers sue their bosses if the rules are violated.

The bill was introduced on May 19, 1993, and congressional hearings were held on June 22, 1993, but as of September 1994 the bill had not passed.

In September 1993 a group of K mart employees sued the company, charging violation of state law and asking for compensatory and punitive damages. The forty-three plaintiffs alleged that their employer put them under surveillance and used private investigators to find out about employees' private lives. The company admitted that the investigation took place, but said that the purpose was to investigate waste and employee theft. The employee unit had recently been unionized, and employee opinions about unions were one of the subjects of investigation, but K mart said that the investigation ended months before the union election.

Free Speech; Communications

That brings us to the question of employees' opinions and what they say—not just their conduct. The National Labor Relations Act guarantees both employers and employees the right to express themselves freely on labor issues—as long as there are no threats or coercive promises, of course. But what about non-union issues?

In mid-1993 the Fifth Circuit ruled that employers do not have a duty to allow their premises to be used for distribution of advocates' views on controversial public issues. The case arose when a group was organized to oppose on-the-job drug testing. One of the members was a Motorola employee who wanted to distribute information about the group at his Austin, Texas, workplace. The employer refused, saying that agreeing to this request would open up the workplace to all kinds of political propaganda. The Fifth Circuit agreed with the employer: controversial material passed out at the job site could lead to hostility or even fights among employees who take different views on the subject—even if the subject is one (like drug testing) that actually relates to the job itself, not just general political expression.

Occupational Safety and Health

Thousands of people are killed or seriously injured at work each year, and a large but hard-to-quantify number of people eventually develop diseases because of the chemicals and other toxic substances they are exposed to at work. Most of these people at risk have low-paid, low-status jobs. As left-wing sociologist Barbara Ehrenreich points out, we would be a lot less blasé if a couple of bank buildings collapsed every year, burying hundreds of executives, than we are when a "few" mines collapse every year, killing the trapped miners.

The year 1992 was the worst for occupational injury and

sickness since 1979. In 1992 about 6.8 million injuries and illnesses were reported (not to mention however many incidents occurred but were not reported), adding up to 8.9 incidents for every 100 full-time workers. (In 1979, things were even worse: 9.5 incidents per 100 workers.) However, the rate of workplace fatalities went down.

There are both state and federal statutes to protect occupational safety and health. The federal statute, the Occupational Safety and Health Act, was passed in 1970. The federal law preempts (replaces) state regulatory measures that are **less** protective of workers than the federal system. States are allowed to maintain their own occupational safety plans as long as they are more protective than the OSHA system. Several of the states do this: Alaska, Arizona, Hawaii, Indiana, Iowa, Kentucky, Michigan, Minnesota, Nevada, New Mexico, North Carolina, Oregon, South Carolina, Tennessee, Utah, Vermont, Virginia, Washington, and Wyoming. (California and New York have state plans that are limited to public-not private-sector, employees.)

But localities have been told not to stick their noses into workplace safety and health: Suffolk County, in New York, passed a county ordinance to promote safety in use of VDTs (computer screens); the bill set standards for VDT safety, required regular breaks for computer operators, and mandated a yearly eye exam for operators, with the employer paying 80 percent of the cost. The county ordinance was struck down by a New York court, under the theory that the OSH Act and state laws cover the whole field of work safety, and that it's not an appropriate area for local lawmaking.

Theoretically, all workplaces with even one employee are covered; there's no minimum number and no exclusion for very small businesses as provided by Title VII, the Age Discrimination in Employment Act, and the Americans with Disabilities Act. On the other hand, every DOL budget since 1977 has refused to include any enforcement money for small farms with fewer than ten employees, or for low-hazard businesses with fewer than ten employees, so there's no way the OSHA inspectors will show up in a three-person direct-mail business office.

OSHA (the Occupational Safety and Health Administration), part of the Department of Labor, is the federal agency in charge of enforcing the OSH Act. It does this by conducting inspections of workplaces. The inspections are unannounced, so employers don't get a chance to make things look good temporarily (just until the inspectors have left). However, if the employer doesn't want to let the inspectors in, they have to go away and apply for a search warrant from a federal magistrate or U.S. district judge. The OSH Act doesn't say anything one way or the other about videotapes, but the Northern District of Illinois decided in 1992 that OSHA inspectors can use videotape to document the conditions in a workplace they inspect, because it is a reasonable inspection tool comparable to the photographs that are specifically authorized by the statute.

OSHA has a lengthy and extensive series of standards, dealing with issues like safe levels of ventilation, respiratory protection, noise levels in the workplace, and safe handling of gases and power tools. Many of these standards were developed by independent testing organizations like the National Standards Association, National Fire Protection Association, and the American Society for Testing and Materials, then officially adopted by OSHA. OSHA also has its own research organization, the National Institute for Occupational Safety and Health (NIOSH).

If the inspectors find that an employer has failed to comply with a standard, then citations are issued, and OSHA proposes penalties. The employer can either agree and pay up, or protest to the Occupational Safety and Health Review Commission, an independent organization that was set up to hear employer challenges. Each time an employer fails to keep records of an occupational injury it is a separate violation, and a separate penalty can be imposed for each, but the overall penalty has to be appropriate in light of the company's size, the seriousness of the violations, and the employer's history of operating in good faith or otherwise.

In a multiemployer workplace—a construction site is a good example—an employer can get off the hook by proving that it neither created nor controlled the hazard that violates the OSH Act, that it's somebody else's fault, and that the particular employer couldn't have known about the violation or did know but took realistic measures to protect its employees. In the appropriate case, the Department of Labor may "pierce the corporate veil"—disregard the corporation, and sue the owner of the corporation, if the corporation is just a legal formality and the owner has all the real responsibility. This was done in a 1992 case, where an employee died because OSHA standards on installation of steel joists were violated.

Employee Rights and Obligations: While it's true that employees have a duty under the OSH Act to comply with OSHA standards—and it makes sense for them to take steps to protect their own safety—they can't be penalized if they fail to do so. Under the OSH Act, employees have a right to initiate inspections, to have representatives (such as union reps) present during inspections, and confer with the inspectors or even sue OSHA, in federal court, if it fails to take action to protect employees against an imminent danger.

What employees **can't** do is sue the employer for maintaining a dangerous workplace—there's no private right of action. On the other hand, if someone besides the employer takes over the duty of providing a safe place to work (let's say, a contractor at a construction site) but doesn't provide a safe environment, the employees may be able to sue that third party.

The OSH Act also makes it illegal to fire, or otherwise retaliate against, an employee who files a complaint or exercises other rights under the OSH Act (for instance, someone who tells an inspector about improper storage of dangerous materials). If you think that you're a victim of retaliation, our advice to you is *hurry up!* That's because federal rules give you only thirty days from the time of the retaliation to make your retaliation complaint to the secretary of labor (check the phone book under Federal Government listings for the nearest office). The thirty-day period will not be tolled (extended) if you also use the grievance procedure under your union contract, or if you file a complaint with another agency that has jurisdiction (such as an environmental regulator, if the problem involves toxic materials). The secretary of labor has a duty to investigate complaints of retaliation; if they are found to be valid, the secretary is also obligated to sue the company in federal court.

The OSH Act also provides legal protection to employees

who refuse, in good faith, to expose themselves to hazardous conditions—as long as a reasonable person would believe that there is a real danger of death or serious injury as a result of the condition. The employer must be asked to correct the situation, if possible; and the danger must be too urgent for employees to go through the normal channels. In 1980 the Supreme Court decided that, while employers can't fire, demote, or otherwise discriminate against workers who refuse to expose themselves to serious danger, it doesn't have to pay them, either, as long as the employees are refraining from the dangerous tasks.

General Duty Clause: The centerpiece of the OSH Act is Section 5(a)(1), the "general duty" clause. This clause requires all employers to provide a workplace that is free of recognized hazards that are serious enough to cause major physical harm or death. The general duty clause applies in all situations where OSHA does not have specific standards (there are specific standards for construction, farming, and mining, but not for most kinds of manufacturing).

In order to bring charges based on a violation of the general duty clause, OSHA has to be able to cite particular steps that the employer could and should have taken to avoid danger. OSHA also has to prove that these measures are feasible and would be likely to solve the problem. The employer can defend itself by proving that employee misconduct caused the situation —for instance, that the employer purchased machinery with adequate guard mechanisms, but that the employees took off the guards despite employer instructions to leave them on.

OSH Act Section 6 imposes a duty on the secretary of labor to adopt standards about toxic materials and harmful physical agents that will make sure, to the greatest feasible extent, and on the basis of the best scientific evidence available, that employees do not suffer "material impairment of health or functional capacity" even if they have long-lasting exposure to the toxic substances. When it's necessary to protect employees from danger, the secretary of labor has the power to impose an emergency temporary standard without going through the rule-making process—but there has to be a real, grave danger, not just a plain old everyday minor hazard.

As you'd imagine, employers—especially small businesses—usually don't like OSHA much. They are apt to point to the standards as a never-ending procession of nitpicky trivialities, a real and costly barrier to business success that often gets well-meaning employers into trouble when there is no meaningful danger.

It's not clear what role cost-benefit analysis is supposed to play in OSHA decision making: that is, whether the expense of meeting safety standards is supposed to be balanced against worker protection. In 1981 the Supreme Court decided that OSHA does not have an obligation to use cost-benefit analysis in making decisions; but an executive order, also dated 1981, tells all federal agencies (not just OSHA) to prepare a regulatory impact analysis for all new or revised rules before they take effect; the analysis is supposed to prove that the agency action provides social benefits that outweigh the cost of complying with the rule.

In 1989 OSHA tightened up the limits on occupational use of hundreds of hazardous substances. However, the Eleventh Circuit ruled that the limits were invalid: OSHA didn't show a significant risk of material health impairment if the limits were violated, and didn't show that obeying the new rules was economically and technologically feasible. OSHA decided not to appeal the case, so the rules went back to the 1971 rules that were amended in 1989.

9

Your Right to Organize: Unions and Labor Law

Every economic system has to find a balance of power between business owners and employees. Usually the owners hold most of the cards. In the United States, for a lot of political and economic reasons, the employees have a lot more power than in other systems. Part of the reason is economic sophistication: complex jobs require educated, trained, willing workers. Shared prosperity is also a factor: you can sell a lot more consumer goods if workers earn a high wage than if they are close to starvation. Another influence is the political and economic muscle fielded by labor unions; this was especially true in the early twentieth century.

American unions once held a proud place in the sun, when "Made in the USA" was the stamp of quality merchandise, and when America had a "labor aristocracy" of skilled and well-paid unionized workers who turned their paychecks into mortgage payments and purchases of enough durable and consumer goods to keep everybody's assembly lines humming.

Today, fewer than one fifth of the U.S. working population belongs to unions. The once-mighty AFL-CIO enrolled only 11 percent of U.S. workers in 1993 (even counting the AFL-CIO's merger with the Teamsters, the country's biggest union with some 1.3 million members). Between 1982 and 1992, unions lost more than a million members.

The greatest growth in union membership was among a group unions traditionally spurned: women. In the earliest history of labor organizing, employers played off men against women, threatening to fire male would-be union members and replace them with lower-wage women workers—a tactic that worked all too well; it took decades for unions to fight their own sexism as well as employer sexism. In 1983 the Bureau of Labor Statistics reported that one third of unionized workers were female; the number has increased to 38 percent, and two thirds of new union members are female.

When collective bargaining agreements (union contracts) come up for renewal, the major topic is not how much more the employer is going to concede, but what givebacks the union will agree to. Maybe the union will accept shortened hours, big layoffs, a wage freeze, even a decrease in wages or a two-tier system in which new hires get paid on a much lower schedule than those already at work. It's likely that the company's medical plan will be cut back—perhaps higher premiums and copayments for active workers, drastic reductions or even elimination of health benefits for retirees. Employees know that without these concessions, the employer is likely to be acquired (with many jobs lost as the new company struggles to pay off acquisition debt), or to file for bankruptcy protection. The newest fear is the worst case scenario: the workers make major concessions and give back a lot, but the employer still goes bankrupt or goes out of business.

The decline in the fortunes of labor unions has many causes. Work itself has changed: there are fewer blue-collar industrial workers, who were comparatively easy to unionize because of their strong loyalties to a particular job and a particular plant. There are more service and knowledge workers, who are hard to organize for many reasons, including low wages that employers are reluctant to raise, language problems, and the prevalence of temporary and part-time work. Deserved or not, unions have gotten a bad reputation. Union leaders are often thought of as self-serving or mob connected. Union demands are often thought of as excessively high, too hard for U.S. employers to meet and still stay competitive in an international market which includes Third World countries where very low wages prevail.

In this chapter we'll explain some basic rules of labor law—including rights to organize a union (if you want, but don't have, one) and your rights as a union member if you are dissatisfied with the job your union is doing, or would rather go it alone without a union. It's simplistic to contrast virtuous unions with evil capitalist exploiters. In the past, each has done some good things for, and some bad things to, workers.

The Right to Organize

Labor unions are no longer considered illegal conspiracies by nature. In fact, federal law specifically gives workers the right to organize into unions. Once a union exists, it becomes the only agent that can bargain for the employees with the employer (although employees can still protest individual grievances). Once a collective bargaining agreement is reached, it governs nearly all facets of the employer-employee relationship. There are limits, of course: for instance, a union and employer can't agree to a contract that says "Don't sweat, we'll never hire a black person in this operation" and expect to have it enforced.

Federal labor laws such as the National Labor Relations Act (NLRA; passed in 1932) and the Labor-Management Relations Act (LMRA, also called the Taft-Hartley Act, 1947) are all-powerful, preempting state laws that might have an impact on the employer-employee relationship.

The National Labor Relations Act applies to all situations that might affect interstate commerce or international commerce. Unlike the antidiscrimination laws (see pages 90–123), there is no exemption for companies that have only a few employees. There is a small-business exception, but it relates to the employer's gross revenues, not the number of workers. The National Labor Relations Board is still using 1959 figures for this purpose, so a company has to be pretty small indeed not to be covered.

Most employees are entitled to protection under the NLRA —in this context, "employees" means ordinary employees, not independent contractors who essentially work for themselves but make contracts to perform certain tasks. At one end of the economic spectrum, farm workers and domestic servants are not covered by the NLRA.

At the other end, supervisors aren't either. Supervisors aren't allowed to take an active role in rank-and-file unions (for obvious reasons of conflict of interest). They can form their own unions if they want to, but employers don't have a duty to bargain with supervisors' unions. The NLRA defines a supervisor as a person who has the authority to exercise independent judgment (not just a clerical or messenger role) in connection with the hiring, firing, transfer, assignment, layoff, recall, promotion, or grievance adjustment of rank-and-file employees. What matters is real authority, not job title—otherwise, employers could flatter everyone (and wiggle out of NLRA compliance) by "promoting" a large number of employees to meaningless so-called supervisory positions, without changing the everyday grunt-work nature of their jobs.

Under the NLRA, employers are guilty of an "unfair labor practice" if they refuse to engage in collective bargaining once a union is in place, if they subject unions to domination, if they discriminate against employees for trying to unionize or otherwise exercising legal rights under the labor laws, or if they retaliate against employees for filing NLRB charges or testifying before the NLRB.

Under the same statute, unions are guilty of unfair labor practices if they engage in "featherbedding" (requiring employers to keep extra workers, who are not necessary to the job, on the payroll), charge excessive union dues, or engage in improper conduct during strikes (for instance, violence, sabotage, and threats to nonstriking workers).

Furthermore, unions are not allowed to call "secondary strikes" or "secondary boycotts"—actions intended to put pressure on an employer who is not directly involved in a dispute (say, unionized carpenters refuse to install a particular brand of window because the window factory is nonunion). Employers who are subjected to secondary strikes or boycotts are entitled to collect damages from the union. Strikes and secondary boycotts are also illegal if the purpose is to compel recognition of one union if the NLRB has certified a different union as the only appropriate bargaining representative for the workers.

The LMRA (Taft-Hartley Act) creates a Federal Mediation and Conciliation Service to intervene in national disputes that threaten the free flow of interstate commerce. Taft-Hartley makes strikes by public employees illegal. If the President of the United States believes that a strike endangers the national health and safety, he can summon a board of inquiry and order the U.S. attorney general to apply for an injunction.

Union Certification

Once a union is in place, the union handles the bargaining process—sometimes just for union members, but usually for all employees within the company. Two kinds of contracts are illegal: a "closed shop" contract that forbids hiring anyone who isn't a union member already, and a "yellow dog" contract that requires employees to promise **not** to join a union.

Between these limits, a company can be a "union shop" (where nonmembers can be hired, but they have to agree to join the union within a certain period of time after hiring) or an "agency shop" (where nonmembers have to pay union dues, but don't have to join; and the union can only use their dues for collective bargaining, administration of the union contract, and settling grievances, not for other purposes—such as organizing other companies' work forces).

In order to become the "authorized bargaining agent" for workers, a union must be "certified," a process that can be lengthy and difficult. The first step is a petition for certification, filed with the NLRB. A person, a group of employees, a union—even the employer—can file the petition. (Why would the employer file? Because it might think the potential union isn't that bad after all—or that if the election is held right away, the union will lose, but a delay could improve the chances of a union victory.)

Even to get to first base, the union has to get an indication of interest from 30 percent of the employees. Acceptable signs of interest are petitions signed by employees, union membership or applications for union membership, and authorization cards signed by employees. A single-purpose authorization card just designates the union as a particular worker's bargaining representative; a dual-purpose authorization also asks the NLRB to hold a certification election.

This 30 percent requirement is only a first step, and it can be a very difficult one for the union to achieve. Employers have a lot of leeway **within** the law to make their case that unionization is a bad idea. They can give honest factual information and express opinions: for instance, they can point to other companies and show the effect of union dues on paychecks, or indicate that they think unionization will force the company to raise its prices, cutting its customer base.

Assuming that the would-be union gets indication of interest from 30 percent or more of the workers who would be in the bargaining unit (explained below) if the union did get recognized, the next step is for the National Labor Relations Board (NLRB) to check out the petition for certification.

If the employer agrees that holding a certification election is appropriate, a "consent election" will be held. But if the employer objects, the NLRB has to decide if there is a case to be made that the union might really represent the interests of the workers. The NLRB makes its decision by holding a hearing; if it decides that an election is proper, the federal agency will supervise the election and try to prevent any monkey business from either side.

To win the election and become certified, the union needs a majority of the votes cast at the election. It isn't necessary to get a majority of the potential voters, so in this case apathy can work for the union, if only the union activists bother to vote and the neutral or promanagement employees don't even cast a ballot.

Certification is important for a union because it gets breathing space—not just against the employer, but against other unions that want to represent the same workers. Once a valid election is held, the NLRB will not grant another election petition for a year—whether the union wins or loses. (If it wins, no other union can come in for that year; if it loses, employees have to wait a year for the next organizing effort.)

If the employees are already working under a valid collective bargaining agreement, an election petition will probably be denied. However, rival unions have a chance to file certification petitions in a "window" period starting ninety days before the contract expires and ending thirty days before expiration (if the contract lasts three years or less). For collective bargaining agreements that last more than three years, the union gets exclusive status for three years; after that, other unions can file petitions and try to get certified.

Bargaining Unit: A union can be set up to cover a particular employer, a particular plant, or a particular "craft" (work specialty). However, the union has to choose an appropriate bargaining unit when it sets out to organize a workplace. Appropriateness depends on the duties, skills, and working conditions of the employees, whether they have been organized in the past, and any history they have with the collective bargaining process.

As mentioned on page 141, supervisors can't form ordinary unions, even if they want to: the theory is that unions bargain **against** management, not on the same side. Employees whose jobs give them access to confidential information about labor relations can be unionized, but they must be in a separate bargaining unit—they can't be in the same unit as the rank-and-file employees about whom they have confidential information. Plant guards also have to have a separate unit if they are organized at all. Professional employees can either have their own unit or be included in a unit of nonprofessional employees—but only if a majority of the professionals vote for inclusion.

For labor law purposes, retirees aren't "employees" anymore, so the union doesn't have a responsibility to bargain on their behalf. This can lead to a real intergenerational brawl, with the union letting the employer cut benefits to retirees in order to sustain benefits for current active workers.

Fair and Unfair Election Conduct

Until the last twenty-four hours before the election, the employer is free to assemble the workers on company time as often as it wants, to give them antiunion speeches. Clear threats are forbidden, but the employer does have the right to present its case that a nonunion shop would be better for the employer and better for the workers.

Of course, this can be taken too far: the NLRB ordered a new election held after a company required employees to show up at a motel for an antiunion speech (attendance at a reception afterward was optional). A prounion employee brought lots of union literature to the meeting. It would have been okay for the employer just to tell her to stop giving the stuff out, but the company was out of line in telling her to collect what was already distributed; there was no prior prohibition, and the company in effect made her participate in its own antiunion activity.

Union Solicitation: The union must be given the right to solicit employees during mealtimes and other breaks—but the employer is not obligated to invite a union representative to "captive meetings" to give an equal-time rebuttal to the employer's antiunion message.

Employees are allowed to wear union buttons if they want to; it's considered a corporate obligation to allow free speech on this point. In fact, even if employees wear union buttons to the polling place, the election will not be invalidated—but it will be if either union or management makes a speech to massed employees on company time within the twenty-four hours just before the election, or if the employer saves up an announcement of new benefits until election day, or if the employer makes an explicit promise of more benefits if the union loses, or an explicit threat of decreased benefits if the union wins.

The NLRB has ruled that it's unlawful for an employer to videotape off-duty employees distributing union literature near (but not blocking) an entrance to the workplace. This was protected union organizing activity, no employees were intimidated, and "something might happen" doesn't constitute adequate justification for interfering with the legally protected right to orga-

nize. Other unfair labor practices include giving oral warnings
about unionization, firing or laying off known union supporters,
and changing work rules to keep a group of prounion workers
out of the break room at a time when they could discuss organization with other workers.

A balance has to be struck between the employees' right to
at least think about unionization, and the employer's right as the
owner of private property. In 1992 the Supreme Court said that
employers usually have the right to prohibit solicitation on private property, so nonemployee organizers can be kept off the
employer's property. The rare exception would be a case where
the employees are so inaccessible that they can't be reached by
ordinary methods of communication (for instance, they're stuck
out on an oil rig in the North Sea). This principle was applied to
allow a hospital with a no-solicitation policy to keep union organizers out of the cafeteria, which was nominally open to the
public but was mostly used by hospital employees. The court's
rationale was that the union could (and did) reach employees by
mailings and holding meetings away from the workplace.

These rules tend to be applied pretty narrowly, restricted to
the situation of an actual union election—not any political issue
that the union wants to become involved in. For instance, the
Fifth Circuit said that the employer did not violate labor law by
banning distribution of materials in the workplace from an advocacy group trying to get a city ordinance passed to forbid
mandatory drug testing. The court said that employees do have
a right to join together in concerted activities, but outside political organizations, not representing the employees, do not have a
right to use the workplace as an arena to pursue their political
goals.

On the other hand, the NLRB said that an employer was
wrong to fire an employee for using the employer's copier, during working hours, to make copies of an article about toxic
waste—the union was opposed to the employer's announced
plan to burn hazardous waste for fuel. The NLRB said that
employees have a right to engage in concerted activity to protect
their safety and health.

Union Security

Once in, the union—like any other institution—naturally wants to **stay** in. This isn't always the best thing for the union members, or for the future of the business as a whole. Federal labor law strikes a balance by forbidding "union shops"—where nobody can be hired unless they are already union members—but allowing "agency shops" (where everybody has to pay union dues as long as they work there), and also allowing states to pass "right to work laws" (letting states outlaw the agency shop, so nonunion members can work alongside union members—in the unlikely case that there are any union members).

In September 1992 the NLRB proposed rules on agency shops. Under the rules, unions have to notify their members once a year of their legal rights with respect to union membership (basically, all it means is that workers have to pay their initiation fees and dues). The rules also require employers to notify workers covered by a union security clause of their right not to join the union, and their right to object to their dues being used for any objective that is not related to union representation (for instance, environmental activism).

If the employees lose confidence in the union, it can be decertified or deauthorized. A deauthorization election can be held at any time; a decertification election can only be performed during specific "windows" defined by federal law. A petition for decertification can be filed by an employee or group of employees. The employer can't file the petition—although it can certainly suggest to employees that getting rid of the union would be a good idea. It takes the signatures of 30 percent of the employees for the decertification petition to become effective, and then an election will be held; it takes a majority vote to decertify a union. But the effect of sheer inertia is that a union may hang on because not enough people feel strongly enough to vote for decertification.

The employer does have the right to file a deauthorization petition if it can allege reasonable cause to believe the union no longer represents a majority of the employees.

Union Representation

The union's major role is negotiating labor contracts, also known as collective bargaining agreements (CBAs). Much of federal law revolves around interpreting CBAs—and, in situations where the CBA **has** to be interpreted, only federal labor law will apply, not state tort or contract law—even if a person who feels aggrieved by something the boss (or the union) has done would rather bring a case in state court because it's faster, cheaper, or offers a better range of remedies or a higher probability of success.

The NLRA requires both employers and unions to bargain in good faith. In fact, if the employer behaves really badly, the National Labor Relations Board has the right to order the employer to bargain with a union—even if the union hasn't won a representation election, or even if the election hasn't even been held. It's also unlawful for an employer to show favoritism—for instance, to bargain with a "sweetheart" union before the election has even been held; in that situation, no one has yet been authorized as the employees' bargaining representative. (A sweetheart union is one that claims to represent workers, but is actually on the management's side.)

While the CBA is in effect, it specifies most of the details of the employer-employee relationship, including work rules, compensation, and benefits. When the CBA runs out, then the union and management have to hammer out a new one. At times, this is a blissfully smooth process, and everyone is happy. More often, the result of hard bargaining fully satisfies neither side, but at least they have a contract to work with. Sometimes, no matter what anyone says or does, they can't agree. In the short run, employees may work without a contract for a while, waiting for the differences to be resolved; in the long run, a strike is the likely result.

Strikes, Walkouts, Lockouts

Technically speaking, a strike is a planned, collective work stoppage authorized by a union; a "wildcat" strike's impetus comes from the workers, contrary to the direction of the union leaders.

(In fact, a wildcat can be just as big an embarrassment and nuisance to the union leaders as it is to the employer.) A lockout is a shutdown by the employer, keeping out employees who are willing to work. According to Section 502 of the Labor-Management Relations Act, a work stoppage is legitimate—and doesn't count as a strike—if workers, acting in good faith, stop working based on abnormally dangerous working conditions. This might happen if, say, there is a spill or discharge of dangerous chemicals. The employer calls for business as usual; the employees want to vacate the premises until adequate cleanup measures have been completed.

Federal labor law sets limitations on strikes and lockouts—both when they can occur, and what conduct is permissible. But the lines can be pretty blurry. What if the employer has a huge overstock of merchandise, and would just as soon close down the place for a while and save on salaries? A smart employer wouldn't engage in an obvious lockout. Instead, it would goad the union into calling a strike.

With any luck, the union would call an **illegal** strike, or engage in unlawful conduct during the strike, thus turning the employer into a hapless victim—possibly entitled to significant damages. Or, the employees might get fed up and stage a wildcat strike, thus forfeiting the sympathy of the NLRB and the courts—and putting them at odds with their own union. For labor law purposes, nobody has employee status, or employee protection, during a wildcat strike. However, a walkout staged in good faith when workers refuse to work in unreasonably dangerous conditions is not considered a strike, and therefore is not subject to legal constraints on strikes.

During the early years of union organizing, before the federal government set a firm policy that unions are legitimate, employers often found it easy to find a court to issue an injunction ordering a union to call off a strike. One important piece of New Deal legislation was 1932's Norris-LaGuardia Anti-Injunction Act, placing strict limits on labor injunctions.

However, in 1969, the U.S. Supreme Court, in the *Boys Market* case, decided that the Norris-LaGuardia Act wasn't really necessary anymore, because unions were well accepted. Therefore, the Supreme Court decided that injunctions could be issued to enforce no-strike clauses in a collective bargaining agreement. The result was that injunctions could be issued to stop a strike that was called over just about any arbitrable issue —and, in effect, making most strikes illegal during the three or four years a union contract is in effect, and legal only during the "window" period when a new contract is being negotiated. Union lawyer Thomas Geoghegan analyzes the impact of the case this way: "Now they [employers] could sit on grievances for years. They could change the safety rules, or fire militants and know that the union couldn't strike, or do anything except wait and wait and wait."

Whenever either side tries to terminate or modify an existing contract, it must give notice to the other side. A sixty-day period is set aside for negotiations, and it's illegal to have either a strike or a lockout during this "cooling-off" period.

Presidential Intervention: If the threat of a strike would be dangerous enough to endanger national health or safety, the Taft-Hartley Act allows the attorney general of the United States to get an injunction against the threatened strike. First, the President of the United States (not of the company) appoints a board of inquiry. That triggers an eighty-day cooling-off period. The board of inquiry reports to the Federal Mediation and Conciliation Service. The President can also instruct the attorney general to apply for the injunction; while the injunction lasts, the parties are supposed to use the FMCS to work out a settlement. In a national emergency dispute, both sides have a legal duty to make "every effort" to settle, but they don't have to accept the FMCS recommendations.

Sixty days after the injunction is issued, the board of inquiry reports to the President about the progress of the settlement talks, and what the employer's last offer was. Then, within the next fifteen days, the NLRB holds a ballot to see if the employees want to adopt the employer's final offer.

The FMCS is not supposed to get involved in disputes that have only a minor effect on commerce. In a nonemergency situation that nevertheless could have substantial impact on interstate commerce, the FMCS can respond to a request from either party, or can volunteer to get involved in settling the dispute.

The procedure is a little different for threatened strikes by railroads and airlines. There, the railroad or airline can call in the National Mediation Board to handle stalled negotiations; the NMB also has the right to volunteer its services when negotiations reach an impasse. If a railroad or airline collective bargaining agreement has to be interpreted, that's usually the job of the National Railroad Adjustment Board, not the NMB.

Economic/Labor Practices: In labor law terms, it makes a big difference if a lawful strike is an "economic strike" or an "unfair labor practices strike." An economic strike is what most people think of as a strike: a work stoppage called by a union in an attempt to get the employer to pay higher wages, enhance benefits, or otherwise provide some kind of economic benefit to the work force.

Someone who strikes because of unfair labor practices remains an "employee" for labor law purposes (including the right to vote in union elections) until and unless he or she is actually fired or denied reinstatement for violence or illegal conduct during a strike. Once the strike is over, and the "unfair labor practices" strikers make an unconditional request for reinstatement, the employer has an obligation to take them back, even if the employer has hired someone else to replace them. In other words, under current law, there can't be "permanent replacements" for unfair labor practices strikers. A recent NLRB ruling says that an employer acts improperly by sending a letter to employees suggesting they would not be reinstated unless they returned to work before the permanent replacements were hired—this was unlawful coercion of union members exercising their right of peaceful organization.

The situation is different for economic strikers. Under current law, employers are allowed to hire new, permanent workers to replace those who go out on strike for economic benefits. After the strike, the employer doesn't have to make a voluntary offer of reinstatement to the economic strikers, because the rights of the permanent replacements are deemed to take precedence. If an economic strike turns into an unfair labor practices strike, the employer doesn't have to get rid of the permanent replacements. The NLRB has also ruled that people hired to be permanent replacements are entitled to that status, even though they don't have time to take their mandatory drug tests or physical exams before the strike ends. The NLRB is the only agency that has the right to deal with questions about permanent replacements: states don't have the power to pass their own laws forbidding hiring of permanent replacements. It's a federal matter, not one that states can decide.

Legislation has been introduced in Congress to ban permanent replacements: the Cesar Chavez Workplace Fairness Act, H.R. 5, was passed by the House, 239 votes to 190, on June 15, 1993—but not by the Senate, so it didn't become law. The bill prohibits an employer from firing or permanently replacing legal strikers, and also from discriminating against strikers in employment terms and benefits. If this bill becomes law, employers will not be allowed to give advantages to workers who cross picket lines to work during a strike.

The term "Laidlaw list" means the list of economic strikers who have unconditionally offered to return to work after a strike, but have been replaced. The employer has an obligation to recall the people on the Laidlaw list and reinstate them as jobs open up—unless the people on the list have gotten equivalent jobs elsewhere, or unless the employer has a legitimate business reason for the failure to recall.

However, the NLRB has the power to order employers to reinstate economic strikers—even if the strikers have gotten other, equivalent jobs but still prefer to return to the old job. Usually, a person stops being an "employee" of one company once he or she gets a substantially equivalent job somewhere else. (A part-time job flipping burgers or clerking in a supermarket clearly wouldn't be equivalent to a full-time, skilled factory job.)

If a strike is called in violation of Section 8(d), the mandatory sixty-day cooling off period required before terminating or modifying a collective bargaining agreement, the strikers lose their status as "employees" as soon as they go out on strike.

Voter Status: Employee status is important because it determines the right to vote in union elections. Both strikers and replacement workers can vote in union elections that are held within twelve months of the start of a strike. This can lead to some pretty bizarre power politics.

Naturally, most people who would take jobs as permanent replacements are going to vote against the union in a certification or decertification election. First of all, they need the employer's good will—as the last hired, they're at risk of being the first fired. Second, they probably don't think a lot of unions anyhow. Third, even if they think unions are a **great** idea, they may have a justified feeling of caution about how their union "brothers" will treat the permanent replacements, who may be scorned (or worse) as "strikebreakers" and "scabs."

From the union standpoint, that makes it crucial to have as many strikers included in the vote as possible—even (or especially) if the strikers don't work there anymore. An ex-worker may take a certain grim pleasure in knowing that the former workplace is unionized: the union will be there to bedevil the boss, and the onetime worker doesn't have to pay dues to the union or suffer any kind of hassles if the union is incompetent or corrupt.

Strike Strategy Pros and Cons: Under the best of circumstances, a strike creates, or at least worsens, strife between workers and management. The best case, from the union viewpoint, is a brief strike that results in enormous gains—a big rise in compensation, dramatic changes in working conditions, or both. The longer a strike drags on, the greater the friction between those who crossed the picket line and those who went out on strike; and the harder it is for the gains of the strike to make up for lost wages and the fear that the wages would never return.

The worst case, for the union, is a strike that ends in defeat, with the workers going back without obtaining much at all—or even having to make givebacks; or jobs disappearing to permanent replacements; or the jobs disappearing entirely. After all, strikes are not an exotic form of unpaid vacation (featuring picketing in the snow rather than basking on the beach), but an attempt to put economic pressure on the employer by cutting off production.

In other words, if you have to make a decision about a strike vote, you have to think about how long the strike is likely to last —and whether the employer really wants to settle it, and how likely the various possible outcomes are.

Who Elects the Union Power Structure?

Well, basically the union officials elect each other. Unions are run about the way the British Parliament was run before World War I: a few influential people make all the decisions. It's true that local union officials are elected by the rank and file, but very few people take much interest in the process . . . and the NLRB doesn't take much interest in preventing ballot-box stuffing and other forms of election fraud.

Once the local officials are elected (with whatever degree of worker participation or funny business), the national leadership of the union is elected at delegate conventions, with no direct input from the rank-and-file members. As you'd imagine, the delegates tend to be the officials of the locals. Don't hold your breath waiting for national campaigns or exciting contests between entrenched union officials and maverick newcomers with new ideas. In fact, you probably won't even be told when your union's national convention is held.

According to the Sixth Circuit, union newsletters are supposed to be an open forum for the members (and often the only way for them to communicate with fellow union members at other job locations). Therefore, a union business manager's refusal to publish a member's Letter to the Editor violated the member's right to free speech within the union.

Grievances and Discipline

The union represents employees in their collective, group concern. However, if there are individual questions, hassles, and grievances that can be settled without interpreting the collective bargaining agreement, the National Labor Relations Act gives employees the right to have the grievances settled without intervention of a bargaining representative from the union (as long as the representative is notified and given a chance to be present at the grievance session).

What usually happens is that collective bargaining agreements contain arbitration clauses. Questions about employee rights, or interpretation of the contract, will usually go to arbitrators, who are selected to be neutral and acceptable to both union and management, and not to courts. NLRB policy calls for recognizing and enforcing arbitration awards; usually, the NLRB won't deal with a charge of unfair labor practices if the matter could have been handled via arbitration.

Work assignments (which group of employees should do what) and job classifications (whether assistant electricians are Level 12 or Level 13 for pay and benefits) are usually arbitrable. If the collective bargaining agreement promises employees that they will only be discharged for just cause, the "justness" of a particular firing is definitely arbitrable. Discharges may even be subject to arbitration when the collective bargaining agreement doesn't say they are—if the employer did something like lying to the employees, saying that it would not close the plant (so they wouldn't quit at inconvenient times), then closing the plant anyway.

Grievance Procedures: In a unionized workplace, a typical grievance procedure might set up an employee committee to handle complaints from employees about things like discipline, layoffs, transfers, promotions, and firing. The committee's task is to talk to the grievant (the complaining employee), the supervisor, maybe other employees, and try to work out an informal agreement. In the meantime, work is supposed to go on as usual —no slowdowns or strikes. If the problem can't be worked out informally, the next step is to go to arbitration under the collective bargaining agreement.

Nonunion Workplaces: Only unionized employees have collective bargaining agreements, and the protection of years of precedent for the arbitration process. But, of course, disputes and problems arise in nonunion workplaces too. Employee handbooks often include a procedure for raising grievances. A typical mechanism is for supervisors to claim that they have an "open door" policy, where they are always ready to hear and adjust disputes in an informal way to prevent them from becoming unmanageable. However, without the protection of a union (and the potential for an unfair labor practices strike) employees often fear that the door is open so the supervisor can drop-kick them back through it!

If the problem is caused by the supervisor (e.g., he is sexually harassing you), or if you are not satisfied with the supervisor's attempt at resolution, there should be a way to complain to a corporate higher-up or the company's human resources department.

Before you take advantage of a nonunion grievance procedure, it pays to make a few discreet inquiries about how objective—and how effective—the policy really is, and whether the promises of no reprisals are kept. In today's lawsuit-happy environment, employers are beginning to realize that it can save lots of money—and always save lots of trouble—if complaints can be resolved speedily and to mutual satisfaction.

An increasing trend, especially among midsized and larger companies, is to have an in-house ombudsman to handle employee complaints. Most of the ombudsmen aren't lawyers; their job is to handle things informally and neutrally. The company's hope is that a nasty and potentially embarrassing and expensive (say, $15,000 to $50,000 for litigation costs, even if the company wins) lawsuit will be headed off.

Disciplinary Interviews: In a sense, labor law parallels criminal law. Someone who is accused of something, and could get into serious trouble as a result, is accorded certain rights. In the labor law context, the equivalent of the law enforcement Miranda warning is the "Weingarten right." An employee who has a "reasonable fear" that an interview with management will result in some disciplinary action (e.g., being demoted; being fired) has the right to have a union representative present at the meeting. (Nonunionized employees do *not* have a comparable right to have a representative of their choice at a disciplinary interview.)

The employer doesn't have to negotiate with the union rep,

but the rep has to be allowed to help the employee present his or her side of the story, and to make additions and clarifications to the record. The Weingarten right applies only to scheduled "investigative interviews" (like the police interrogation covered by Miranda)—there's no right to have a representative present if a spontaneous argument escalates, or if the interview exists only to tell the employee about a disciplinary decision that management has already made.

This protection was extended in 1993, when the Sixth Circuit held that it's an unfair labor practice for the employer to prevent the employee from consulting a shop steward before an interrogation about alleged misconduct.

The Right to Know

Labor recognizes that there are some things that are management prerogatives. It's up to the management to decide what products or services the company will offer, who it will do business with, and similar big strategic decisions. (See pages 167–169 for a discussion of "decision bargaining" about shutdowns and relocation.) But unions can't do an effective job of bargaining unless they have the relevant information, and there are circumstances where the union must communicate important data to its members.

For example, collective bargaining agreements may give unions the right to examine the company's financial records to see if wage and hour laws are being followed. If, in the course of collective bargaining, a company says that it can't pay a wage increase because it can't afford any more money, the union may be entitled to look at the employer's books (or have them audited) to test out the reality behind the statement.

The NLRB has ruled that unions have a right to ask for the employer's general records that involve the health and safety of employees; the employer can't wriggle out by claiming that giving the union the information would violate the privacy rights of employees mentioned in the records.

The general rule is that the union is also allowed to find out the names of chemicals used in the employer's manufacturing operations. One possible exception is chemical formulas that are trade secrets; but even then, the employer has an obligation to bargain in good faith to work out a way to keep the secrets but still give the union a chance to find out about the potential health impact of the chemicals. If the union wants an outside expert (such as an industrial hygienist or a safety expert) to have access to a plant, the employer will probably have to allow it— although the outsider can be restricted to reasonable access (e.g., during normal working hours) and the expert and the union will probably have to sign a confidentiality agreement to prevent disclosure of proprietary processes.

Worker Ownership

There wouldn't be any products, or any profits for business owners, if there weren't any employees. An argument could be made that this gives employees the right to have input into important decisions that affect their health, their working conditions, and the future of their jobs.

In the United States, employees don't exactly own most businesses, but pension funds own huge amounts of stock, often stock of the company where the union's members work. Corporate law allows stockholders (including pension funds) to propose topics to be voted on at the corporation's annual shareholder meeting. So far, few of these proposals (such as limitations on top executives' compensation, changes in working conditions) have actually won a majority of shareholder votes, but the prospect of a battle at the shareholder meeting changes the corporate balance of power.

Stockholders can also vote on corporate issues such as whether a corporation will merge with another corporation. Pension funds (especially public-employee pension funds) have become so powerful that companies will often negotiate with the pension fund, and make substantial concessions, just to avoid a public struggle and lots of bad publicity. Pension-fund shares can often be the deciding factor in a takeover battle between companies, and a company that wants to fight a takeover may have to make significant promises to get the support of the pension fund and stockholding employees.

Some of the union contracts negotiated in mid-1993 reflected the concept of "employee empowerment": more control for workers (but sometimes in return for economic givebacks by unions). Inland Steel, for instance, has a union-nominated seat on its board of directors; some airlines offered a big chunk of stock to unions in return for concessions. Other companies may let unions have a say in big decisions such as how the company should invest its capital, whether a merger should take place—maybe even who should be hired for senior management posts.

For many years corporations have granted shares of stock and options to buy stock to their top managers, as a perquisite of executive status. Ordinary employees are often given a chance to buy employer stock as an option for investing their retirement accounts. (If you're in this category, remember to balance your loyalty to the corporation with a sensible intention to diversify your portfolio; don't let all your retirement security, as well as your current employment security, depend on the performance of the employer's stock.) Another possibility, often used as a defense against an unwanted corporate takeover, is the ESOP—Employee Stock Ownership Plan. In late 1993 there were almost 10,000 companies with ESOPs, and about 11 million participating employees.

A more recent development is for employees to actually gain control of corporations and their stock. Generally speaking, this happens when the trained professional managers have run the company into the ground; the employees get to take it over, more or less by default, because the alternative is shutting up shop. Or, to quote a pithy East European proverb, "When a poor man gets to eat a whole chicken, one of them is sick."

10

The Terminators: Losing Your Job

The Chinese term for firing someone (or quitting a job) is "breaking the rice bowl": that says a lot about the connection between work and survival. When you lose your job, unless you step immediately into a much better one with superior career prospects, you face economic risk (ranging from the minor to the catastrophic), possible derailment of career plans (sometimes a gap on the resume is viewed with as much suspicion as a forthright "1980–1995: In stir"), and very likely anxiety and self-doubt.

At one end of the continuum, everyone agrees that losing your job was not your fault in any way, was completely beyond your control, and doesn't reflect badly on you. Indeed, there are situations where your job ceases to exist. The whole **factory** where you worked might cease to exist. You may have rights to notice or substantive rights to benefits, such as unemployment compensation (if you were without fault in losing a job) or

Workers' Compensation benefits (if you were injured in connection with work, irrespective of whose fault, if anyone's, it was).

At the other end of the scale, your ex-employer thinks you're lucky not to end up in prison. So the question is, what is the most favorable, yet still accurate, way to describe the situation? Do you have any negotiating options? What is your one-time employer allowed to say about you when asked for a reference? And if there's something improper or unlawful about the circumstances of your departure, what are your remedies?

In the first "Terminator" film Arnold Schwarzenegger played an unstoppable killing machine. In the sequel he played a pretty nice . . . well, not guy, but a pretty nice all-around killing machine. Who knows? Losing your job could be a blessing in disguise.

Wrongful Termination

The rule used to be simple, easy to understand, but brutal: employers could hire people for any reason, at any time, and fire them the same way. The first step in eroding this legal rule of "at-will employment" (the employee works at the will of the employer) was recognition of employment contracts. If an employer agreed to hire you for seven years, then you couldn't be fired for those seven years except under the circumstances spelled out in the contract.

Today, the doctrine of at-will employment still has some legal validity, but it's been shot full of holes. First of all, employers are not allowed to fire employees for any reason that would be illegal under federal or state law. You can fire someone who **is** a member of a minority group, a woman, over forty, pregnant, or handicapped—but you can't fire that person **because** of that reason. These forms of wrongful termination are dealt with by Title VII, the ADEA, and the ADA (see Chapter Seven), and there are intricate technical rules that must be followed to make the case.

There are many other kinds of unlawful firing that can become the subject of suits in state courts. Not all states have uniform rules, so we suggest that you see an attorney who has relevant experience as soon as you determine that you may have a valid case. The lawyer will explain the rules that apply in your jurisdiction, and what you have to do to enforce any contract or tort rights that you have under local law.

Termination is not wrongful if the employer has a valid cause, such as poor performance. But a recent Third Circuit case holds that, where a customer complaint results in employee discipline, the employee is entitled to the name, address, and phone number of the angry consumer, unless the complainer requests, or the employer offers, confidentiality.

In at least some of the states, you can win a wrongful termination action based on these claims:

- That you were fired for a reason that violates public policy. Examples would be going on jury duty when your employer doesn't want to give you time off, engaging in lawful conduct to organize a union at work, filing a legitimate Workers' Compensation claim that will increase your employer's insurance rate unless you get fired in time, being ordered to work weekends after your doctor tells you to "take it easy" after hospitalization, or "blowing the whistle" on illegal conduct by your employer. About half the states recognize some kind of public policy exception to the at-will doctrine. This may be your only source of remedy if you work for a company that is so small that it isn't covered by Title VII or the state antidiscrimination law.

- That your employer promised you continued employment in a formal way short of a written employment contract. The most prominent example is an employee handbook that assures employees that they will only be fired for good cause, and after an investigation giving them a chance to state their side of the story. Sometimes courts will require employers to live up to the language in the handbook. If this is true, employees will also have to live up to the language of the handbook; if it describes a grievance arbitration program, for instance, the employee will have to go through the whole process instead of skipping straight off to the courthouse to file a complaint.

However, other cases hold that the handbook is only an informal internal document, not a promise—especially if the employer had enough sense to include a disclaimer in the handbook saying that the text of the handbook does not restrict the employer's right to fire. Needless to say, employers have gained sophistication on this issue over time.

- "Promissory estoppel"—if an employer induces you to take a job, and you undergo some kind of loss to accept it (moving your family cross-country, quitting a job that would otherwise have continued), courts may keep the employer from firing you without good cause, on the theory that your sacrifice binds the employer.
- A few states (usually, states that don't have a public policy exception) imply a "covenant of good faith and fair dealing" in all employment relationships, so it may be possible to sue the employer for dastardly deeds that violate this covenant.

But one thing to watch out for in these tough economic times: if you lose your job in a budget cutback or out of economic necessity, you won't have a wrongful termination claim even if your employer has agreed not to fire you without good cause. In effect, economic factors always constitute good cause (unless, of course, it could be proved that the employer used them as an excuse to practice unlawful race, sex, age, or handicap discrimination).

Preemption: By now, you may have gotten the idea that when ERISA horns in, employees get booted out of state court, because ERISA preempts the claim. This is true in ERISA Section 510 cases (where an employee charges that he or she was fired so the employer could avoid paying ERISA benefits), even if the employee says that it's a violation of public policy to fire him or her for this reason.

If a wrongful termination claim requires interpretation of a collective bargaining agreement, then state-law claims are preempted for another reason: those claims are covered by the Labor-Management Relations Act (LMRA) Section 301.

Whistle-blowers: People who are fired for detecting and reporting wrongdoing are a special case. Employees of government contractors who detect and report fraud against the government can feel all the satisfaction of saving money for the taxpayers. They can also feel another kind of satisfaction: the whistle-blower can receive 15–25 percent of the amount of the fraud if and when the federal government charges the employer with filing false government claims. According to the Justice Department, several whistle-blowers have gotten multimillion-dollar bounties; the man who revealed $150 million in fraudulent billing for military helicopters was awarded $22.5 million. The laboratory employee who exposed $150 million in claims for unnecessary blood tests was awarded $15 million to be paid by one lab and $8 million from another.

Many states have whistle-blower acts to protect people against wrongful termination by the "whistle-blow-ee." In 1993, for instance, a nurse received an award of $703,000 for lost wages and benefits, plus attorney's fees, after she was fired in retaliation for reporting a doctor's fraudulent statement on four patients' charts that he had performed a particular procedure. The nurse pointed out that there was no evidence that the procedure had been performed, there were no consent forms in the file, and the necessary equipment for performing the procedure had not been checked out.

Most of the states (thirty-five, at last count) have some kind of statutory protection for whistle-blowers, but only eleven cover private employees, not just public employees who tell the public about government improprieties.

Sometimes whistle-blower laws are interpreted very narrowly: for instance, a requirement may be imposed that the whistle-blower expose conduct that is unlawful, not just unsafe or improper. It may also be required that a report be made public or made to a law enforcement agency, not just disclosed internally within the organization. This seems unfair, since one of the basic principles of employment law is that people are expected to "go through channels," and many cases are dismissed precisely **because** the plaintiff was too impatient to use the internal grievance procedures (or believed that it was pointless to complain to the person who created the problem in the first place). Incidentally, a Florida court recently ruled that even someone who has participated in the wrongdoing can take advantage of the whistle-blower act if, after repenting of the action, he or she voluntarily reports it.

Corporate Transitions

The effect of an employer's merger, acquisition by another company, or bankruptcy can be as brutal—and as sudden—as an earthquake or explosion. If there's no company, your job may vanish along with it; and, very possibly, your right to sue disappears too, if there's no legal entity still responsible—or if someone is certainly responsible and can be sued, but the money to pay the judgment has vanished.

When two corporations merge, or if one corporation acquires another, the way the deal is structured determines whether the buying corporation takes over legal responsibility for the selling corporation's debts, obligations, and lawsuits.

For the employees of the now-vanished company, the issue is "successor liability": who can be found to take the responsibility and, in appropriate cases, the blame? Usually the new company has at least some responsibilities. Sometimes, especially if the corporation had no real existence except as a front for its owner, the owner of the dissolved business is on the hook (but he or she seldom has enough assets to pay all the claims). Unfortunately, in some cases, nobody is liable.

Successor Liability: U.S. Can acquired the stock to purchase four plants from Continental Can. Continental Can had a master agreement with a union. The master agreement included a hiring preference at its other plants for workers who got laid off or lost their jobs in a plant closing. (See page 170 for a discussion of the WARN Act and notice of plant closings.)

In January 1993 the Seventh Circuit treated U.S. Can as if it had assumed the entire contract—even though U.S. Can adamantly insisted just the contrary to the unions—because U.S. Can also told the unions it would adopt the terms of the collective bargaining agreement. The agreement included the hiring preference. U.S. Can also acted as if it accepted the agreement. For instance, it performed "dues checkoff" (deducting union dues from employees' paychecks) and abided by the contract's union security clause. The court basically said that a company has to either accept all the provisions of a union contract (in this case, including the hiring preference) or none of them (so it can't follow the dues checkoff or union security clause). Companies can't pick and choose the contract provisions they're willing to honor.

Collective Bargaining Agreements: A company is considered a successor, with an obligation to bargain with the former company's union, as long as there is continuity of operations. The most important factor is whether a majority of the workers used to work for the old company. In other words, if Joe's Home-Style Cookie Co. is bought out by a conglomerate, but they keep on making the same cookies in the same way with pretty much the same staff, there is continuity of operations. If the conglomerate buys the company, sells the machinery to a postmodern sculptor, and turns the building into a ten-plex movie theater, there isn't.

This sounds like a bigger deal for the employees than it really is. The successor has to bargain with the union, and the union is presumed to still represent a majority of the workers after the change in control (although the employer can prove that this is no longer the case)—but all they have to do is bargain. The general rule is that the successor can just reject the former company's union contract and set its own terms and conditions of employment; the union has to start from scratch in negotiating a new contract with the new owner.

In a unionized company, the duty to arbitrate claims under the collective bargaining agreement continues after the company is sold, or after a merger, as long as there is substantial continuity of operations. And if the company goes bankrupt and is completely terminated (many bankrupt businesses are allowed to continue their operations), the obligations under the collective bargaining agreement die along with the business.

Pension Plans: Because pension plans are usually set up as independent trusts, it often doesn't matter when the company is sold or merged; the plan can continue on its merry way, with the new employer making the necessary contributions. If it's a defined-benefit plan, the new employer maintains the same PBGC insurance as the old employer.

On the other hand, pension plans can be terminated for various reasons, including a company sale or shutdown. In order for a plan to be qualified for tax purposes, the plan documents must provide that a plan's merger with another plan will not reduce the benefits that employees receive when the plan terminates. (In this case, the merger is the merger of pension plans, not of companies.) As soon as a plan is terminated, all participants must become 100 percent vested in their account balances or their accrued benefits.

When an employer sells a business, but keeps up pension plan contributions, it can be held liable for underfunding the plan for up to five years from the date of the last payment to the plan—not the date of the sale (which would get the employer off the hook earlier). The Third Circuit adopted this approach in 1993 to close a potential loophole, under which companies could squeeze out of making pension payments by transferring an underfunded plan to another company that has too little capital to make the payments. Employees aren't considered "separated from service" (risking potential loss of pension payments) if their employer sells a division and transfers the pension plan to the buyer. The original employer has an obligation to transfer enough money to take care of benefits, including the early retirement benefits that employees would have been able to qualify for if the employer had kept the division and the original plan.

Decision and Effects Bargaining

In many circumstances, the management of a company has an absolute right to make major decisions about corporate directions and strategy. Legally speaking, the board of directors is responsible, but often the board is made up of prominent people who don't have much day-to-day involvement. Sometimes the union has one or more seats on the board of directors, but usually it won't be represented.

Labor law obligates the employer to engage in collective bargaining with the union over subjects like employees' working conditions, hours, and compensation package. The employer has an obligation to bargain with the union about the effects of an economically oriented decision to close down operations at a particular location (see page 170 for a discussion of the WARN Act's notice requirements when there is a plant closing)—but the Supreme Court says there is no obligation to bargain over the **decision** to shut down. Employers have a right to terminate an entire business for any reason, or no reason (even if they are motivated by hostility to the union). However, if an employer operates multiple plants, then it's not permitted to shut down one of the plants if the motivation is to keep the other plants from unionizing.

The employer does have an obligation to tell the union about the planned shutdown, so the union can attempt to bargain over changed working conditions (but not over the decision itself). The employer may also have to give the union information about its financial condition—possibly including information the company would prefer to keep to itself.

However, the NLRB doesn't accept the Supreme Court's distinction between shutdowns (no need to bargain) and lesser decisions (bargaining required)—so an employer may find itself hauled before the NLRB, or even ordered to cease and desist from threatening to move a plant. If the plant has actually been moved, it probably goes beyond the NLRB's powers to make the employer move back (the NLRB isn't allowed to make any unreasonable demands on employers), but the NLRB might order the employer to offer jobs to workers at the old plant and pay their relocation expenses if they move to take the new jobs.

In August 1993 the D.C. Circuit set some new standards for bargaining about relocation of jobs from one plant to another (say, from a plant in a high-wage city to another one in a low-wage rural area). The court says that the decision to relocate is a management prerogative, with no need to bargain, as long as there is a basic change in the operation, scope, and direction of the business. A basic change requires that the work at the new location is significantly different—and that work is discontinued at the old location, not just transferred to a new one. But even if the relocation is not a basic change, the employer won't have to bargain with the union if it can show that labor costs were not a factor in the relocation. Furthermore, bargaining is not required if the employer can prove that it would be futile—in other words, the union won't (or can't) make enough concessions for the employer to change its mind about the relocation.

Even if the employer doesn't have to bargain over the decision itself, the effects will probably have to become a subject of bargaining: things like severance pay and seniority rights after the transfer.

Labor Law and Bankruptcy

Many employers resent the terms of their union contracts. If the business is in financial trouble, it has a powerful incentive either to get someone else to take over the union contract (and the rest of the business) or to find a way to cancel the union contract without breaking the law. The bankruptcy system is designed to give debtors a breathing space and a chance to regain financial health. Sometimes that means that bankruptcy can be used to reject a collective bargaining agreement.

In 1984 the Supreme Court gave bankrupt employers the chance to rip up their union contracts. Congress thought that was going a little too far, so the Bankruptcy Amendments of 1984 (PL 98-353) impose some not-too-stringent controls on a company's ability to use bankruptcy to repudiate union contracts. Under the Bankruptcy Amendments, employers can't discard a union contract unilaterally. Court approval is required.

Before rejecting a contract, the employer has to disclose its plan to the union; come up with a proposal for modifying the contract; and meet with the union and confer in good faith. If the union and management can't come to an agreement, the employer can petition the bankruptcy court for permission to repudiate the contract. The court's job is to "balance the equities" if the employer can demonstrate that the union's refusal to accept the proposed modifications was made without good cause.

The union doesn't have a lot of great choices; turning down an unfavorable contract modification may result in outright termination of the contract. If the employer's dire economic predictions come true, it won't really matter if the contract is affirmed—if the company goes under and there aren't any jobs to be covered by the agreement.

The court balances the equities by determining if it is clearly fair for the employer to back out of the contract, based on the impact of contract rejection on the employees; the effect that keeping the contract in place would have on the company's creditors; and the likelihood that the company will have to be liquidated if the contract is affirmed.

Hanging On

In effect, if your company is acquired or participates in a merger, you may have to "audition" for your own job. The company may have an urgent need to downsize (because even friendly mergers are expensive; a prolonged acquisition battle costs billions of dollars, and the "winning" company will have enormous debts to pay off). There may be a desire to merge two headquarters, thus tossing out half the people.

Career counselors suggest that you be prepared to justify your retention, by showing that you can outperform rivals (within the old company as well as the newly merged company) and fit into the corporate culture of the acquiror or the new corporate culture that will be created.

The WARN Act

In order to protect workers who lose their jobs, through no fault of their own, when an entire plant or other business operation shuts down, Congress passed a federal law, the Worker Adjustment Retraining and Notice Act (WARN Act), 29 USC Section 2101, in 1988. The statute requires certain employers to give sixty days notice to employees, unions, and the government before a plant is closed or mass layoffs are implemented. A covered employer is one with one hundred or more full-time employees—or one hundred or more employees (with part-timers included in the count) working 4,000 or more straight-time hours per week.

If an employer wants to claim that the work is "seasonal," it is still required to give WARN Act notice unless it can prove that the shut-down facility was a temporary one—and that hiring was done on that basis. There must be objective evidence that the project had a defined and limited period with an announced end point—not just the employer's claim of seasonality.

A plant closing is defined as a situation in which fifty or more full-time employees suffer "employment loss" (detailed below) within a thirty-day period because an employment site, or part of an employment site, is shut down. A mass layoff is a reduction in force that doesn't add up to a plant closing, but causes employment loss of at least one third of the work force, adding up to fifty or more full-time employees in a thirty-day period. Employment loss for 500 or more employees also constitutes a mass layoff, even if this is actually less than one third of the work force.

There are three kinds of employment loss potentially covered by the WARN Act:

- Outright, involuntary termination other than resignation, termination for cause, or retirement.
- A layoff extending more than six months.
- Cutting hours in half (or reducing them even further) for each month in a six-month period.

Notice has to be given to supervisory and management employees, and to other laid-off workers who have a reasonable expectation of recall after the layoff (as determined by industry practice).

There are also other limitations on employers' WARN Act obligations. Notice isn't required if job loss is caused by an event that is defined as either a strike or a lockout under the National Labor Relations Act. Nonstrikers at a job site who suffer employment loss are covered—but it's not required that notice be given to economic strikers who lose their jobs to permanent replacements.

Nor is notice required if the employer is defined as a "faltering business"—one needing more capital to stay in operation, with the risk that publicizing the impending closing will blow the deal. (Employers claiming this defense have the obligation of proving it.) Of course, employers don't have to (and can't) give two months' notice of closure caused by natural disaster or act of God, and they don't have to give notice if less drastic but sudden, unforeseen circumstances prevent them from giving notice. An unpredictable decline in business, or a strike at a major supplier, might fall into this last category. In April 1993 a Florida federal court ruled that notice was not required when a plant shut down temporarily, then reopened with a single fifty-five–hour working shift to replace the previous two forty-hour shifts. The change led to eighty-one layoffs. The court applied the business circumstances exception because the company thought the decline in lumber prices would be temporary and the original work pattern could be restored eventually.

When a business is sold, all of its full-time employees are considered to become employees of the buyer company as soon as the sale takes place. Until the date of the sale the selling company is responsible for notices; afterward, it becomes the buyer's responsibility. Employees aren't considered to have "employment loss" as defined by the WARN Act if they are offered a transfer to another work site within reasonable commuting distance, and their involuntary time off lasts six months or less. Nor is there any employment loss under the act if the employee is offered a transfer beyond reasonable commuting distance (thus forcing a relocation), and accepts the offer within thirty days, or within thirty days of the closing or layoff—whichever is later.

If an employer fails to meet its obligations, the only remedy is for the employees to sue for damages and a penalty. There is no federal agency that can hassle or punish employers for falling down on the job (the way the EEOC can do in cases of employment discrimination), and employees can't ask for punitive damages or criminal penalties. Each employee is entitled to up to sixty days' back pay plus benefits if proper WARN Act notice is not given, and a civil penalty, payable to the federal government, of up to $500 can be imposed for each day of violation. Courts have reached contradictory decisions about what the statute of limitations (the time to bring a claim before it becomes too stale to pursue) is: your court could place it at anywhere between six months and six years.

It's clear, though, that the individual employees are the ones who have the right to bring the suit: a union can't bring the suit without the participation of the workers.

Results: What with one thing and another, the WARN Act has not been very effective. Neither the Democrats' self-congratulations about granting a huge victory to Labor, nor Republican shrieking about the crippling effect on Management, has proved to have more than a grain of truth.

Two economists at the University of South Carolina, pointing out that many industries are dominated by small exempt shops with fewer than one hundred workers, noted that between 1988 and 1991, when the WARN Act was in full effect, 8.2 percent of all laid-off workers received more than a month's notice of a layoff. Pretty swell, right?

Well, before the act was passed, 8.6 percent of laid-off workers got a month or more of notice. The U.S. General Accounting Office (GAO), investigating plant shutdowns occurring in 1990, found that more than half of employers in this situation failed to give proper notice to employees and state regulators; more than a quarter of those who bothered to give notice at all gave less than the required two months' worth.

Plant Closings and Incentives

A large factory or other business that employs many people casts a long shadow in a small town; in fact, even a city as large as New York can be powerfully affected by a major employer's decision to move. So it's not uncommon for cities and states to offer incentives for major employers to stay put (and avoid massive layoffs). The employer may be given a break on its corporate taxes or real estate taxes; the taxes may even be waived entirely.

A recent decision spells bad news for cities that hope their incentive programs will carry out their stated objectives. General Motors was allowed to close down its Ypsilanti, Michigan, plant even though the city had agreed to cut the company's taxes in half. A Michigan appeals court said that that was just too bad for the city—there had been no specific, formal agreement that

GM was obligated to keep the plant open for a specific period of time in exchange for the tax breaks.

After the Pink Slip

If you've been let go for whatever reason, you're undoubtedly facing rough times. However, you do have some options. Get full information before you make up your mind; decisions can have serious consequences. In particular, don't sign anything until you're sure that you understand it, and that it represents the best deal you're going to get. For unionized workers, the union should be active in providing information. Otherwise, if a whole department, division, or company is involved, it often makes sense for a group of workers affected by the decision to join together to hire an experienced attorney to explain the implications of various options. Some choices that may be available:

- If you're in mid-life, your company may want you to retire early instead of being officially considered unemployed. Find out if there's a package of early retirement incentives, and what lump-sum or continuing payments are available. But if you think that you are being pushed out because of age, sex, race, or any other forbidden category of discrimination, get legal advice before you sign a release. Sometimes you can sue even though you did sign a release (see page 114—for instance, if you only signed the release because the company deliberately lied to you about a crucial factor), but don't sign a release until you understand all its legal and practical implications.
- If you're a person with seniority, the company may provide some degree of outplacement assistance. This is often fairly useless—like a resume-writing workshop when the problem isn't the quality of your resume but the absence of decent jobs—but it may have at least some psychological value. What's really important is whether the company will allow you the use of desk, phone, fax, copier, and support staff for a while, so you can conduct your job hunt on more solid

ground. In 1993 the IRS decided that outplacement benefits do not constitute taxable income to those who receive them.

- The timing of your departure may make a big difference. Staying on for a few extra months may qualify you for an early retirement incentive program, or for a pension formula that enhances your retirement income significantly.
- See if you can get an agreement about your reference letter. A warm, gracious letter explaining that you did an outstanding job but had to be let go as part of an economy drive can be just the incentive a new employer needs to hire you.
- There may be another job available. Perhaps your boss didn't mention it because it's a demotion, or pays less, or involves commission sales to the worst territory.

Continuing Health Coverage: Don't forget to check your benefit options. Employers have to let you buy "continuation coverage": you take over the premium that the employer paid for your health coverage, perhaps with a small (not more than 2 percent) administration fee payable to the employer. Depending on your age and circumstances, you may be entitled to continuation coverage for a period lasting anywhere from eighteen to thirty-nine months. You may be entitled to continuation coverage even if you were discharged for cause; and even if you're not entitled, your missteps won't block your spouse's and children's right to health insurance.

Continuation coverage is required by a federal statute called COBRA—the Comprehensive Omnibus Budget Reconciliation Act. You must decide whether to accept or refuse the COBRA option within forty-five days. The period for continuation coverage begins at the date of the triggering event (such as a layoff or dismissal), not when insurance benefits under the non-COBRA part of the policy stop, if there's a difference.

You won't have to bother with continuation coverage if you have adequate coverage provided by your spouse's employer (but you take the risk that his or her family coverage will be reduced or eliminated in the future, before you become covered under a new employer's plan—or, even worse, you may both be out of work at the same time). You may be able to buy coverage cheaper as an individual or a member of a group (such as a professional association) than you can get it through continuing the employee policy, but that's pretty unlikely.

COBRA also applies to families where an offspring is about to lose coverage under the parent's health insurance because he or she is no longer a student. The recent grad can take over payments under the policy for up to eighteen months; the expectation is that he or she will find a first job within that time and get covered by the employer's plan. There may also be less expensive options for new graduates who are still job hunting. Some insurers sell inexpensive short-term (up to six months) coverage at low premiums. The problem is that they may exclude preexisting conditions, so a policy of this type would be a poor choice for someone with a chronic disease or lingering effects of an injury. New grads can also get group coverage under affinity plans (e.g., alumni groups) or individual policies —if they can afford the price.

Severance Pay

Usually, except in cases of firing for good cause, employees will get severance pay in addition to the money owed to them (salary plus things like unused vacation days). A typical arrangement is an extra day's or week's pay for every year of service with the company. Severance pay is often considered a substitute for getting long-range notice that the job will end, so if you get a lot of lead time, you may get less or no severance pay on the theory that you have a long time to stay on the payroll while searching for a new job opportunity.

What if you have to sign a release to get your severance pay? A recent case says that the lump sum severance won't be considered "earnings" that increase a pension based on average earnings.

Another question is your bonus. In many companies, the stated salary is far from the whole story: top performers, or indeed all employees, may get big bonuses once or twice a year. Employers tend to use these bonuses to ensure loyalty, by casting broad hints that bonuses will only be paid to people who stick around all year—or even who stick around for months afterward, until the bonus is actually paid. There may be legal theories that entitle a terminated employee to a percentage of the bonus based on the number of months worked; the employee may even be entitled to the whole bonus. A court might very well decide that getting two bonuses a year was part of the job. Even if it's impossible to calculate the hypothetical bonus exactly, the employee may be entitled to an amount based on adjustments to bonuses paid in the past. The employer, of course, will claim that giving bonuses is a purely discretionary function, and that it's improper for a court to interfere—but the court may very well decide that that argument is bogus if the employer's "discretion" leads to bonus grants year after year.

Parachutes, Golden and Otherwise

A "golden parachute" is a very generous benefit package that becomes payable to a top executive when his corporation is taken over. For a while in the 1980s, they were very popular as a takeover defense. The theory was that nobody would do a hostile takeover because it would be too expensive to satisfy all the big shots under the parachute arrangement. It has been held that a company policy of making lump-sum payments to executives who are discharged within two years of a change in control of their employer corporation is not a "plan" subject to ERISA, because it's a one-time arrangement, not the kind of long-range, ongoing relationship that ERISA is supposed to regulate.

In 1984, at the height of the takeover madness, Congress added Section 280G to the Internal Revenue Code. This section imposes a 20 percent excise tax (on top of the income tax due on the money) on "excessive" golden parachute payments made after June 14, 1984. An excess payment is one that's more than three times the "base amount," and the base amount is the executive's average annual compensation for five years (or his or her whole stay at the company, if it was less than five years). Amounts that constitute "reasonable compensation" are not considered parachute payments—the parachute is pure severance, not employee compensation.

Tin Parachutes: Four states (Maine, Massachusetts, Pennsylvania, Rhode Island) decided that it was unfair for the top executives (who, presumably, had managed to save a few bucks out of their six- and seven-figure incomes) to get parachutes, while the ordinary workers got nothing. And if an acquiror had to pay off the whole work force, the disincentive to stage a hostile takeover would be even greater!

One of these statutes, the Maine law, was upheld by the Supreme Court in *Fort Halifax Packing Co. v. Coyne,* 482 U.S. 1 (1987), because it just called for a one-time payment for employees not otherwise covered by severance pay. The Massachusetts statute wasn't so lucky: the First Circuit said that it is preempted by ERISA, because Congress wanted nationwide uniformity in complex situations that add up to an ERISA plan.

Unemployment Insurance

It's getting tougher all the time to qualify for unemployment benefits. According to the General Accounting Office (the federal government's investigative agency), only 39 percent of unemployed people qualified for unemployment benefits in the 1989 recession; in 1980, 43 percent of the jobless qualified for benefits.

Tax Funding: Unemployment insurance benefits are funded by taxes that employers pay. (In a few states—Alaska, New Jersey, and Pennsylvania, employees also have to contribute to the unemployment insurance tax fund; and California, Hawaii, New York, and Rhode Island require employee contributions, but just for disability benefits, not unemployment insurance.)

There is a federal tax, called FUTA, for the Federal Unemployment Tax Act. Employers are subject to the tax if, for the current year or the year before, they had at least one employee in at least one day of each of twenty weeks, or paid wages to everybody of $1,500 or more in any quarter of the year.

The definition of "employee" for FUTA purposes is pretty much the same as for income tax and other purposes, but some agent-drivers and traveling salespersons who are not considered employees for other purposes, are employees for FUTA purposes. Both federal and state law exempt insurance salespersons from unemployment tax, though (which, of course, means they can't get unemployment insurance benefits).

FUTA tax is one of the smaller hassles facing employers. For one thing, the tax is due only on the first $7,000 of an employee's wages. Theoretically, the federal tax rate is 6.2 percent (scheduled to decrease to 6 percent in 1997), but really most employers pay less than 1 percent of the $7,000 taxable amount per employee to the federal government, because they get a credit for the taxes they pay to the state unemployment insurance systems. The federal share of the tax is used to pay administrative costs; the state share actually pays the unemployment benefits.

States have a lot of different ways of imposing the tax burden on the employer. Usually, they use an "experience rating" system: that is, employers that fire a lot of employees generate more people who can claim unemployment checks, so these employers pay more.

Collecting Benefits: In order to collect unemployment insurance benefits, you need to meet several criteria:

- You have to be totally or partially unemployed—if you're working full time, no matter how miserly your paycheck, you don't qualify; but self-employment usually doesn't reduce your eligibility.
- You have to be available for work—i.e., if you're a full-time college student or have family responsibilities that keep you from accepting a suitable job, you don't get benefits.
- You have to be legally entitled to work in the United States, so an undocumented alien can't collect unemployment benefits.
- You must have enough "work experience" in covered employment during the "base period" (generally the year before you apply for benefits). However, temporary and part-time workers are usually eligible for unemployment (though they may receive checks even smaller than the usual ones). Disability benefits and severance pay are not considered "remuneration for work"—so weeks when you don't work but do get these benefits can't be counted toward determin-

ing whether you have enough weeks of work to qualify for benefits.
- A "waiting period" must pass between the time you lose your job and the time you can collect benefits—usually, this is just a week or two.
- You must have lost your job through no fault of your own. In other words, you didn't quit voluntarily, and you weren't fired for misconduct.

Federal law was amended by the Unemployment Compensation Amendments of 1976, which prevents states from denying benefits solely on the basis of pregnancy or termination of pregnancy. The 1976 law also says that unemployment compensation can't be paid to anyone who is getting a pension based on previous employment, unless the unemployment check is reduced by the pension. With the reduction, at least employers don't have to pay twice (once to provide the benefit, once to furnish unemployment compensation).

On the other hand, a Pennsylvania court decided in the summer of 1993 that payments employees get because their employers failed to give proper notice under the WARN Act (see page 170) are not "remuneration" for work. Therefore, a person who gets these benefits doesn't lose eligibility for unemployment compensation, and the WARN Act payments aren't deducted from the unemployment check.

The Check: The size of the benefit usually depends on the amount earned in your highest-paid quarter of the benefit period (remember, that's usually a year), but some states use a percentage of your annual wages or an average weekly wage for the calculation. Many states use a sliding scale: the lower your earnings, the higher the percentage of your earnings that can be replaced by unemployment insurance.

Nobody gets rich from unemployment benefits. Each state has a minimum and maximum benefit. The very highest maximum benefit is $335 a week in the District of Columbia. Alaska, Connecticut, the District of Columbia, Illinois, Indiana, Iowa, Maine, Maryland, Massachusetts, Michigan, New Jersey, Ohio, Pennsylvania, and Rhode Island provide additional dependents' allowances for people on unemployment who have families to support—but even then, the highest possible dependents' allowance is $78 a week.

Duration of Benefits: Except for the emergency extensions discussed below, the usual maximum length of time anyone can collect benefits is twenty-six weeks. After that, you have to be employed and start a new benefit period in order to be entitled to any more benefits.

TIP   A few states—Illinois, Massachusetts, Oklahoma—have a special health plan for unemployed people; the premiums are deducted from the unemployment check. If you live in one of these states, and you've used up your COBRA continuation coverage, or can't afford it, the state health plan may be a worthwhile alternative to a superexpensive individual health plan.

There are economic cycles when just about anybody who really wants a job can get one—and cycles when people with decades of high-caliber experience get nothing but a scornful laugh when they apply for jobs. This fact has been recognized by Congress since 1970, when the Employment Security Amendments of 1970, PL 91-373, created a joint federal and state extended benefits program for workers who have used up their benefits at a time when there are few available jobs. The program usually provides an extra thirteen weeks of benefits in states whose unemployment rate is more than 20 percent above the national average.

In 1991 and 1992, Congress passed four laws dealing with Emergency Unemployment Compensation (EUC) (PL 102-164, -182, -244, -318). Some states have an extra thirteen-week period of benefits; some have a twenty-week extra benefit period, if the state's total unemployment rate is over 9 percent, or its unemployment rate, adjusted for certain economic indicators, is over 5 percent. PL 102-244, which was passed February 7, 1992, increased the amount of EUC benefits available: the thirteen-week states went up to twenty-six weeks of benefits, and the twenty-week states went to thirty-three weeks of benefits.

PL 102-318, dated July 3, 1992, extended EUC to March 6, 1993, but cut back the number of weeks of available benefits to twenty or twenty-six weeks. This law, the Unemployment Compensation Amendments of 1992, imposed a trade-off for the longer benefits: for the first time, income tax withholding was imposed on pension payments (except for amounts rolled over to an IRA or another company's pension plan). The amount of income tax that pension recipients had to pay was not increased, but the effect was to speed up payments by collecting taxes at the source instead of waiting for pensioners to pay their taxes.

In October 1993, the Senate voted to extend EUC again, but added some conditions that were expected to cause political problems in the House of Representatives.

Misconduct: In order to keep the system honest, unemployment benefits are limited to situations where the employee was not at fault for losing the job. Misconduct will therefore disqualify an applicant from getting unemployment benefits. Some kinds of misconduct are pretty obvious: getting caught committing a crime, industrial espionage, sexually harassing other employees. Other situations are more ambiguous.

As an example of disqualifying misconduct, consider a recent New York case. The claimant for benefits showed up five days late for work after her vacation, causing a lot of hassles for her employer. It's true that her car broke down while she was on vacation—but she didn't call her employer until she arrived back in New York, and she took her own sweet time about getting the car fixed anyway. A more responsible employee would have notified the boss about the delay, and tried to get back ASAP.

It's disqualifying misconduct not to respond to a request made by the employer that is reasonable and doesn't impose undue burden on the employee.

There are various things that a person can do that are bad enough to justify the employer in firing the person (so the wrongful termination issues we discuss on pages 161–164 won't apply), but not bad enough to make unemployment compensation unavailable. Two recent examples from cases: tearing up a written warning from the employer about poor performance; an isolated use of profanity in a telephone conversation with a supervisor.

Voluntary Quits: Alas, the unemployment system does not exist to provide checks to people who are fed up and need a few months to find themselves or seek a new career direction. The simplest formulation is that, if you quit your job, benefits will not be available. But that's an oversimplification. If you are "constructively discharged" (forced out of your job), benefits may still be available. It pretty much depends on the way a reasonable person would behave in the situation.

For example, a 1993 New York case denied benefits to an employee who was told that her employer was dissatisfied with her performance, but didn't want to terminate her. She quit on the spot—not, under the circumstances, a reasonable response: she could have kept her job by improving her work results.

Even if the employee definitely quits, and is not constructively discharged, unemployment compensation may be available if the employee had good cause for leaving the job—and the cause can reasonably be blamed on the employer.

Sexual harassment would be a case in point. A 1992 Vermont case lets the employee collect benefits, even though she didn't report the harassment. The theory was that the employer should have known that harassment was a possibility, and taken steps to prevent it. Just drafting an official policy isn't enough; there have to be real-world, not just paper, steps to prevent harassment and redress it if it occurs.

Employees can also collect benefits if they quit because of a personal emergency so compelling that disqualifying them would violate fairness and good conscience. Family needs are also recognized. For instance, if a worker's spouse gets a new job 300 miles away, it's considered only reasonable for the worker to quit and follow the spouse to the new job location, where unemployment benefits will probably be available. Massachusetts extends the same treatment to an unmarried cohabitant who joined her live-in mate at a new job site.

Suitable Work: People collecting benefits are required to make an active search for new work, and to accept suitable jobs when they are offered. Suitability depends on the worker's physical condition, work history, and salary history, as well as any risk of the new job; but unemployment claimants are expected to lower their expectations and look for work lower down on the economic scale the longer the job search lasts; but federal law forbids states to deny benefits if somebody turns town a job offer whose wages and working conditions are substantially less attractive than those prevailing in the area for similar jobs.

Unemployment programs try to stay neutral in labor disputes. However, most states will pay benefits to employees who are not participating in a strike. Under the Federal Unemployment Tax Act, Section 3304(a)(5), benefits can't be denied because someone has refused to be a strikebreaker, or if taking a job that is offered would either require joining a corrupt "sweetheart" union or limit the worker's right to join or remain in a legitimate union.

Workers' Compensation Effects: A few states (California, Hawaii, New Jersey, New York, Rhode Island) have state disability benefit plans that provide cash benefits when individuals lose wages because they are sick or injured, and the problem is not job related. These plans fill the gap between Workers' Compensation and state unemployment benefits. About half the states disqualify people who get Workers' Compensation (WC) benefits from getting unemployment—either by denying unemployment benefits in any week in which WC payments are received, or by subtracting the WC payments from the unemployment check.

Workers' Compensation

All of the states have Workers' Compensation systems, designed for speedy, efficient resolution of cases where work-related disease or injury causes temporary or permanent disability. Applying for WC benefits is simple and not too bureaucratic. Many cases are uncontested, so benefit payments begin quickly. The downside is that the existence of the WC system forbids workers from suing their employers. So people who are unable to work are limited to the amount of the WC benefits (usually equivalent to one half to two thirds of their average weekly wage, plus reimbursement for medical bills)—even if the employer was guilty of serious negligence, and even if the combination of injury and negligence would be enough to yield a multimillion-dollar settlement or recovery if the employee did have the right to sue.

The WC system bars suits against the employers, not against negligent third parties, so when there is a serious injury, there is also usually a hunt for a "deep pocket" that can be held responsible. For instance, if someone loses a limb or is crippled in a machinery accident, it may be possible to blame the manufacturer of the equipment. Of course, that won't work if the employee disregarded warnings, or disabled safety devices to make the machine easier to use.

Workers' Comp, like unemployment insurance, is funded by the employer. States vary in their approaches. A few states (such as Texas) let employers opt out of the WC system entirely. In those states, injured workers can sue their bosses. In the other states, employers must participate in WC, but get a choice about how they'll handle it. About a third of the states have a state-run fund, so employers can buy in to the state fund, get private insurance, or self-insure (keep the money someplace safe for when it's needed). If there's no state fund, then self-insurance and private insurance are the choices.

WC rates depend on the amount of risk in the job, so construction work generates higher rates than paper shuffling. The nationwide average is 2.57 percent of payroll, which doesn't seem all that ruinous, especially when you consider that one whacking good lawsuit could eat up 10 percent or more of payroll if the WC system weren't there to limit the employer's exposure.

According to the New York firm Actuarial & Technical Solutions, the states with the best Workers' Comp benefits were Michigan, Rhode Island, Vermont, Massachusetts, and Connecticut. The states with the lowest costs to employers were Indiana, Oregon, Virginia, Maryland, and South Carolina. (Southern states usually adopt proemployer laws.)

Covered Events: WC systems provide benefits for personal injuries suffered in the course of employment. That seems simple enough, but creates some questions. The basic rule is that the employee actually has to be at work when the damage is caused. Commuting to and from work usually doesn't count, but traveling inside the workplace does; so does driving that is an essential part of the job (such as making deliveries).

Then again, employees have to be doing something that is part of their job. If a supervisor goes to the stockroom to get some supplies, trips on a carton, and knocks out two teeth, that would be covered. But WC probably wouldn't cover the same accident if he were sneaking into the stockroom for a forbidden smoke.

If the boss sends an employee on a personal errand, and the employee is injured while doing the errand, WC will probably cover it. Also covered, under most circumstances, will be a good-faith attempt to help another employee with the other employee's work. Bad-faith actions probably won't be covered. If horsing around at work results in injuries, participants probably won't be covered, but unlucky bystanders will be.

Usually, it doesn't matter for WC purposes if the employer, the employee, both, or neither were negligent—WC is a no-fault system. But one exception is a situation in which the real problem was caused by the employee's own negligence after an occupational injury. Let's say that an employee hurts his knee at work. That would be covered; but if he knows that his sore knee makes it unsafe to lift heavy objects, and persists in moving packages instead of using a hand truck or getting someone else to do it, he won't be covered if his knee gives out and he falls, injuring his back and cracking two ribs as heavy cartons land on him. Another exception: many states reduce (but don't eliminate) benefits if the injury is caused by the employee's failure to use safety equipment.

WC is usually thought of in connection with injuries, but it also covers occupational disease. It's clear that the disease will be covered if it is purely a product of the work environment. The employee has to be able to demonstrate a close connection. For instance, a casino pit boss lost his WC claim based on lung disease that he blamed on the smoke-filled condition in the casino. The Nevada Supreme Court said that passive smoke isn't closely enough related to the casino worker's job to give rise to a comp claim for occupational disease.

What about a disease that the employee already had, that

got worse because of conditions at work? Most states will cover it but only if work conditions contribute to, or aggravate, the disease. In a few states (California, Florida, Kentucky, Maryland, Mississippi, North Dakota, South Carolina), WC benefits will be cut back, so that only the percentage of disability attributable to the work-related worsening of the condition will be covered.

Occupational disease creates difficult regulatory problems: it may take years, even decades, for the ravages of exposure to dangerous substances to manifest themselves. Therefore, workers are not required to file occupational disease claims until they have symptoms of the disease; until some disability has resulted (for instance, inability to walk more than a block or so due to shortness of breath); and the employee could reasonably be expected to draw a connection between the symptoms and occupational disease.

Four Categories: There are four categories of disability for WC purposes: permanent total, permanent partial, temporary total (the most common category), and temporary partial. A "schedule injury" is the loss of a finger, toe, arm, eye, or leg; there is a fixed schedule of the number of weeks of benefits payable in this situation. A nonschedule injury (such as back strain) requires an individual case-by-case determination of just how serious it is, and when the injured worker can be expected to get back to work. The comp system also includes death benefits payable to survivors of people fatally injured at work.

Tax and Related Issues: About half the states deduct Social Security disability benefits from WC benefits. (In order to get Social Security disability, you have to be completely incapable of gainful work.) Some private pension plans also provide that WC benefits will be subtracted from the pension if the employee has to retire early because of occupational injury or disease. The Supreme Court has held that it doesn't violate ERISA to offset the pension to take WC benefits into account.

WC benefits (including survivor's benefits) generally aren't taxable income, unless:

- Benefits are payable to someone who is back at work, but restricted to light duties.
- The payment is made for nonoccupational disability.
- The payment offsets Social Security benefits; the "overlap" is taxable income.

Claims Process: WC works a lot like unemployment insurance. There is a waiting period before benefits begin (to screen out very minor occurrences), and the benefit is usually defined as a percentage of the worker's wages, with a minimum and maximum amount payable per week (sometimes increased if the worker has dependents) and a maximum amount payable over- all. There is a separate limit for claims based on a worker's occupationally related death.

Employers have to file injury reports with the state WC board or commission. (They have an incentive not to do this— their insurance rate goes up if they have a lot of accidents.) The worker is given a certain amount of time to file a claim.

In an uncontested case, where the employer agrees as to the severity of the injury and that it was work related, most states have an "agreement system": the employer (or the employer's insurance company) and the employee agree on a settlement. States vary in their procedures: sometimes the settlement is enough, sometimes the WC board has to approve the settlement before it becomes effective.

In a contested case, a referee or hearing officer hears the case and makes a decision. If either employer or employee is dissatisfied, they can appeal to the whole WC commission, and if they're still dissatisfied, they can go to court but few take this option.

Noncompetes

Some situations are clear. If you're a file clerk or production- line worker, and you leave your job (willingly or unwillingly) there probably won't be much hassle about your knowledge of company information, contacts, or techniques. At the other end of the continuum, if you are a scientist, designer, major execu- tive, or top salesperson, an important part of negotiating a separation will involve "covenants not to compete"—especially if the business is a fairly easy one to enter, or if your soon-to-be-ex-employer has hated rivals.

The employer has reasonable concerns, of course. A celebrity hairdresser can lead clients out of a salon and to a rival faster than a snake charmer can put the moves on a cobra. A marketing vice president with intimate knowledge of a company's new product line would be . . . well, *interesting* to a company trying to sell the same stuff. Insight into a customer's buying pattern would be useful to a salesperson trying to set up as an independent consultant, or ready to bring the Rolodex to a competitor.

The legal system recognizes the basic reasonableness of this concept, and a covenant not to compete will be enforceable as long as the agreement itself is reasonable. After all, people have to earn a living once they leave a company. A covenant that kept somebody from ever working again would not be enforceable; neither would one that covered a geographic area so broad that the ex-employee wouldn't have a hope of doing business throughout it. Covenants will be enforced if they prevent the departing employee from taking the employer's trade secrets, customer lists, or other proprietary information, but not if they prevent the employee from using his or her creativity in the future.

As the economy gets more precarious, employers are more likely to insist on noncompete agreements farther down the employee ladder, and are more likely to go through the trouble and expense of litigating in the case of fairly ordinary former employees. Factors in determining whether information belongs to the employer, so use by the ex-employee can be controlled, include:

- The extent to which the information is known outside the business—it's not too tough to find out who is the president of Xerox, for instance.
- The extent to which the information is known inside the business—there's no need for disloyal employees to hand over information that the new employer knows perfectly well.

- The company's security measures to protect the information —a departing employee should get a clue that information protected by security measures is a little more secret than stuff discussed in the mimeographed employee newsletter.
- The effort and money required to develop the customer list.
- How hard it would be for someone to duplicate the list independently, without relying on inside information.

Even if employers can get a lid put on information, it's unlikely that courts will enforce a covenant not to compete that prevents the employee from using his or her experience and skills in a new job. The point is to protect the employer's trade secrets and related information, not to take away the employee's livelihood.

Communications About Ex-employees

As we mentioned in connection with the prehire process (see page 18), employers are usually pretty reticent about talking about their current and ex-employees. A certain degree of hostility may develop if an employee is terminated for cause, and thus employers may say some negative things. Are the employers guilty of slander, libel, or interference with a potential new employment relationship?

Recent state-law cases say that a performance evaluation is just an opinion, and therefore it can't be libelous unless it includes a deliberate false accusation of dishonesty or other serious negative trait. Just saying that somebody didn't do a very good job doesn't add up to defamation—even if somebody else might disagree with the characterization. However, a Maine court held that damage to a person's reputation within a company can be devastating, and therefore a corporation can be liable for defamation even in an internal communication that is never divulged to anyone outside the company.

An employer has a qualified privilege to make statements about employees (even ones that are negative enough to injure the employee) as long as the employer acts in good faith. An employer may also have a duty to make the statements—or at least an interest in making them—and appropriate limitations are placed on the scope of the statement and the audience to which it is made. But if the employer recklessly publishes the material—and if the employee can show malice, not just carelessness—then the employee may be able to win.

For example, an employee with twenty-three years of experience with the employer lost his job because of negative statements in a performance appraisal; he was awarded $465,000 in compensatory and punitive damages. Another employee got $250,000 in damages when he was given a negative reference that implied firsthand knowledge of his character and job performance, but was really based on secondhand gossip.

Interference

Another possibility is that the ex-employer, by preventing the discharged employee from getting another job, is tortiously interfering with the employee's right to form a contract (with a new employer). This has to be intentional; there's no legally recognized cause of action for negligently messing up someone's chance at a new job. Of course, there has to be improper interference—not an appropriate warning.

Usually, this claim can only be made if three parties are involved (employee, ex-employer, potential new employer), because an employer can breach its own contracts, but can't tortiously interfere with them. There's at least a chance that a supervisor can be sued if he acts for improper motives, and not in the corporation's best interests.

11

Retirement:
What Are You Doing
the Rest of Your Life?

Retirement, of course, is a pretty new concept in human societies. Prior versions of the concept included "complete debilitation" and "death." The picture-perfect image of the retiree is the devoted grandmother or happy golfer. But current conditions may mean thirty or even forty years of retirement. In fact, the length of postemployment life may exceed the length of work life—especially in high-stress jobs like police and the military that promise "twenty and out."

Thirty or forty years is a lot of golf. You may not get a real choice about when to retire; but if you do, there are many factors in the decision. It makes a lot of sense to get professional advice about the legal and financial consequences of the options that face you, and this chapter is not a substitute for that personal advice. We hope that we'll lay out the basic issues, though, so you can ask the right questions and get maximum benefit from the advice.

Retirement Timing

If you do get to pick the time to retire, consider these factors:

- How do you feel about your job? You may discover that you miss it. Even if you hate your job, at least you have a professional identification; you may feel very deprived if you give that up.
- What are your employment prospects if you want a new job? Are your plans for a second career unrealistic? Nobody may want to hire a middle-aged or older person with your package of skills; the business you dream of launching may become a casualty of economic conditions (or your own overestimation of your entrepreneurial skills). Eighty percent of retirees who are reemployed go to work for smaller, less prestigious companies, earning less money. Some face a precipitous drop from high-paid executive positions to door-to-door peddling or low-paid retail sales work.
- How good are the retirement incentives offered to you? Just as companies are now downsizing and cutting benefits for active employees, they often provide packages for retirees that are far less generous than those of even a few years ago.
- If you're married, how do your retirement plans fit with your spouse's plans? Many husbands are several years older than their wives, and his retirement comes at the peak of her career (especially if she took several years off to raise kids).
- Do you have enough enthralling activities planned to keep you occupied as long as you remain healthy and vigorous?
- What will your postretirement income be (considering your Social Security benefits, employer pension, IRAs and Keoghs, and investments)?
- What will your income be, after paying taxes? There are tax factors that may affect retirement timing.
- Would your Social Security benefits be lower or higher if you changed your retirement timing?
- What will your postretirement expenses be—lower or higher? Will there be a shortfall that will force you to ex-

haust your savings (and thus further lower your investment income)?

■ How will you take care of your health care needs? Medicare benefits are not available until age sixty-five; and, as we discuss below, retiree health benefits often can't be counted on. It might make more sense to remain an active employee and take advantage of the job-related health plan.

Of course, if you decide that you retired too early, it may be possible to "unretire" and reenter the work force. But sociologist Mark Hayward found that, while about one third of early retirees did go back to work (especially professionals and people with a history of self-employment), three quarters of the returning workers made the decision in the first year of retirement. Almost nobody returned to the work force more than three years after getting the gold watch.

Early Retirement Plans

Picture the situation of a company desperate to downsize. There just isn't enough market for its products to keep churning them out at the same old rate. Cutting the payroll would help the bottom line immensely, but wholesale firing generates hostility at best.

So the company wants to find people who won't go away mad . . . they'll just go away. Early retirement incentives developed for just this reason. Find a bunch of people who really want to retire, but haven't reached the plan's normal retirement age. Cut a special deal for them: they can retire right now, and start to draw a pension (although almost always a reduced one).

The employer's ironic plight is that early retirement programs can be awfully expensive—almost as expensive as keeping people around, when presumably they would accomplish at least some valuable work.

The company may hope that the program will serve to prune the deadwood, with the worst workers happily heading for the rocking chair. But just the reverse often happens. The best workers, who have been the subject of constant recruitment efforts, may make a rational decision to take the incentives and then accept one of the job offers. The company has spent a lot of money to lower the quality of its work force.

The people who qualify for the retirement incentives may sue anyway, claiming that they were pushed into unwanted retirement, or that they were deceived about the real nature of the incentive program, or that other people got a better retirement package than they did, or that they weren't given enough time to think it over. (See page 111 for a discussion of age discrimination issues in early retirement, and the Older Workers' Benefit Protection Act.) And the people who didn't qualify sometimes sue, saying that they should have gotten a shot at the incentives.

Early Retirement Trends: In 1993 University of Michigan scholars studied early retirement offers made to about 13,000 people. The study found that about one worker in sixteen was offered an early retirement package—but 60 percent turned down the offers, which averaged $29,000 in one-time cash bonuses and $4,000 additional income a year. The people who did take the offer often got another job (at least half did so), but usually cut back their hours in the second, "postretirement" job.

In 1986 the law on age discrimination changed, also changing the distribution of normal and early retirement. Before 1986, it was okay for companies to stop making pension contributions once a worker reached normal retirement age. That cut down on the incentive to stick around. The amendments, effective as of January 1, 1988, required employers to apply the same contribution or accrual rules to all employees, regardless of their age. There are some loopholes, though. An employer can impose a limit on overall contributions, or overall number of years of service that will affect benefits (as long as these limits are applied to employees of all ages). Corporate officers and people earning over $75,000 (or over $50,000, if they are in the top 20 percent of employee pay) can also be shut out from this protection.

Court Cases: ERISA preempts (crowds out) state-court cases when employees make claims about retirement plans, including claims that employers misrepresented the terms or effects of the plan in order to induce the employees to retire early.

So angry ex-employees get the advantages of the federal system (potential for big wins) and its disadvantages (long waits; high costs).

Some claims are ruled out right away: the court may say that an ex-employee is no longer a plan "participant," and only "participants" can sue under ERISA. But courts take different approaches to the issue: in early 1994 the First Circuit allowed a former employee to sue based on his claim that he stopped being a participant because his employer misrepresented the terms of the retirement plan.

Another group of retirees lost an ERISA claim based on their not being informed about the unfavorable tax consequences of taking an early retirement lump-sum benefit—especially since the employer did tell the employees to get tax and financial planning advice from an impartial source before making a decision about their benefits. Employees who signed a release eventually went to court, claiming that the employer defrauded them by making inaccurate oral statements that their jobs would be eliminated if they didn't take the early retirement deal. They lost, too: the text of the release said that they were not relying on any representations other than the ones spelled out in the release itself. So even if the employer did make oral statements, and even if the oral statements were utter lies, the employees couldn't have relied on them, and couldn't use them as the basis of a lawsuit.

The retiree team did win one in 1992: some people retired early, relying on benefits staying at the specified level in the early retirement incentive package. They made out an "equitable estoppel" claim (i.e., it would be unfair not to make the employer live up to its promises). The retirees could get the difference between the promised and actual benefits from the employer in its role as plan administrator. Interestingly, they could not get the shortfall from the plan itself, because ERISA forbids plans to make payments contrary to the written terms of the plan. (Estoppel is a legal concept that stops a party to a suit from taking advantage of its own wrongdoing, or otherwise getting something unfair. For instance, an employer that concealed facts about a plan from an employee might be estopped from claiming that the employee's claim about the plan was filed too late.)

An early 1994 federal decision from Pennsylvania says that, although employers must give accurate information about the terms of their current early retirement programs, they do not have a duty to inform employees about early retirement programs that will be offered in the future (even though employees might stick around longer if they knew about the future plans).

The Three-Legged Stool

Okay, it's corny, but the traditional way of thinking about after-retirement income is still the best. Your retirement security rests on a "three-legged stool": your Social Security benefits, the pension from your employer, and your own savings and investments.

The most financially conservative approach is to keep your investments intact, and live on the income, so the capital sum can be left to your spouse or children. Unfortunately, most people aren't affluent enough, or successful enough investors, to be able to do that, so they'll have to "dis-save": spend some of their accumulated assets. After all, the rainy day you were saving for has arrived. The trick is to control the spending so that you don't run out of money, and so that your surviving spouse (if any) will be reasonably comfortable once insurance and other death benefits are taken into account.

As for Social Security benefits, they are extremely valuable in keeping low-income people from dire poverty, but most people would hate to have to rely on them completely as a source of income. The size of a person's Social Security benefit depends on a laborious calculation. First the person's earnings for each year are compared to the national average earnings; that provides a figure called the AIME, for Average Indexed Monthly Earnings. (The 1994 average wage is $22,936.42.) Then the AIME is used to compute the PIA, or Primary Insurance Amount. For people who reach age sixty-two in 1994, PIA equals 90 percent of the first $422 of AIME, plus 32 percent of AIME between $422 and $2,545, and 15 percent of any higher amount of AIME. The average 1994 benefit was $674 a month

—let's hope you have a bigger Social Security benefit and lots of other income.

Right now, the "normal" Social Security retirement age is sixty-five; the age is gradually being increased, until it will become sixty-seven in the year 2022. People who retire early have their Social Security benefits decreased (perpetually—not just until normal retirement age); people who retire after normal retirement age get their benefits increased. In either situation, the maximum adjustment is about 20 percent.

Other people in a worker's family can also get benefits based on the worker's benefit: spouse, divorced spouse, widow/ -er, surviving ex-spouse, sometimes children or parents. A married woman can collect either a Social Security benefit based on her own earnings history or one based on her husband's earnings—she gets whichever benefit is bigger, but not both.

Money earned after age seventy will not affect Social Security benefits—you still get your full benefit. But if you retire early, your benefit will be reduced $1 for every $2 you earn above the permitted maximum amount; if you retire at normal retirement age, each $3 earned takes $1 off your Social Security check.

How Big Will Your Pension Be?

Unlike Social Security, which has a complicated (but nationwide) formula for figuring out benefits, pensions have a rich variety of approaches. In a defined-contribution plan, the size of your benefit depends on the investment success of your pension account. Defined-contribution plans were touted in the eighties as a way to allow retirees to participate in the booming stock market, and to protect them from the traditional curse of being limited to a fixed income. True, as far as it went—but today's retirees may face a climate with attractively low inflation but a parsimonious pension because their individual defined-contribution account doesn't earn very much.

Defined-benefit plans have formulas, based on average compensation, or on compensation for a few years (usually the highest-paid, or the latest in your career, which tend to be highest-paid). The benefit may be a uniform percentage, or may be a certain percentage of, say, the first twenty years of service, a higher percentage of any additional service.

Pensions plans don't have to offer a lump-sum option; if your plan does, then the question is whether you think you will do a better job managing the after-tax portion of the money (you have to pay taxes on the lump sum in the year you receive it, although there are some special tax relief provisions) than you would do if you left the money in the pension plan and got regular monthly annuity payments.

Here Today, Gone Tomorrow

At first, without really thinking it through, companies promised to pay the full freight of lifetime health benefits for their retirees. Several factors coincided to make this a bad move for companies. First, health costs exploded, then companies soon discovered that the worse the employee's health, the more likely he or she was to want to retire early. That meant that the sickest people, the ones who could be expected to rack up the highest medical bills, left the work force earlier than healthier people. This had the effect of raising the employer's health insurance premiums.

As we discuss on page 70, health benefits don't vest. Ever. That means that employees can never use ERISA to challenge an employer's decision to limit, or indeed completely do away with, their health benefits. There may be some non-ERISA remedies, such as proof of breach of a contract, for angry employees. The upshot is that employers generally have a legal right to stop providing retiree health benefits; to tell current retirees that they have these benefits, but future retirees will not; or to make retirees pay for their benefits, or pay more if they already pay part of the premium or have responsibilities for deductibles and coinsurance.

Retirees have won some recent courtroom victories with respect to their health plans. Just after Christmas 1993 a group of Curtiss-Wright retirees won, because the Third Circuit said that Curtiss-Wright reserved the right to amend its benefit plan, but didn't specify a **procedure** for making a valid amendment. Therefore, the company couldn't eliminate its retiree health benefits unless it amended the plan "by formal action of those who possess the sponsor's final management authority"; an informal management decision wouldn't be enough.

In early 1994 a Michigan court told General Motors that it couldn't make 50,000 early retirees and spouses pay part of the cost of their health care coverage because they were promised lifetime health benefits at no cost to them. The promise was made to induce them to retire early, so in effect GM made a contract with them that was separate from the company's health plan.

Cutbacks: The issue is an important one for employees and retirees, because many companies use (or at least try) reductions in retiree health benefits as a way to save money. The financial consulting firm William H. Mercer asked big companies how they dealt with retiree health plans in 1992. More than one fifth of the survey respondents said they eliminated retiree health benefits; 44 percent made employees pay more, an average of 10 percent per year in additional premiums, deductibles, and coinsurance. The average retiree had to pay $1,719 a year for coverage for himself or herself and spouse, which can represent a painful bite out of a retiree's pension income.

Cuts were even more dramatic for smaller and midsized companies. Accounting firm KPMG Peat Marwick found that the percentage of gigantic companies (5,000 or more workers) offering retiree health benefits held steady at 72 percent between 1991 and 1992. But companies with 200–999 workers went from 44 percent offering retiree health plans in 1991 to only 37 percent in 1992. The report's sobering conclusion was that retiree health benefits are "eroding at a considerable pace and in many ways"—for instance, bigger premiums. In 1988, retirees aged sixty-five and over paid about one quarter of the premium for family health insurance coverage; in 1992, they paid 41 percent (a higher percentage of what was probably a bigger premium).

Some other approaches employers took to cutting retiree health benefit costs include limiting full health benefit coverage to workers with thirty years of service, with shorter-stay workers getting only a percentage of the full benefit—someone who worked twenty years before retirement would get two thirds, for instance. Of course, there are many factors (such as transfers, corporate acquisitions, and layoffs) that make it awfully hard for even the most loyal worker to hang in for thirty years.

Employers may adopt a "defined contribution" approach (not the same as a defined contribution pension plan). The employer simply decides how much it will spend per retiree for health benefits; any health care required over what that amount will bring simply doesn't get covered by the employer's plan, and the retiree is stuck. Employers may also keep the retiree health benefit plan in effect for people who are already retired, but announce that benefits will be limited or removed for people who retire in the future.

Summary

It all comes down to choices. Perhaps there won't be as many as there would be in a more robust economy. You may decide to stick with a tedious job and a despicable boss because you don't think that you can get a better one anytime soon. You might fear "job lock": the tendency to stay put because getting a new job could result in loss of health care coverage, or at any rate generate a new preexisting condition waiting period and the risk of big expenses without coverage.

But even the crummiest job gives you access to meaningful legal rights. Unless exempt, you're entitled to overtime pay; after meeting minimal requirements, you're entitled to participate in whatever pension plans are offered by your employer. You can join a union or help organize one—or help get rid of a union that is corrupt or simply not doing its job. If you're a victim of sexual harassment or wrongful termination, it can take a long time and a lot of effort to secure justice, but the rewards of victory can be sweet (and numbered in seven figures).

You have a right to combine work and the obligations and joys of family life. You have a right to reasonable privacy at work; to be hired or fired based on meaningful qualifications, not the fantasies of bigots; to make full use of employee benefits.

For many years, Congress has been adding to the protection offered to workers. State laws play their part. There are court cases on your side (as well as court cases that make it tough or impossible to make your point). Although new ways to work are spreading, most people, for years to come, will continue working in offices, stores, or factories. This book shows you how much has already been done to define and safeguard your rights at work. The next step is up to you.

Notes

These notes are the sources we used to research this book. You may want to refer to them if a topic intrigues you, or if you want more information to cope with a problem.

We found many helpful newspaper stories. *NYT* is our abbreviation for the *New York Times*. *WSJ* stands for the *Wall Street Journal*. *NYLJ* is the *New York Law Journal*, a daily newspaper for lawyers. *LW* is *U.S. Law Week*, a newsletter that summarizes legal developments. (Many big public libraries subscribe to *Law Week*, if you want to do some research of your own.)

Chapter 1

p. 5 Discouraging trends in employment: see Peter T. Kilborn, "A Labor Day Message No One Asked to Hear," *NYT,* September 5, 1993, p. F1.

p. 6 Effects of restructuring: Gilbert Fuchsberg, "Why Shake-Ups Work for Some, Not for Others," *WSJ,* October 1, 1993, p. B1.

p. 7 National Study of the Changing Workforce: this survey is discussed in Sue Shellenbarger, "Work-Force Study Finds Loyalty is Weak, Divisions of Race and Gender are Deep," *WSJ,* September 3, 1993, p. B1; Barbara Presley Noble, "Dissecting the 90's Workplace," *NYT,* September 19, 1993, p. F21.

p. 7 Growth in help-wanted ads: Lucinda Harper, "Despite Big Layoffs, Employment Grows," and "Employer Survey May not Provide Best Jobs Measure," *WSJ,* October 8, 1993, p. A2.

p. 7 Pay gap lower: Valerie Reitman, "It's All Relative," *WSJ,* April 13, 1994, p. R7; Top Fortune 500 jobs for women: Joann S. Lublin, "Firms Designate Some Openings for Women Only," *WSJ,* February 7,

1994, p. B1; Black employment trends: Dorothy J. Gaiter, "The Gender Divide," *WSJ*, March 8, 1994, p. A1.

p. 8 Effect of recession on black workers: Rochelle Sharpe, "In Latest Recession, Only Blacks Suffered Net Employment Loss," *WSJ*, September 14, 1993, p. A1. The study was done by the *Journal*'s news system editor, Edward P. Foldessy; he used data compiled by the federal government.

p. 9 Bad job climate for graduates: Julie Amparano Lopez, "College Class of '93 Learns Hard Lesson: Career Prospects Are Worst in Decades," *WSJ*, May 20, 1993, p. B2; William Celis 3d, "Current Crop of College Graduates Finds Job Market Painfully Tight," *NYT*, June 6, 1993, p. A30; Tamar Lewin, "Low Pay and Closed Doors Confront Young Job Seekers," *NYT*, March 10, 1994, p. A1.

p. 12 Temporary factory workers: Louis Uchitelle, "Temporary Workers Are on the Increase in Nation's Factories," *NYT*, July 6, 1993, p. A1.

p. 13 Short-term professional and management jobs: Mary Rowland, "Temporary Work: The New Career," *NYT*, September 12, 1993, p. F15.

p. 13 Disposable workers: Peter T. Kilborn, "New Jobs Lack the Old Security in a Time of 'Disposable Workers,'" *NYT*, March 15, 1993, p. A1.

p. 16 Topless dancers: *Reich v. Circle C Investments Inc.*, 62 *LW* 2144 (5th Cir. August 24, 1993). Perhaps if the dancers had been ruled to be independent contractors, the Federal Trade Commission would have investigated the price-fixing aspects.

p. 17 Liability of employers of temps: John F. Furfaro and Maury B. Josephson, "Temporary Employees," *NYLJ*, May 7, 1993, p. 3. Relevant cases include *Amarnare v. Merrill Lynch*, 611 F.Supp. 344 (SDNY 1984) [temp worker was an employee of both the employment agency and the job-site employer for Title VII purposes]; *Magnuson v. Peak Technical Services Inc.*, 808 F.Supp. 500 (E.D. Va. 1992) [sexual harassment at job site].

Chapter 2

p. 19 Misrepresenting salary: Julie Amparano Lopez, "The Big Lie," *WSJ*, April 21, 1993, p. R6.

p. 20 Resume fraud bars discrimination suit: *Johnson v. Honeywell Information Systems*, 955 F.2d 409 (6th Cir. 1992); *Milligan-Jensen v. Michigan Technological University*, 61 *LW* 2203 (6th Cir. September 17, 1992).

p. 20 Employer prevails if employee would have been fired absent discrimination: *Washington v. Lake County, Illinois,* 61 *LW* 2055 (7th Cir. July 10, 1992), even if the employee's misconduct was not severe or pervasive, as long as it would be enough to justify the discharge: *O'Driscoll v. Hercules,* 62 *LW* 2450 (10th Cir. January 5, 1994) or if the employee wouldn't have been hired: *Welch v. Liberty Machine Works Inc.,* 62 *LW* 2696 (8th Cir. May 6, 1994). *Van Deursen v. U.S. Tobacco Sales & Marketing Co.,* 62 *LW* 2451 (D. Colo. December 16, 1993) says that it's irrelevant whether the employee intended to mislead; the important point is whether the company would have fired her if it knew the real facts.

p. 20 Resume fraud limits remedies: *Wallace v. Dunn Construction Co.,* 61 *LW* 2120 (11th Cir. August 17, 1992); *Smith v. Equitable Life Assurance Society,* 61 *LW* 2515 (SDNY January 8, 1993); *Kristufek v. Hussmann Foodservice Co.,* 61 *LW* 2531 (7th Cir. February 10, 1993); *Massey v. Trump's Castle Hotel and Casino,* 62 *LW* 2115 (DNJ July 30, 1993).

p. 23 Legal and illegal questions under ADA: see 62 *LW* 2732 (May 31, 1994).

p. 24 Arrest record checks: see William J. Quirk, "Questions You Can and Cannot Legally Ask in an Employment Interview," New York: Panel Publishers, 1993.

p. 24 Tougher interview tactics: Julie Amparano Lopez, "Firms Force Job Seekers to Jump Through Hoops," *WSJ,* October 6, 1993, p. B1.

p. 27 States receptive to truth in hiring: Jonathan M. Moss, "Employers Face New Liability: Truth in Hiring," *WSJ,* July 1, 1993, p. B1. Also see Richard J. Reibstein, "The Emergence of 'Truth in Hiring' Claims," *NYLJ,* May 19, 1993, p. 1, discussing cases like *Stewart v. Johnson & Nash,* 976 F.2d 86 (1992); *Backer v. Levit,* 584 NYS2d 480 (1st Dept. 1992); *Wilder v. Cody County Chamber of Commerce,* 62 *LW* 2531 (Wyo.Sup. January 25, 1994).

p. 27 Lying about financial prospects: *Berger v. Security Pacific Information Systems,* 795 P.2d 1380 (Colo.App. 1990).

p. 27 Smoking gun: *Dowie v. Exxon Corp.,* 12 Conn.L. Trib. 1 (July 28, 1986), discussed in the Quirk Special Report cited above.

Chapter 3

p. 32 Okay to pay fixed salary plus additional 50 percent for overtime hours: 29 CFR §778.114; *Condo v. Sysco Corp.,* 62 *LW* 2107 (7th Cir. August 4, 1993).

p. 32 Lag payrolls violate FLSA: *Biggs v. Wilson,* 62 *LW* 2107 (9th Cir. August 12, 1993).

p. 33 DOL cases: Richard B. Schmitt, "Employers' Overtime Liability Expanding," *WSJ,* November 5, 1993, p. B8.

p. 33 Partial day leave and exempt status: *Abshire v. County of Kern,* (9th Cir. 1990); *Michigan Supervisors' Union v. State of Michigan,* 125 Labor Cases ¶35,820 (D.Mich. 1993).

p. 35 Journalists not exempt: *Reich v. Newspapers of New England,* 62 *LW* 2323 (D.N.H. November 3, 1993).

p. 36 Title VII case can be won after losing EPA case: *Miranda v. B&B Cash Grocery Store Inc.,* 61 *LW* 2331 (11th Cir. October 28, 1992).

p. 36 Willfulness is a jury issue: *Fowler v. Land Management Groupe,* 61 *LW* 2289 (4th Cir. October 28, 1992). *Note:* The company really is called "Groupe," not "Group."

p. 36 Every unequal paycheck is a separate EPA violation: *Gandy v. Sullivan County,* 62 *LW* 2763 (6th Cir. May 24, 1994).

p. 37 Skill-based pay: Mary Rowland, "It's What You Do that Counts," *NYT,* June 6, 1993, p. F17, and "For Each Skill, More Money," *NYT,* June 13, 1993, p. F16.

p. 38 Two-tier wage scales: Clifford J. Levy, "An Idea Whose Time May Have Passed," *NYT,* September 17, 1993, p. D1.

Chapter 4

p. 40 Plans for top management: Ellen E. Schultz, "More-Equal Benefits Go to Some Top Executives," *WSJ,* May 25, 1993, p. C1.

p. 44 OK to terminate a plan: *Seaman v. Arvida Realty Sales,* 61 *LW* 2555 (11th Cir. March 29, 1993)—see *Employee Benefits Alert*, March 31, 1993, and *Nat'l Law J.,* March 29, 1993, p. 22. Also see *Pickering v. USX Corp.,* 1992 U.S. Dist. LEXIS 17242 (D. Utah 1992), *Employee Benefits Alert,* November 25, 1992, p. 3.

p. 47 Government report on PBGC worries: GAO/T-HRD-93-1, "Assessing PBGC's Short-Run and Long-Run Conditions" (February 1993). For more information on underfunded pensions, see Albert R. Karr, "Pension Plans' Underfunding Worsened in '92," *WSJ,* November 23, 1993, p. A3, no byline, "Government Finds Wider Gap on Financing of Pensions," *NYT,* November 23, 1993, p. D12, Leslie Scism, "Agency Reunites People and Their Pensions," *WSJ,* February 17, 1994, p. C1, and Deborah M. Rankin, "How Safe is Your Retirement Cache?" *NYT,* June 11, 1994, p. A35.

p. 48 Statistics on 401(k) plans: the numbers come from a Gallup poll, quoted in Mary Rowland, "Small-Company Retirement Goals," *NYT,* May 16, 1993, p. F17.

p. 49 401(k) investment choices: Leonard Sloane, "Saving at the Office: New Choices Near," *NYT,* May 15, 1993, p. A33.

p. 49 Deposit insurance on retirement accounts: Kenneth H. Bacon, "Saving for Retirement? Don't Bank on It," *WSJ,* June 15, 1993, p. C1.

p. 49 SERPs: Mary Rowland, "Making Pension Promises Secure," *NYT,* February 21, 1993, p. F19.

p. 50 Cross-testing and age-weighting: see Ellen E. Schultz, "Small Firms Turn Retirement Plans Into Owners' Gains," *WSJ,* August 15, 1993, p. A1. After merger, participants can't divide surplus funds: *Malia v. General Electric,* 62 *LW* 2714 (3d Cir. May 13, 1994).

p. 54 Overly enthusiastic assumptions: Susan Pulliam, "Aggressive Rate Assumptions Put Pension Funds at Risk," *WSJ,* March 25, 1993, p. C1, and "Hopeful Assumptions Let Firms Minimize Pension Contributions," *WSJ,* September 2, 1993, p. A1. Also see Albert H. Karr, "Risk to Retirees Rises as Firms Fail to Fund Pensions They Offer," *WSJ,* February 4, 1993, p. A1, and his update, "Pension Plans' Underfunding Worsened in 1992," *WSJ,* November 23, 1993, p. A3.

p. 58 Outplacement assistance: see Rev.Rul. 92-69, 1992- IRB 36.

p. 59 Golden parachutes: *Fontenot v. NL Industries,* 953 F.2d 960 (5th Cir. 1992).

p. 60 Vacation benefits: however, vacation benefits paid from an employer's general assets aren't considered an ERISA plan—so workers who lose vacation benefits because of a strike can't use that as the basis of an ERISA claim: *United Automobile, Aerospace & Agricultural Implement Workers of America v. R.E. Dietz Co.,* #92-9368 (2d Cir. June 18, 1993).

p. 61 Plans of midsized firms: Jan M. Rosen, "Step Up Savings Goals, Pension Experts Urge," *NYT,* June 5, 1993, p. A36.

p. 61 "Spouse" must be legally married: *Rovira v. A T & T,* 61 *LW* 2612 (SDNY March 24, 1993).

p. 61 Gay and other unmarried domestic partners: David J. Jefferson, "Gay Employees Win Benefits for Partners at More Corporations," *WSJ,* March 19, 1994, p. A1; Ian Fisher, "Cuomo Decides to Extend Domestic-Partner Benefits," *NYT,* June 29, 1994, p. B4.

p. 63 Advice about plan choices: Ellen E. Schultz, "How to Get the Most Out of Your Benefit Plan," *WSJ,* July 9, 1993, 7993 p. C1.

p. 64 Consultants not liable as fiduciaries: *Mertens v. Hewitt Associates,* #91-1671, 62 *LW* 4510 (Sup.Ct. June 1, 1993).

p. 64 Participants and beneficiaries have the right to sue trustees and administrators: *Bixler v. Central Pennsylvania Teamsters Health & Welfare Fund,* 62 *LW* 2428 (3d Cir. December 28, 1993).

Chapter 5

p. 66 Does managed care save money for employers? See GAO/T-HEHS-94-91, "Managed Health Care: Effect on Employers' Costs Difficult to Measure" (February 2, 1994).

p. 68 Coordination of coverage: also see *Broatz v. Labor & Industry Review Comm'n,* 61 *LW* 2586 (Wisconsin March 16, 1993). A collective bargaining agreement forced married employees whose spouses also had health coverage to choose between their own health plan and the spouse's health plan. The state court said this was an unlawful requirement—it was illegal marital status discrimination, in violation of the state's Fair Employment Practices Act. The rationale was that unmarried employees with access to another source of coverage would not have to surrender that entitlement—only married employees did. By the way, an earlier Wisconsin case, *Phillips v. Wisconsin Personnel Commissioner,* 482 N.W.2d 121 (Wis.App. 1992) ruled that it was not illegal marital status discrimination to deny health insurance to unmarried people living together, under the theory that married people have a duty to support each other (including paying for their medical care), and unwed partners don't.

p. 69 Career planning and health insurance: Barbara Presley Noble, "Surprise: Bigger Isn't Always Better," *NYT,* June 19, 1994, p. F21; no byline, "Availability of Health Insurance Affects Job Mobility," HHS *Research Activities* No. 174 (January/February 1994) p. 1. Downside of little white lies: Ellen E. Schultz, "Fudging Medical Claims Can Backfire," *WSJ,* June 29, 1994, p. C1.

p. 70 Federal preemption: according to *Pilot Life Insurance v. Dedeaux,* 481 U.S. 41 (Sup.Ct. 1987), ERISA preempts state law claims dealing with breach of contract or bad faith, because, although states are allowed to regulate the "business of insurance" without federal interference, bad faith claims for employment-related policies are ruled out by ERISA.

p. 70 Discretion in ERISA plans: *Firestone Tire & Rubber v. Bruch,* 109 S.Ct. 948 (1989).

p. 71 Insurance purchase plan: *Randol v. Mid-West National Life Ins. Co.,* 61 *LW* 2708 (11th Cir. April 12, 1993).

p. 71 HMO cases: *Kohn v. Delaware Valley HMO Inc.,* 60 *LW* 2560 (E.D. Pa. February 4, 1992) [no preemption]; *Kuhl v. Lincoln Nat'l Health Plan,* 62 *LW* 2099 (8th Cir. July 7, 1993) [case is preempted].

p. 71 Bankruptcy of self-insured plan: *Lee v. Burkhart,* 1993 U.S. App. LEXIS 8687 (2d Cir. 1993).

p. 72 Wellness programs: see Employee Benefits Alert December 9, 1992, p. 3.

p. 73 Reduction in AIDS benefits: *McGann v. H&H Music Co.,* 946 F.2d 401 (5th Cir. 1991), cert. denied #91-1283, 61 *LW* 3355 (November 9, 1992).

p. 73 Eleventh Circuit case on "discrimination relating to the plan in general": *Owens v. Storehouse Inc.,* 61 *LW* 2542 (11th Cir. February 25, 1993).

p. 73 ERISA preemption in Indiana: *Westhoven v. Lincoln Foodservice Products Inc.,* 62 *LW* 2058 (Ind.App. 7/6/93).

p. 73 Fiduciary duty to reveal cancellation: *Rucker v. Pacific FM Inc.,* 61 *LW* 2111 (N.D. Cal. 7/2/92).

p. 74 Multiemployer plan: *Carparts Distrib. Ctr. Inc. v. Automotive Wholesaler's Ass'n of New England,* 62 *LW* 2083 (D.N.H. July 19, 1993).

p. 74 Article in the *New York Law Journal:* Daniel Wise, "Excluding AIDS Coverage in Medical Plans Violates ADA," *NYLJ,* February 8, 1993, p. 1. Also see Jeffrey S. Klein and Lawrence J. Baer, "Employment Law," *Nat'l Law Journal,* May 9, 1994, p. B5, summing up later cases, including *EEOC v. Connecticut Refining Co.,* 62 *LW* 2595 (EEOC settlement). The case that was settled at the end of 1993 is *Estate of Kadinger v. IBEW Local 110,* 62 *LW* 2436 (D. Minn. December 21, 1993).

p. 74 Pending cases: see Milt Freudenheim, "Patients Cite Bias in AIDS Coverage by Health Plans," *NYT,* June 1, 1993, p. A1.

p. 74 Summary judgment motion denied: Milt Freudenheim, "Disabilities Act Wins a Round in AIDS Case," *NYT,* November 23, 1993, p. D2.

p. 75 Employer didn't know about disability: *Phelps v. Field Real Estate Co.,* 61 *LW* 2691 (10th Cir. April 16, 1993).

p. 75 Privacy rights and HIV status: *Estate of Urbanek v. Newton,* 226 Cal.App.3d 1128 (1991); *Doe v. Borough of Barrington,* 729 F.Supp. 376 (D.N.J. 1990). See the Corenthal article cited above. The New York case involving the subpoena is *Doe v. Roe, M.D.,* 61 *LW* 2796 (N.Y. A.D. May 28, 1993).

Chapter 6

p. 76 For background on work-family issues, see Barbara Presley Noble, "Interpreting the Family Leave Act," *NYT,* August 1, 1993, p. A23 and "Dissecting the 90's Workplace," *NYT,* September 19, 1993, p.

F21; Susan Chira, "Census Data Show Rise in Child Care by Fathers," *NYT,* September 22, 1993, p. A20; Sue Shellenbarger, "Work and Family," *WSJ,* October 13, 1993, p. B1. A book by Deborah J. Swiss and Judith P. Walker, *Women and the Work-Family Dilemma* (John Wiley & Sons, 1993) shows the difficulties faced by graduates of elite law and medical schools in combining career and family; in "Even Women at the Top Still Have Floors to Do," *NYT,* May 31, 1993, p. A1, Marian Burros quotes U.S. Senator Dianne Feinstein saying that her daughter could run a successful campaign for district attorney, "But she'd still have to go home and clean."

p. 77 Incidence of caregiving experience: Alan L. Otten, "People Patterns," *WSJ,* August 17, 1993, p. B1.

p. 77 FMLA: the citation for this statute is 29 USC §2612(a)(1) et.seq.

p. 77 The states with family-leave provisions when the FMLA was passed are California, Colorado, Connecticut, Hawaii, Iowa, Kansas, Kentucky, Louisiana, Maine, Massachusetts, Michigan, Minnesota, Montana, Nevada, New Hampshire, New Jersey, New York, Ohio, Oregon, Pennsylvania, Rhode Island, Tennessee, Vermont, Washington, and Wisconsin.

p. 78 Figures come from Susan Chira, "Family Leave Is Law: Will Things Change?" *NYT,* August 15, 1993, p. E3.

p. 78 Getting around the FMLA: Jeanne Saddler, "Small Firms Try to Curb Impact of Leave Law," *WSJ,* August 5, 1993, p. B1.

p. 78 Eligibility rules: Department of Labor interim final rules published on June 4, 1993, in 58 Federal Register 31794.

p. 80 Definition of comparability for reinstatement: under Wisconsin state leave law, it was inappropriate to reinstate a manager who supervised four employees in a job involving 25 percent clerical work and only one subordinate—even though the hours, pay, and benefits of the new job were the same as the old job: *Kelley Co. v. Marquardt,* 61 *LW* 2383 (Wis.Sup. December 16, 1992).

p. 80 Rights on reinstatement: see 29 USC §2614(a)(1); for employee benefits, see §2614(a)(2), and 2614(c)(2) for group health plans.

p. 81 Health insurance rules: see 29 CFR §825.103, .200, .212, .213, and .701, as amended by the June 1993 DOL rules printed at 58 Federal Register 31794.

p. 82 This obligation is spelled out in 29 USC §2612(e)(2)(A).

p. 83 Expected duration of family leave: Jeanne Saddler, "Small Firms Try to Curb Impact of Leave Law," *WSJ,* August 5, 1993, p. B1 and Barbara Presley Noble, "We're Doing Just Fine, Thank You," *NYT,* March 29, 1994, p. F25.

p. 86 Track record on work-family issues: Sue Shellenbarger, "Concerns Fight to be Called Best for Moms," *WSJ*, September 14, 1993, p. B1 and " 'Best' List for Working Mothers Shows New Faces: Midwest Firms, Oil Giants," *WSJ*, September 16, 1993, p. A8; Rochelle Sharp, "Family Friendly Firms Don't Always Promote Females," *WSJ*, March 29, 1994, p. B1.

p. 87 Percentage of workers taking care of elderly relatives: see Sue Shellenbarger, "Firms Try Harder, but Often Fail, to Help Workers Cope with Elder-Care Problems," *WSJ*, June 23, 1993, p. B1.

p. 87 Employees in caregiver role: see Sue Shellenbarger, "Work and Family," *WSJ*, November 9, 1992, p. B1; June 29, 1993, p. B1.

Chapter 7

p. 91 Sexual orientation discrimination: federal Courts of Appeals have rejected Title VII claims based on workplace harassment stemming from a person's sexual orientation (or perceived sexual orientation): see, for instance, *Dillon v. Frank,* #90-2290 (6th Cir. January 26, 1992).

p. 92 42 USC §1981 extends white citizens' right to make and enforce contracts to citizens of other races. In 1989 the Supreme Court ruled that this statute cannot be used to sue for any conduct occurring after hiring, because the contract has already been formed: *Patterson v. McLean Credit Union,* 485 US 617. One of the objectives of the Civil Rights Act of 1991 was to overturn this decision. But some courts say that the broader remedies under CRA '91 are themselves enough to keep plaintiffs from suing under §1981 or a related statute, §1983 (which don't require all the Title VII rigmarole)—they can get a complete remedy under Title VII: *Marrero-Rivera v. Department of Justice of Puerto Rico,* 61 *LW* 2119 (D.P.R. July 23, 1992). It sure gives you a nice safe warm feeling: the plaintiff was suing her employer for sexual harassment—she worked for the Department of Justice.

p. 93 Caps on damages: according to an EEOC Staff Policy Memo dated July 7, 1992 (see 61 *LW* 2029), the caps on damages apply on a per-employee basis: that is, each plaintiff can get the full amount recoverable from an employer of that size. The policy memo also approves of the inclusion of medical expenses (for example, therapy) as part of the compensatory damages in a discrimination case.

p. 95 Administrative remedies: claimants have to be careful what they ask for. In late 1992 a trial court awarded $4 million in punitive damages under New York's Human Rights Law in a case of quid pro quo sexual harassment. When the employer appealed, New York's highest court ruled that the Human Rights Law only allows punitive damages in housing cases—and even then, punitive damages are limited to $10,000. So the plaintiff didn't get any punitive damages, much less the $4 million the jury thought she was entitled to: *Thoreson v. Penthouse Int'l Ltd.*, 61 *LW* 2395 (N.Y.App. December 21, 1992).

p. 95 Propriety of suits against individuals: compare *Miller v. Maxwell's International Inc.*, 61 *LW* 2649 (9th Cir. April 19, 1993) [plaintiff could not sue company's CEO, two restaurant managers, or three lower-level employees—especially since she had already gotten adequate relief by settling with the corporate employer]; *Berry v. North Alabama Electric Coop*, 61 *LW* 2763 (N.D. Ala. May 10, 1993) [additional remedies added by Civil Rights Act of 1991 don't entitle plaintiff to bring a Title VII suit against the person who retaliated against him when he opposed sexual discrimination against a coworker], *Smith v. Capitol City Club of Montgomery*, 62 *LW* 2681 (M.D. Ala. April 12, 1994) [even after CRA '91, individuals can't be sued under Title VII] and *Grant v. Lone Star Co.*, 62 *LW* 2763 (5th Cir. May 27, 1994) [branch manager charged with sexual harassment can't be sued under Title VII], with *Elias v. Sitomer*, 61 *LW* 2420 (S.D.N.Y. December 7, 1992) [age discrimination plaintiff can sue the president of the now-bankrupt employer company, when the president is the one who forced him out of his job; court suggests that a Title VII case could not be brought against an individual] and *Vakharia v. Swedish Covenant Hospital*, #90 C 6548 (N.D. Ill. June 8, 1993). [An agent of an institution can be personally liable under Title VII, the ADEA, and 42 USC §1981 for discriminatorily impeding the plaintiff's access to employment opportunities—as long as the plaintiff is blamed for his own actions as distinct from policy set by the employer itself.]

p. 96 Ezold case: 983 F.2d 509 (3d Cir. December 30, 1992).

p. 97 Disadvantages of arbitration: Steven A. Holmes, "Some Employees Lose Right to Sue for Bias at Work," *NYT*, March 8, 1994, p. A1; Margaret A. Jacobs, "Men's Club," *WSJ*, June 9, 1994, p. A1.

p. 98 Brown case: 61 *LW* 2732 (5th Cir. May 4, 1993).

p. 98 Racial harassment: In 1992, there were over 6,000 racial harassment complaints filed with the EEOC. See Michael Janofsky, "Race and the American Workplace," *NYT*, June 20, 1993, first Business page.

p. 98 Reverse discrimination against a white male: *Notari v. Denver Water Department*, 61 *LW* 2128 (10th Cir. July 23, 1992) and *McNabola v. Chicago Transit Authority*, #92-1133 (7th Cir. 1993); see Benjamin A. Holden's "Law" column in the *WSJ*, November 30, 1993, p. B8.

p. 98 Discrimination by black against black: *Hansborough v. City of*

Elkhart, 61 *LW* 2267 (N.D. Ind. September 30, 1992). The plaintiff lost his case though—he failed to produce evidence of anything except personal animosity and interpersonal conflict with a supervisor.

p. 98 Standing for testers: *Fair Employment Council of Greater Washington Inc. v. BMC Marketing Corp.,* 62 *LW* 2005 (D.D.C. June 18, 1993).

p. 98 Honeywell case: *Dep't of Labor v. Honeywell, Inc.,* 61 *LW* 2793 (DOL June 2, 1993).

p. 99 Lucky's Supermarket settlement: Jane Gross, "Big Grocery Chain Reaches Landmark Sex-Bias Accord," *NYT,* December 17, 1993, p. A1.

p. 99 Modification of Lucky Stores settlement: news item, "$60 Million Sex-Bias Pact," *NYT,* April 22, 1994, p. A15. Safeway case: news item, "Safeway, Inc. Agrees to Settle a Lawsuit on Sex Discrimination," *WSJ,* April 4, 1994, p. B4 [mentioning December 1993 agreement by American Stores to pay over $100 million to settle sex discrimination case, and $29.5 million race/sex discrimination settlement by Albertson's, another California grocery chain]; A T & T settlement: news item, "A T & T Settles Sex-Bias Lawsuit for $3.3 Million," *NYT,* June 6, 1994, p. B8; ABC judgment: news item, "ABC to Pay Over $300,000 to Settle Bias Lawsuit," *NYT,* June 16, 1994, p. B10.

p. 99 Hostile environment: Arab employee, *Boutros v. Canton Regional Transit Authority,* 62 *LW* 2063 (6th Cir. June 30, 1993); Chicano employee, *Ugalde v. W. A. McKenzie Asphalt Co.,* 61 *LW* 2748 (5th Cir. May 12, 1993).

p. 100 Albertson's settlement: see Margaret A. Jacobs's Law column in the *WSJ* issue of November 23, 1993, p. B12.

p. 100 Protestant teachers only: *EEOC v. Kamehama Schools,* 61 *LW* 2624 (9th Cir. March 31, 1993).

p. 101 Accommodation to worker with Saturday Sabbath: *Wright v. Runyon,* 62 *LW* 2151 (7th Cir. August 10, 1993).

p. 101 Sabbath observer's vacation days: *Cooper v. Oak Rubber Co.,* 62 *LW* 2579 (6th Cir. February 9, 1994). Religious harassment guidelines: Richard B. Schmitt, "EEOC May Pit Church vs. State at Work," *WSJ,* June 8, 1994, p. B8.

p. 101 Discrimination against smokers: Junda Woo, "Employers Fume Over New Legislation Barring Discrimination Against Smokers," *WSJ,* June 4, 1993, p. B1. According to a January 11, 1993, arbitration ruling, a company violated its collective bargaining agreement by charging smokers a higher health premium than nonsmokers. The agreement referred to only two premiums (one for single workers, one for workers with spouses and/or children)—not to high and low health risks. The arbitrator made the company give back the extra premiums it collected: *Equitable Gas Co. v. IBEW Local Union 1956,* 62 *LW* 2048.

p. 102 Asthmatic employee and workplace smoking: *Harmer v. Virginia Electric & Power Co.,* 62 *LW* 2199 (E.D. Va. September 20, 1993). Also see *Gupton v. Virginia,* 62 *LW* 2441 (4th Cir. January 13, 1994) [an employee who is allergic to smoke is not "disabled" as defined by the Rehabilitation Act unless the allergy keeps her from working at all in her own occupation, not just keeps her from holding a particular job; if she isn't disabled, the employer's failure to provide a smoke-free workplace doesn't violate the Rehab Act].

p. 102 CRA '91 is not retroactive: two related cases were decided April 26, 1994, *Rivers v. Roadway Express,* #92-938 (62 *LW* 4255), and *Landgraf v. USI Film Products,* #92-757 (62 *LW* 4255).

p. 103 PDA: the statutory cite is 42 USC §2000e(k).

p. 103 Temporary disability: nurses—*EEOC v. Detroit-Macomb Hospital Corporation,* 1992 U.S. App. LEXIS 1208 (6th Cir. 1992); cops—*Adams v. Nolan,* 1992 U.S. App. LEXIS 7627 (8th Cir. 1992).

p. 104 Increase in pregnancy discrimination complaints: Sue Shellenbarger, "As More Pregnant Women Work, Bias Complaints Rise," *WSJ,* December 6, 1993, p. B1.

p. 104 Unsolicited statement about no more children: *Lysak v. Seiler Corporation,* 62 *LW* 2006 (Mass.Sup.Jud. Ct. June 21, 1993).

p. 104 Okay to fire pregnant employee for lateness: *Troupe v. May Dep't Stores Co.,* 62 *LW* 2632 (7th Cir. March 31, 1994). Gaps in maternity coverage: Deborah Lohse, "Prospective Parents Should Look Out for Gaps in Maternity Health Coverage," *WSJ,* May 5, 1994, p. C1.

p. 104 Fleming v. Ayers & Associates, 948 F.2d 993 (6th Cir. 1991).

p. 106 Cite for *EEOC v. Johnson Controls:* #89-1215 (March 1991). January 24, 1990 EEOC guidelines require the employer to prove that efforts have also been made to protect the children of male workers from genetic damage. If the employer only applies its fetal protection policy to women, the employer has the burden of proving that only pregnant women, not fathers, risk transmitting genetic damage—and that no pregnant woman can do the job without risking transmission of genetic damage.

p. 107 In 1992 the EEOC got 10,577 sexual harassment claims; a little less than 10 percent were filed by men. The largest reported award to a man was a $1 million jury verdict in May 1993 on behalf of a onetime manager of a manufacturing company who charged daily harassment from a female supervisor. No byline, "Man Wins $1 Million Sex Harassment Suit," *NYT,* May 21, 1993, p. A15. The Center for Women in Government (Albany, N.Y.), using figures from the EEOC, reported that in 1993 U.S. workers won 1,546 sexual harassment cases, and were awarded a total of $25.2 million—twice the 1992 level of damages. See news item, *New York Law Journal,* May 25, 1994, p. 1.

p. 107 Supervisor or coemployee: these are the usual "suspects" involved in sexual harassment cases, and the supervisor's power makes it more likely that the employer will be held responsible for the supervisor's acts. However, the employer may be responsible under other circumstances. If waitresses have to wear sexually provocative uniforms as a condition of their job, for instance, the employer may be held liable for harassment by customers. If the employer creates the hostile environment, it can be held liable for the conduct of the employees of other companies: e.g., auto workers harassing the employees of a food-service company. *King v. Chrysler Corp.,* 61 *LW* 2502 (E.D. Mo. February 5, 1993). Sexual harassment was found in *Chiapuzio v. BLT Operating Corp.,* 62 *LW* 2084 (D. Wyo. July 29, 1993) where a supervisor both repeatedly propositioned a female worker and belittled her husband as an inadequate lover unable to satisfy his wife; the court found that, in both cases, the harassment was gender based.

p. 108 Reactions to work environment: "Reasonable woman" standard used in *Andrews v. City of Philadelphia,* 895 F.2d 1469 (3d Cir. 1990); *Ellison v. Brady,* 924 F.2d 872 (9th Cir. 1991); *Robinson v. Jacksonville Shipyard,* 760 F.Supp. 1486 (M.D. Fla. 1991), and in the lead New Jersey case of *Lehmann v. Toys 'R' Us,* described in "New Jersey Court Rules on Sex Harassment in Workplace," *NYT,* July 15, 1993, p. B6, but rejected in *Radtke v. Everett,* 61 *LW* 2771 (Mich.Sup. June 2, 1993). On July 13, 1993, the EEOC issued proposed guidelines reflecting the "reasonable person" standard. The guidelines are proposed regulations that, if adopted, will appear at 29 CFR Part 1609.

p. 108 Nevada gambling casino case: *Powell v. Las Vegas Hilton Corp.,* CV-5-91-359-PMP (D.Nev. May 7, 1992), discussed in Stephen A. Ploscowe and David W. Garland, "Scope of Harassment Liability Expands," *Nat'l Law J.,* February 8, 1993, p. 23. Hooters case: see Andrew Blum, "Assumption of Risk Tested in *Hooters* Suit," *Nat'l Law J.,* May 24, 1993, p. 7.

p. 108 In a later casino case, a former blackjack dealer was allowed to proceed with a hostile environment case based on constant sexually explicit insults from her onetime floor manager. The lower court believed the casino's defense—that he abused everyone, men and women alike, with profane insults; but the Ninth Circuit said that using degrading epithets toward men does not "cure" linguistic harassment of women. See Junda Woo, "Harassing Both Sexes Equally Isn't Excuse," *WSJ,* June 16, 1994, p. B5.

p. 108 Suit usually against the employer: for an exception, see *Bridges v. Eastman Kodak,* 61 *LW* 2159 (S.D.N.Y. September 1, 1992), permitting suits against harassers as individuals, based on an interpretation of CRA '91 as expanding remedies to include the kind of money damages usually sought against individuals as well as the earlier "employer-type" remedies like reinstatement and back pay. However, *Grant v. Lone Star Co.,* 62 *LW* 2763 (5th Cir. May 27, 1994) forbids suit against a supervisor charged with harassment.

p. 109 Constructive discharge when supervisor failed to listen to woman: *Cortes v. Maxus Exploration Co.,* 61 *LW* 2375 (5th Cir. November 18, 1992).

p. 109 Burden on the employer: see, e.g., *Sparks v. Regional Medical Center Board,* 1992 U.S. Dist. LEXIS 6729 (N.D. Ala. 1992) and *Emery v. Chicago Transit Authority,* 1992 U.S. Dist. LEXIS 7222 (N.D. Ill. 1992); *Reynolds v. Avalon, New Jersey,* 61 *LW* 2100 (D.N.J. August 5, 1992). The employee doesn't have to suffer actual economic loss to prove quid pro quo harassment by a supervisor; a threat of economic loss is sufficient. See *Karibian v. Columbia University,* 62 *LW* 2477 (2d Cir. January 25, 1994), which also finds the employer liable in a hostile work environment case, even if it sets up a complaint procedure and takes timely action on complaints, as long as the person who commits the harassment is an agent of the company who appears to have the power to take action on behalf of the company.

p. 109 LMRA §301 preemption: *Mumphrey v. Jones River Paper Co.,* 777 F.Supp. 1458 (W.D. Ark. 1991).

p. 110 EPA cite: 29 USC §206(d)(1).

p. 110 1993 Tennessee case: *Gandy v. Sullivan County,* 125 Labor Cases ¶35,821 (D.Tenn. 1993).

p. 110 EPA Act effects: Joan E. Rigdon, "Three Decades After the Equal Pay Act, Women's Wages Remain Far From Parity," *WSJ* June 9, 1993, p. B1.

p. 111 ADEA cite: 29 USC §621.

p. 111 People over forty: *Hamilton v. Caterpillar, Inc.,* 59 FEP Cases 504 (7th Cir. July 16, 1992) defines "age discrimination" to mean discrimination based on the fact that someone is forty or older, not any action taken because of age; the court thought that Congress perceived and tried to remedy widespread discrimination against older people, not younger people. It looks like one effect of the economic downturn of the 1990s is to make age discrimination more fashionable than ever. Each year in the 1990s, the EEOC saw a significant increase in the number of age discrimination complaints (about 20,000 in 1993 alone). Overall damages awarded also rose sharply, nearly doubling between

1992 and 1993; the 1993 level was about $100 million. See Thomas J. Lueck, "Job-Loss Anger: Age Bias Cases Soar in Region," *NYT,* December 12, 1993, p. A1. Analysts suggest that one factor in the larger number of suits is the aging of the baby boom—an assertive, and perhaps pampered, group of people well used to standing up for actual or perceived rights.

p. 112 Age discrimination complaints and verdicts: Thomas J. Lueck, "Job-Loss Anger: Age Bias Cases Soar in Region," *NYT,* December 12, 1993, p. A1; Milo Geyelin, "Age-Bias Cases Found to Bring Big Jury Awards," *WSJ,* December 17, 1993, p. B1.

p. 112 Overqualified older employees: Compare *Stein v. Nat'l City Bank,* 924 F.2d 1062 (6th Cir. 1991) [refusal to hire/discharge based on legitimate market factors] with *EEOC v. Francis W. Parker School,* 61 *LW* 2618 (ND Ill. March 23, 1993).

p. 114 1992 case showing complexities: *EEOC v. Boeing Services Int'l,* 61 *LW* 2137 (5th Cir. August 19, 1992).

p. 115 Giving up rights under the ADEA: They don't give up all rights, even if the release is valid. The release covers only claims that arose before the date of the document, not future claims; and the employee still retains the right to file an EEOC charge (as distinct from a lawsuit) and to participate in EEOC investigations (after all, citizens have an obligation to assist in law enforcement).

p. 115 Okay to keep consideration for defective release: *Oberg v. Allied Van Lines Inc.,* 61 *LW* 2159 (N.D. Ill. July 22, 1992); *Collins v. Outboard Marine Corp.,* 61 *LW* 2219 (N.D. Ill. August 24, 1992).

p. 116 Deferral state: the states in this category are Alaska, California, Connecticut, Delaware, Florida, Georgia, Hawaii, Idaho, Illinois, Iowa, Kentucky, Maryland, Massachusetts, Michigan, Minnesota, Montana, Nebraska, Nevada, New Hampshire, New Jersey, New Mexico, New York, Oregon, Pennsylvania, South Carolina, Utah, West Virginia, Wisconsin. These states are also called "referral" states, because if the person charging age discrimination goes to the EEOC first, the charge is supposed to be referred to the state agency so they can investigate it. In Massachusetts, Michigan, New York, and Ohio complainants have another choice: they can file with the state agency or bring a suit right away in state court. In Arizona, Colorado, Kansas, Maine, Ohio, Rhode Island, South Dakota, and Washington, "conditional referral" applies because the state statutes cover different conditions than the federal law. Claims are referred if they are covered by both federal and state law, but handled only by the federal agency if they cover situations that are unlawful under federal law but permitted by state law.

p. 116 Effect of bad evaluation: *Gustovich v. A T & T Communications Inc.,* 61 *LW* 2176 (7th Cir. August 18, 1992).

p. 117 Rehab Act cite: 29 USC §793. *Buckingham v. U.S.,* 62 *LW* 2068 (9th Cir. July 13, 1993) says that under the Rehab Act (and therefore, even more strongly, under the more protective ADA), reasonable accommodations may include transferring the employee to another location, where better medical care is available; in this reading, the need for accommodation can prevail over seniority rules for transfers. ADA claims have to go through collective bargaining agreement grievance procedure: *Austin v. Owens-Brockaway Glass Container Inc.,* 62 *LW* 2483 (W.D. Wa. January 14, 1994).

p. 118 Six months' worth of ADA complaints: Randall Samborn, "First ADA Trial Marks Beginning of Enforcement," *Nat'l Law J.,* March 22, 1993, p. 17. A lawyer claimed that his law firm (which had only ten employees) fired him because he had AIDS. He was still allowed to bring an ADA case because his firm did 90 percent of its work for the leasing and brokerage firms with which it shared office space, and the employees from those firms were added in to meet the twenty-five employee minimum prevailing at the time—a strategy that might work for other employees of small companies that are related to other companies: *Doe v. William Shapiro Esq. P.C.,* 62 *LW* 2771 (E.D. Pa. April 16, 1994).

p. 118 Definition of handicap: people who are *not* handicapped are not allowed to bring "reverse-discrimination" claims when a handicapped person gets a job they want: *Ortner v. Paralyzed Veterans of America,* 61 *LW* 2181 (D.C. Super. September 11, 1992). The court's analysis was that the law was necessary to protect people against discrimination for being handicapped (a real risk), not against discrimination for not being handicapped (which the court didn't think was a big problem). A point that could have been made: the job was recreation director for an organization of handicapped people; using a wheelchair might well have been a bona fide occupational qualification.

p. 119 Alcoholism as disability: see *Ellenwood v. Exxon Shipping Co.,* #92-1473 (1st Cir. January 14, 1993). After the environmental disaster caused by the *Exxon Valdez,* Exxon barred anyone who had ever been in an alcohol rehabilitation program from holding certain jobs. An engineer was fired because of his participation in Exxon's own alcohol rehab program. The First Circuit let him sue under state law for handicap discrimination; the court didn't think that either the law of the sea nor the Rehabilitation Act preempted the case. The court didn't note, but should have, that it's very bad policy to discourage people with alcohol problems from getting help. They shouldn't keep drinking and keep working—they should not be penalized for seeking sobriety before they hurt someone!

p. 119 Obesity as a disability: *Cook v. State of Rhode Island,* #93-1093 (1st Cir. 1993); see Wade Lambert, "U.S. Court Ruling Bars Hiring Bias Against the Obese," *WSJ,* November 23, 1993, p. B12. *Cassista v. Community Foods, Inc.,* 62 *LW* 2159 (Cal.Sup. September 2, 1993) allows California's Fair Employment and Housing Act to be used to bring a claim of weight discrimination as a handicap claim, but only if it can be proved that the weight problem is caused by a physiological condition that affects at least one basic body system; otherwise the weight condition is not considered an impairment.

p. 119 Theoretical risk of transmission: *Chalk v. U.S. District Court,* 840 F.2d 701 (9th Cir. 1988). The plaintiff was a teacher removed from classroom duties. See Richard Corenthal, "Balancing Interests Under the ADA," *NYLJ,* July 2, 1993, p. 1.

p. 120 EEOC guidelines on ADA and health plans: see 61 *LW* 2761.

p. 122 First ADA jury award: *EEOC v. A/C Security,* 2 AD Cases 561 (N.D. Ill. March 18, 1993).

p. 122 Reduction in punitive damages: *EEOC v. A/C Security Investigations Ltd.,* 61 *LW* 2770 (N.D. Ill. June 7, 1993).

p. 122 Effectiveness of ADA: see Carl Quintanilla, "Disabled People Aren't Getting More Job Offers," and Joann S. Lublin, "Law Does Help Some Managers to Move Ahead," both *WSJ,* July 19, 1993, p. B1.

p. 123 Title VII damages are taxable income: *U.S. v. Burke,* 112 S.Ct. 1867 (1992). Punitive damages: *Reese v. U.S.,* 62 *LW* 2730 (Fed. Cir. May 16, 1994), *Maleszewski v. U.S.,* 62 FEP Cases 361 (N.D. Fla. June 4, 1993). IRS ruling: Rev.Rul. 93-88 (December 20, 1993). Also see *Stender v. Lucky Stores,* 62 *LW* 2431 (N.D. Cal. December 15, 1993), finding that settlement payments in a class action charging racial and sex discrimination are not taxable income. ADEA damages: *Downey v. Commr,* 100 T.C. No. 40 (Tax Court June 29, 1993), *reversed* 63 *LW* 2142 (7th Cir. August 30, 1994).

Chapter 8

p. 125 Preemption by LMRA: see, e.g., *Schlacter-Jones v. General Telephone of California,* 936 F.2d 435 (9th Cir. 1991); *Clark v. Newport News Shipbuilding and Dry Dock Co.,* 937 F.2d 934 (4th Cir. 1991).

p. 125 Benefits of drug testing: Joseph B. Treaster, "Testing Workers for Drugs Reduces Company Problems," *NYT,* October 10, 1993, p. A1.

p. 126 Impairment testing: William L. Holstein, "Finding a Better Way to Test for Drugs," *NYT,* November 28, 1993, p. F11. Also see Anne Newman, "Drug-Testing Firms Face Pluses, Minuses in New Rules," *WSJ,* March 15, 1994, p. B4.

p. 127 Drug testing is a violation of privacy right: *Semore v. Pool,* 217 Cal.App. 3d 1087, 266 Cal.Rptr. 280 (1990); compare this with cases holding notice to the employee rules out this argument, such as *Jennings v. Minco Technology Labs Inc.,* 765 SW2d 497 (Tex.App. 1989); *Baggs v. Eagle-Picher Industries Inc.,* 750 F.Supp. 264 (W.D. Mich. 1990), aff'd 957 F.2d 268 (6th Cir. 1992).

p. 127 Standards for drug testing: see, e.g., *Skinner v. Railway Labor Executives' Ass'n,* 489 U.S. 602 (1989); *Employees' Union v. Von Raab,* 489 U.S. 656 (1989). *Electrical Workers v. Nuclear Regulatory Comm'n,* 61 *LW* 2047 (9th Cir. June 24, 1992) holds that the Nuclear Regulatory Commission was correct in including clerical, warehouse, and maintenance employees in nuclear plants' industry-wide drug-testing program, because the union failed to establish that these fellow-employees of Homer Simpson's were not in safety-sensitive jobs.

p. 127 Management rights and unilateral policy: *Chicago Tribune v. NLRB,* 61 *LW* 2184 (7th Cir. September 10, 1992).

p. 128 Arbitrating unilateral drug policy that was not part of the contract: *United Steelworkers or America v. ASARCO Inc.,* 61 *LW* 2171 (5th Cir. September 8, 1992). For more on arbitration, see Michael Janofsky, "Drug Use and Workers' Rights," *NYT,* December 28, 1993, p. D1.

p. 128 Firsthand investigation results aren't "credit reports": *Hodge v. Texaco Inc.,* 61 *LW* 2259 (5th Cir. October 7, 1992).

p. 128 EAP confidentiality issues: Milt Freudenheim, "Corporate-Paid Psychotherapy: At What Price?" *NYT,* April 12, 1994, p. A1; Ellen E. Schultz, "If You Use Firm's Counselors, Remember Your Secrets Could be Used Against You," *WSJ,* May 26, 1994, p. C6.

p. 130 Liability of polygraph operator: *Rubin v. Tourneau Inc.,* 61 *LW* 2058 (S.D.N.Y. July 9, 1992).

p. 130 Rhode Island state law: *Carr v. Mulhearn,* 125 CCH Labor Cases ¶57,394 (R.I. Supreme Court 1993).

p. 130 Arbitration of securities claims (including polygraph violations of privacy): *Saari v. Smith Barney,* 61 *LW* 2039 (9th Cir. June 29, 1992).

p. 131 Employee surveillance and proposed legislation: see Peter Blackman and Barbara Franklin, "Blocking Big Brother," *NYLJ,* August 19, 1993, p. 5.

p. 132 K mart privacy case: Stephanie Strom, "K mart is Sued by

43 Workers in a Privacy Case in Illinois," *NYT,* September 15, 1993, p. D5.

p. 132 Employer can restrict distribution of advocacy materials: *NLRB v. Motorola,* #92-4317, (5th Cir. 1993). See Edward Felsenthal and Richard J. Schmitt, "More Limits Set on Workplace Activism," *WSJ,* June 3, 1993, p. B2.

p. 133 Occupational injuries in 1992: no byline, "Workplace Injuries, Illnesses Rose Sharply in 1992, U.S. Reports," *WSJ,* December 16, 1993, p. A18. Also see Barbara Presley Noble, "Breathing New Life Into OSHA," *NYT,* January 23, 1994, p. F25.

p. 133 County can't regulate VDTs: *ILC Data Device Corp. v. Suffolk County,* 61 *LW* 2197 (N.Y.A.D. September 14, 1992).

p. 134 Videotapes okay: *In re Inspection of Kelly-Springfield Tire Co.,* 61 *LW* 2358 (N.D. Ill. November 30, 1992).

p. 134 Each failure to report is a separate violation: *Sec'y of Labor v. Caterpillar, Inc.,* 61 *LW* 2513 (OSHA February 5, 1993).

p. 135 Piercing the corporate veil: *U.S. v. Cusack,* 61 *LW* 2309 (D.N.J. November 5, 1992).

p. 136 Employers don't have to pay: *Whirlpool Corp v. Sec'y of Labor,* 445 U.S. 1 (Sup.Ct. 1980).

p. 137 Cost-benefit analysis: *American Textile Manufacturers' Association v. Donovan,* 452 U.S. 490 (1981); Executive Order 12291.

p. 137 OSHA rules for hazardous substances: *AFL-CIO v. OSHA,* 965 F.2d 962 (11th Cir. 1992); see 61 *LW* 2594-5 for OSHA decision not to appeal.

Chapter 9

p. 139 AFL-CIO: Kevin G. Salwen, "What, Us Worry? Big Unions' Leaders Overlook Bad News, Opt for Status Quo," *WSJ,* October 5, 1993, p. B1.

p. 139 Women in unions: Elisabeth Ginsburg, "Gains Seen by Women in Unions," *NYT,* September 5, 1993, p. NJ1.

p. 139 Negotiation for givebacks: These are some stories that were current at press time; there will no doubt be lots more in the newspapers at the time you read this. See, e.g., Robin Toner, "Striking Coal Miners Fight to Protect Shrinking Power," *NYT,* June 8, 1993, p. A16; Robert L. Rose, "Northwest Air's 'Giveback' Pact Faces Rejection," *WSJ,* June 9, 1993, p. A3, "Airlines' Woes Make Pushing for Labor Hard," *WSJ,* June 25, 1993, p. B1, and "Northwest Airlines Machinists Appear to be Backing Revised Concessions Plan," *WSJ,* July 27, 1993, p. A3; Thomas J. Lueck, "Jet-Engine Workers Accept Harsh Reality,"

NYT, June 25, 1993, p. B6; Michael deCourcy Hinds, "Notice the Steel Strike? 48 Hours Sum Up a Slide," *NYT,* March 4, 1994, p. A16; Peter T. Kilborn, "California Strike Becomes a Battle Over Permanent Job Replacements," *NYT,* April 17, 1994, p. A22.

p. 141 Discrimination: The NLRB can order the employer to reinstate a worker, give him or her back pay, or both. If the employee was fired for cause, the NLRB can only order back pay if it decides that the primary reason for the discharge was to discourage union activity. Back pay doesn't have to be provided if the plant was shut or the job eliminated—or if the employee was given an unconditional offer of reinstatement, but turned it down. If the employee doesn't make reasonable efforts to get a new job, that will affect the NLRB's decision about back pay.

p. 145 Election invalidated: *Curtin Matheson Scientific, Inc.,* 1992-3 NLRB ¶17,806.

p. 145 Videotaping is wrong: *F.W. Woolworth Co.,* 1992-3 NLRB ¶17,817. On the other hand, the Eighth Circuit refused to throw out election results that favored the union just because the union sent a TV cameraman to videotape employees taking or rejecting union literature at a rally; the employees didn't know that the cameraman was sent by the union, and therefore couldn't feel pressured: *Millard Processing Services v. NLRB,* 62 *LW* 2132 (8th Cir. July 30, 1993).

p. 146 Unfair labor practices: *Quality Asbestos Removal, Southeast Inc.,* CCH NLRB ¶17,822; *Miller Group, Inc.,* 1992-3 NLRB ¶17,825.

p. 146 On-premises solicitation: *Lechmere Inc. v. NLRB,* 60 *LW* 4145 (Sup.Ct. 1992); *Oakwood Hospital v. NLRB,* 62 *LW* 2425 (6th Cir. January 6, 1993).

p. 146 Materials from advocacy group: *NLRB v. Motorola, Inc.,* 61 *LW* 2741 (5th Cir. May 26, 1993).

p. 146 Toxic waste policy: *Blue Circle Cement Co. Inc.,* 1992-3 NLRB ¶17,901.

p. 147 NLRB agency shop rules: 29 CFR Part 103; see 61 *LW* 2174 (September 22, 1992). Also see *Electrical Workers Local 444,* 1992–3 NLRB ¶17,898.

p. 150 Labor lawyer Geoghegan: the quote comes from p. 31 of his book, *Which Side Are You On? Trying to Be for Labor When It's Flat on Its Back* (Farrar, Straus & Giroux, 1991)—which is highly recommended.

p. 150 Strikes that could be hazardous: NLRA §8(g) also requires unions to give ten days' notice of intention to strike—or even picket—a health care institution.

p. 151 Letter to strikers: *Gibson Greetings, Inc.,* 1992–3 NLRB ¶17,833.

p. 152 Economic to unfair labor practices strike: *Hormigonera Del Toa, Inc.,* 1992–3 NLRB ¶17,930.

p. 152 Status of permanent replacements: *JMA Holdings Inc.,* 1992–3 NLRB ¶17,837. States can't pass laws forbidding permanent replacements: *Midwest Motor Express Inc. v. Teamsters,* 62 *LW* 2592 (Minn.Sup. March 11, 1994).

p. 155 Employer lies may trigger arbitration: *Mason v. Continental Group Inc.,* 763 F.2d 1219 (11th Cir. 1985).

p. 156 Nonunion grievance procedures: for more information—or if your job includes grievance adjustment—see David W. Ewing, *Justice on the Job,* Harvard Business School Press, 1989.

p. 156 Weingarten right: the name comes from *NLRB v. J. Weingarten Co.,* 420 U.S. 251 (Sup.Ct. 1975).

p. 157 Right to consult shop steward: *U.S. Postal Service v. NLRB,* 61 *LW* 2024 (D.C. Cir. June 30, 1992).

p. 158 Pension fund stockholder activism: Leslie Scism, "Labor Unions Increasingly Initiate Proxy Proposals," *WSJ,* March 1, 1994, p. C1.

p. 159 Swapping concessions for union entry into decision making: Kevin Kelly and Aaron Bernstein, "Labor Deals that Offer a Break from 'Us Vs. Them,' " *Business Week,* August 2, 1993, p. 30.

p. 159 ESOP figures: The figures come from the National Center for Employee Ownership. See Adam Bryant, "Can Unions Run United Airlines?" *NYT,* December 9, 1993, p. D1. Also see Mary Rowland, "Rare Bird: Stock Options for Many," *NYT,* August 1, 1993, p. A14; Ronald L. Rose, "Employee Ownership is Catching on in Airline Industry," *WSJ,* July 23, 1993, p. B4.

Chapter 10

p. 161 Validity of at-will doctrine: see *Robinson v. Christopher Greater Area Rural Health Planning Corp.,* 207 Ill.App.3d 1030, 566 NE2d 768 (1991). An employee who signed an interoffice memo accepting a new job that was projected to last three years was still an at-will employee, not one hired under a three-year contract. The memo itself said that the duration of the job was uncertain, and not guaranteed: *Griffen v. Elkhart General Hospital,* 125 CCH Labor Cases ¶57,387 (Ind.App. 1993).

p. 162 Identity of complainer: *Resorts Int'l Hotel Casino v. NLRB,* 62 *LW* 2042 (3d Cir. July 1, 1993).

p. 162 Union organizing: *Davies v. American Airlines Inc.*, 61 *LW* 2128 (10th Cir. July 13, 1992).

p. 162 Discharge for Workers' Compensation claim: even then, the employee may be out of luck. See *Moran v. Washington Fruit and Produce*, 125 CCH Labor Cases ¶57,388 (Wash.App. 1993), saying that the employee has no tort claim against the employer even if that was the reason for the discharge, and the employee's only remedy is through administrative Workers' Comp appeals, not the court system. Of course, Workers' Comp appeals **never** result in seven-figure judgments, and court cases occasionally do. On the other hand, *Michaels v. Anglo America Auto Auctions Inc.*, 62 *LW* 2561 (N.M.Sup. February 10, 1994) says that the state law, which forces employers to rehire employees who were fired in retaliation for filing Comp claims, is not the only remedy: the aggrieved employees can still file civil suits and seek damages.

p. 162 Weekend work: *Wilcox v. Niagara of Wisconsin Paper Corp.*, 61 *LW* 2031 (7th Cir. June 4, 1992).

p. 162 Very small employers: *Kerrigan v. Magnum Entertainment Inc.*, 61 *LW* 2347 (D. Md. August 31, 1992).

p. 162 Employee handbook: a basic case is *Duldulao v. St. Mary of Nazareth Hospital*, 115 Ill.2d 482, 505 NE2d 314 (1987), which defines an implied contract as one whose language is clear enough to make the employee think that there was an offer of lasting employment; was communicated to the employees; and where the employees do in fact work, thus accepting the implied contract. *Durtsche v. American Colloid Co.*, 958 F.2d 1007 (10th Cir. 1992), says that the disclaimers in the employee handbook were not strong enough to allow termination at will. *Cummings v. South Portland Housing Authority*, #92-1611 (1st Cir. January 21, 1993), says that an employee manual stating that all employment actions would be based on merit and ability created a Constitutionally protected interest in continued employment, so the plaintiff (a government worker) could bring a 42 USC §1983 suit charging violation of Constitutional rights by the state. See *Nat'l Law J.*, March 8, 1993, p. 38.

p. 162 Grievance procedure must be followed: *Fregara v. Jet Aviation Business Jets, Inc.*, 764 F.Supp. 940 (D.N.J. 1991).

p. 163 Handbook is not an implied contract: typical cases include *Johnson v. Morton Thiokol Inc.*, 818 P.2d 997 (Utah 1991); *Leatham v. Research Foundation*, 658 F.Supp. 651 (E.D.N.Y. 1987). But to be effective, the disclaimer must be conspicuous: a disclaimer printed in ordinary type as part of a "welcome aboard" letter to a new employee was not given effect in *Arellano v. Amax Coal Co.*, 125 CCH Labor

Cases ¶57,411 (D. Wyo. 1993), because it was not set apart from the rest of the text.

p. 163 Promissory estoppel theory: accepted by *Sheppard v. Morgan Keegan & Co.,* 218 Cal.App.3d 61, 266 Cal.Rptr. 784 (1990), but rejected by *Tolmie v. United Parcel Service,* 930 F.2d 579 (7th Cir. 1991). An employee who claims oral promises by the employer leading to promissory estoppel may run into a problem with the "Statute of Frauds," a legal doctrine requiring written evidence of any contract that is supposed to last a year or more: see *Crenshaw v. General Dynamics Corp.,* 940 F.2d 125 (5th Cir. 1991).

p. 163 Covenant of good faith and fair dealing: In early 1994, a Wyoming court said that there is an implied covenant of good faith and fair dealing in every employment contract, and damages are available if the employer breaches the covenant when there is a relationship of trust and reliance between employer and employee: *Wilder v. Cody County Chamber of Commerce,* 62 *LW* 2531 (Wyo.Sup. January 25, 1994). But watch out—cases in Hawaii, Illinois, Minnesota, Missouri, New York, South Carolina, Texas, Vermont, Virginia, Washington, and Wisconsin reject this theory.

p. 163 Economic factors add up to good cause: *Reisman v. Regents of Wayne State University,* 125 CCH Labor Cases ¶57,404 (Mich.App. 1993).

p. 163 ERISA §510 preemption: *Felton v. Unisource Corp.,* 940 F.2d 503 (9th Cir. 1991). A claim by someone who says he's a whistleblower disclosing ERISA violations is also preempted by ERISA: *McLean v. Carlson Cos. Inc.,* 777 F.Supp. 1480 (D. Minn. 1991).

p. 163 Preemption by LMRA §301: the basic concept of contract interpretation comes from *Lingle v. Norge,* 486 U.S. 399 (1988); the employee's task is to show that the claims don't involve contract interpretation.

p. 164 Awards to people revealing fraud in federal contracts: John Holusha, "A Whistle-Blower is Awarded $22.5 Million," *NYT,* April 1, 1994, p. D1; Calvin Sims, "Trying to Mute the Whistle-Blowers," *NYT,* April 11, 1994, p. D1.

p. 164 $703,000 award to nurse: *Kraus v. New Rochelle Hospital Medical Center, NYLJ,* July 29, 1993, p. 27 col. 4 (Sup.Ct., Westchester County). She was awarded a large sum of money instead of reinstatement in her job because the court thought that reinstating her would lead to tensions that could compromise patient care.

p. 164 Conduct must actually be illegal: *Hancock v. Express One Internat'l Inc.,* 125 CCH Labor Cases ¶57,418 (Tex.App. 1993) [infractions of federal aviation rules punishable only by civil penalty]; *Kay v.*

Windsor Home Care Inc., NYLJ, May 21, 1993, p. 32 col. 5 (Sup.Ct. Nassau County) [falsified nursing notes to further a scheme of insurance fraud—deemed not to be a threat to public health and safety]; *Birthisel v. Tri-Cities Health Services Corp.,* 61 *LW* 2499 (W.Va.App. December 29, 1992) [ordering worker to add missing information to treatment plans, so facility could pass accreditation, was not illegal, so wrongful discharge claim denied].

p. 164 Report to law enforcement agency required: *Roxberry v. Robertson & Penn, Inc.,* 125 CCH Labor Cases ¶57,412 (1993); *Wright v. Shriners Hospital,* 60 *LW* 2699 (Mass.Sup. Jud.Ct. April 16, 1992).

p. 165 Participant can use whistle-blower act: *Edenfield v. Martin County,* 125 CCH Labor Cases ¶57,408 (Fla.App. 1993).

p. 166 Hiring preference in can factories: *U.S. Can Co. v. NLRB,* 61 *LW* 2473 (7th Cir. January 28, 1993).

p. 166 Successor employer's obligation to negotiate: *Fall River Dyeing & Finishing Corp. v. NLRB,* 482 U.S. 27 (1987).

p. 166 Continuity of operations: *John Wiley & Sons v. Livinston,* 376 U.S. 543 (Sup.Ct. 1964). For more information see J. Allen Miller and Eve I. Klein, "Labor Woes May Arise After a Merger," *Nat'l Law J.,* January 20, 1994, p. 21.

p. 166 Bankrupt business: *Johnson v. England,* 356 F.2d 44 (9th Cir. 1966).

p. 167 Pension plan underfunding: *PBGC v. White Consolidated Industries Inc.,* 62 *LW* 2027 (3d Cir. June 30, 1993).

p. 167 No break in service: *Hollingshead v. Burford Equipment Co.,* 809 F.Supp. 906 (M.D. Ala. 1992); *Gillis v. Sargeni,* 62 *LW* 2180 (3d Cir. September 7, 1993).

p. 169 Relocation bargaining: *United Food & Commercial Workers v. NLRB,* #91-1290 (D.C. Cir. August 10, 1993). See *Employment Alert,* August 26, 1993, p. 1.

p. 169 Decision bargaining and effects bargaining: Philip A. Miscimarra and Dale L. Deitchler, "Restructuring Missteps Can Be Costly," *Nat'l Law J.,* May 19, 1993, p. 19. The two Supreme Court cases are *Fibreboard Paper Products v. NLRB,* 379 U.S. 203 (1964) and *First National Maintenance Corp. v. NLRB,* 452 U.S. 666 (1981). Employees who are transferred to a new employer, without going through a period of unemployment, are still entitled to severance benefits from the first employer if they lose pension credits for some years of service: *Bedinghaus v. Modern Graphic Arts,* 62 *LW* 2596 (11th Cir. March 9, 1994).

p. 170 Surviving corporate transition: Joann S. Lublin, "Don't Assume Merit Protects Your Job After a Takeover," *WSJ,* September 22, 1993, p. B1.

p. 172 Unpredictable decline in business: *International Ass'n of Machinists v. General Dynamics Corp.,* 61 *LW* 2742 (E.D. Mo. May 24, 1993), excuses the defense-contractor employer from giving WARN Act notice when 3,000 workers were laid off. The Navy warned the company that its contract to produce a warplane would be canceled if performance failed to improve. Performance didn't improve; the contract was canceled, but the court ruled that, in the wacky world of defense contracting, that was so surprising an event that it counted as a unforeseeable business circumstance. See Andrea Adelson, "Ruling Seen to Weaken Layoff Law," *NYT,* May 27, 1993, p. D1.

p. 172 Change to single long shift: *Chestnut v. Stone Forest Industries Inc.,* 61 *LW* 2691 (N.D. Fla. April 1, 1993).

p. 172 WARN Act damages: A Missouri court has ruled that when the damages are paid, they are to be deducted from the employee's unemployment compensation; the payments are "wages" for services rendered, even though the services were rendered in the past. *Labor & Industrial Relations Comm'n v. Div. of Employment Security,* 62 *LW* 2116 (Mo.App. July 6, 1993).

p. 172 Statute of limitations: *Newspaper & Mail Deliverers' Union v. United Magazine Co.,* 61 *LW* 2371 (E.D.N.Y. November 27, 1992) and *Halkins v. General Dynamics Co.,* 62 *LW* 2064 (N.D. Tex. June 24, 1993) set the statute of limitations at six months—the time period for bringing a claim under the National Labor Relations Act. But *United Paperworkers Int'l Union v. Specialty Paperboard Inc.,* 62 *LW* 2057 (2d Cir. July 19, 1993) applies the state (Vermont) statute of limitations for contracts and torts—six years—under the theory that the WARN Act doesn't have anything to do with collective bargaining, so the NLRA time period shouldn't count.

p. 173 Union can't bring the suit: *Food & Commercial Workers Local 751 v. Brown Group Inc.,* 61 *LW* 2691 (E.D. Mo. April 12, 1993).

p. 173 WARN Act a toothless tiger: Kevin G. Salwen, "Most Firms Fail to Warn Workers of Plant Closings," *WSJ,* February 23, 1993, p. A2; Barbara Presley Noble, "Straddling the Law on Layoffs," *NYT,* March 28, 1993 p. F37; Sylvia Nasar, "Layoff Law is Having Slim Effect," *NYT,* August 3, 1993, p. D1.

p. 174 Okay to close plant despite tax breaks: Krystal Miller and Edward Felsenthal, "GM Can't be Forced Into Keeping Plant Open, Appeals Court Says," *WSJ,* August 5, 1993, p. B8.

p. 175 Employee fired for cause: see, e.g., *Conery v. Bath Associates,* Employee Benefits Alert November 11, 1992, p. 1; *MLSNA v.*

United Communications, Inc., 1993 U.S. Dist. LEXIS 9076 (N.D. Ill. 1993).

p. 175 COBRA timing: *Phillips v. Riverside Inc.,* 796 F.Supp. 403 (E.D. Ark. 1992); *Gaskell v. Harvard Co-Op Society,* 62 *LW* 2162 (1st Cir. August 25, 1993).

p. 176 Health insurance choices for new graduates: Stephen Frank, "Jobless Grads Need to Pick Health Plans," *WSJ,* August 18, 1993, p. C1.

p. 176 Severance benefit not used to calculate pension: *Licciardi v. Kropp Forge Division Employees' Retirement Plan,* 61 *LW* 2638 (7th Cir. April 9, 1993).

p. 177 Tactics for getting bonuses: David B. Wechsler and Leonard B. Pack, "Do Terminated Employees Forfeit Their Rights to a Bonus?" *NYLJ,* March 16, 1993, p. 1.

p. 177 Parachutes are not an ERISA plan: *Fontenot v. NL Industries,* 953 F.2d 960 (5th Cir. 1992).

p. 178 Massachusetts statute preempted: *Simas v. Quaker Fabric Corp. of Fall River,* 62 *LW* 2226 (1st Cir. October 6, 1993).

p. 178 Declining unemployment insurance eligibility: Christopher Conte, "Labor Letter," *WSJ,* October 12, 1993, p. A1.

p. 180 Disability, severance payments don't count as work weeks: *Claim of Katz,* 595 NYS2d 133 (A.D. 1993); *Claim of Barrett,* 595 NYS2d 143 (A.D. 1993).

p. 180 WARN Act payments not an offset: *Georgia-Pacific Corp. v. Unemployment Compensation Board of Review,* 62 *LW* 2168 (Pa. Comm. August 18, 1993).

p. 182 Extension of EUC benefits: Michael Wines, "Senate Amends, Then Passes, Bill on Extra Jobless Benefits," *NYT,* October 29, 1993, p. A22.

p. 182 Okay to fire the employee, but unemployment benefits available: *Benitez v. Girlfriday Inc.,* 609 So.2d 665 (Fla.App. 1992); *Nelson v. Burdines, Inc.,* 611 So.2d 1329 (Fla.App. 1993).

p. 183 Not a constructive discharge: *Claim of Bradley,* 593 N.Y.S.2d 596 (A.D. 1993).

p. 183 Benefits granted although harassment not reported: *Allen v. Department of Employment and Training,* 618 A.2d 1317 (Vermont 1992).

p. 183 Personal emergency: *Dannenfelser v. Employment Security Board of Review,* 844 P.2d 41 (Kan.App. 1992). The employee still has a responsibility to preserve work before quitting.

p. 183 Marriage not required: *Reep v. Commission of Employment and Training,* 61 *LW* 2028 (Mass.Sup.Jud.Ct. June 11, 1992).

p. 185 Workers' Comp bars lawsuit: see, for instance, *Juarez v. Ameritech Mobile Communications,* 957 F.2d 317 (9th Cir. 1992), where an employee charging sexual harassment was not permitted to sue her employer for intentional infliction of mental distress. The Ninth Circuit treated exposure to harassment as an inherent risk of employment, and thus preempted by Workers' Comp—even though the whole purpose of sexual harassment law is to make it clear that the employer's duty is to prevent harassment from becoming an element of the work environment.

p. 186 Aggravation of past injury: on a similar issue, see *Huisinga v. Opus Corp.,* 61 *LW* 2419 (Minn.Sup. December 31, 1992). A carpenter, who was partially disabled by a back injury, applied for another job, but lied about his past medical and WC history. When he was injured again on the new job, he made another WC claim, and the administrative law judge said that his lies freed his employer of any liability. But the state Supreme Court disagreed heartily, pointing out that the state's Human Rights Act forbids any prehiring questions about disability. Asking employees if they have ever had a back injury is not allowed, because the question is too broad—a proper question would be narrowly tailored to identify employees who aren't capable of doing the job. It's also forbidden to ask about past WC claims unless the question is limited to permanent disabilities that affect potential job performance.

p. 186 Passive smoking not related enough to lung disease: *Palmer v. Del Webb's High Sierra,* 61 *LW* 2157 (Nev.Sup. September 1, 1992).

p. 187 Survivors' benefits: Kansas had a state law setting the death benefit at $750 for dependents who are nonresident aliens, versus a much higher entitlement for other dependents, but the statute was found unconstitutional by *Jurado v. Popejoy Construction Co.,* 61 *LW* 2761 (Kan.Sup. May 28, 1993), because there was no compelling state interest to justify the disparity. If a state provides any benefits at all to aliens, it can't claim that there is an excessive administrative burden in providing full-scale benefits.

p. 187 Social Security benefits deducted from comp: *Harris v. Washington,* 61 *LW* 2479 (Wash.Sup. January 21, 1993), also upholds the state's policy of deducting Social Security retirement benefits from the comp benefit.

p. 190 Performance appraisals: *Jensen v. Hewlett-Packard Corp.,* 61 *LW* 2676 (Cal.App. March 30, 1993); *Schauer v. Memorial Care Systems,* 61 *LW* 2676 (Tex.App. March 18, 1993).

p. 190 Internal communication can be defamatory: *Staples v. Bangor Hydro-Electric Co.,* 62 *LW* 2152 (Maine 1993); but see *Bale v.*

Verduzco, 564 N.E.2d 307, saying that an employee evaluation that is only communicated to managers has not been published.

p. 191 Qualified privilege for employer: see, e.g., *Yetter v. Ward Trucking Corp.,* 585 A.2d 1022 (Pa. Super. 1990); *Hunt v. University of Minnesota,* 465 N.W.2d 88 (Minn.App. 1991).

p. 191 $465,000 damages: *Cary v. A T & T Technologies,* #@-027817-87 (N.J. Superior Court 1991); $250,000 award: *Siegel Construction Corp. v. Stanbury,* 586 A.2d 1204 (D.C.App. 1991).

p. 191 Suing the supervisor: *Giordano v. Aerolift, Inc.,* 818 P.2d 950 (Ore.App. 1991); *Nickens v. Labor Agency of Metropolitan Washington,* 600 A.2d 813 (D.C.App. 1991).

Chapter 11

p. 193 Retirement timing factors: Julie Amparano Lopez, "Many Early Retirees Find the Good Deals Not So Good After All," *WSJ,* October 25, 1993, p. A1.

p. 194 Reemployment after retirement: Alan L. Otten, "People Patterns," *WSJ,* March 17, 1993, p. B1. Statistics on early retirement: "Labor Letter" column, *WSJ,* June 15, 1993, p. A1.

p. 195 Study of 13,000 workers' early retirement options: Kevin G. Salwen, "Labor Letter," *WSJ,* September 28, 1993, p. A1.

p. 195 ERISA preempts state cases: *Barr v. American Cyanamid,* 61 *LW* 2408 (W.D. Wash. December 8, 1992).

p. 195 Ability to sue under ERISA: *Raymond v. Mobil Oil Corp.,* 61 *LW* 2474 (10th Cir. January 20, 1993). First Circuit allows suit: *Vartanian v. Monsanto,* 62 *LW* 2509 (1st Cir. February 2, 1994). Pennsylvania case about disclosure of future early retirement incentives: *Taylor v. Peoples Natural Gas Co.,* 62 *LW* 2515 (W.D. Pa. January 27, 1994).

p. 196 Tax consequences of lump sum: *Farr v. U.S. West Inc.,* 61 *LW* 2436 (D. Oregon December 24, 1992).

p. 196 Even if the employer lied orally: *Astor v. IBM,* 62 *LW* 2296 (6th Cir. October 20, 1993).

p. 196 Equitable estoppel: *Thesenvitz v. Kaiser Engineers,* 61 *LW* 2048 (E.D. Wash. May 26, 1992).

p. 199 Non-ERISA remedies: see, e.g., *Bidlack v. Wheelabrator Corp.,* 61 *LW* 2776 (7th Cir. May 18, 1993).

p. 200 Curtiss-Wright didn't explain method: *Schoonejongen v. Curtiss-Wright Corp.,* 62 *LW* 2468 (3d Cir. December 28, 1993). GM not allowed to make retirees pay for health benefits: *Sprague v. GM,* 62 *LW* 2532 (E.D. Mich. February 2, 1994).

p. 200 Negative changes in retiree coverage: Julie Amparano Lopez, "Many Early Retirees Find the Good Deals Not So Good After All," *WSJ,* October 25, 1993, p. A1.

   p. 200 KPMG Peat Marwick study: Robert L. Rose, "Retiree Health Coverage Erodes at Small, Midsize Firms," *WSJ,* April 16, 1993, p. B2.

Index